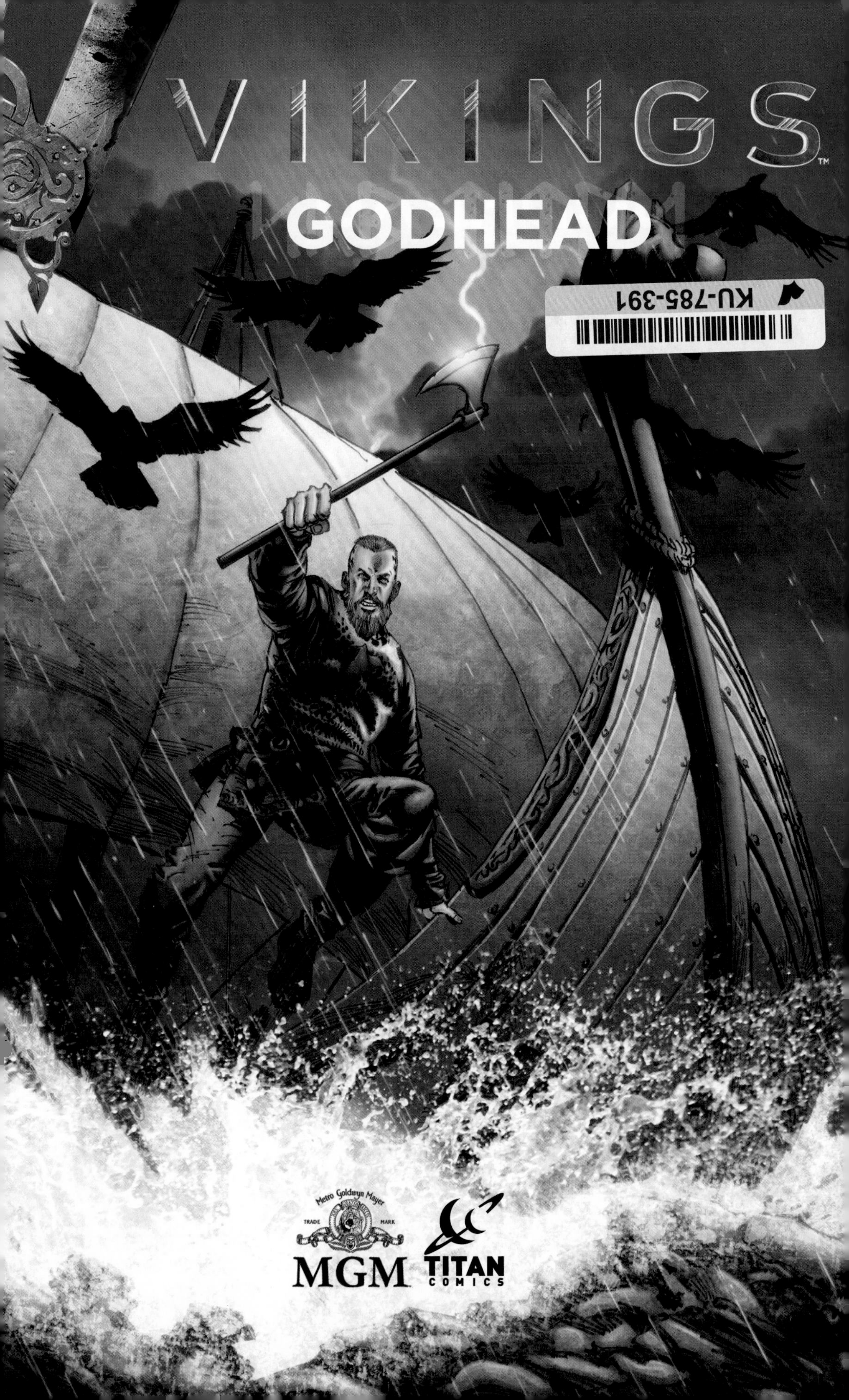
VIKINGS™
GODHEAD
Metro Goldwyn Mayer
TRADE MARK
MGM
TITAN COMICS

VIKINGS™

GODHEAD

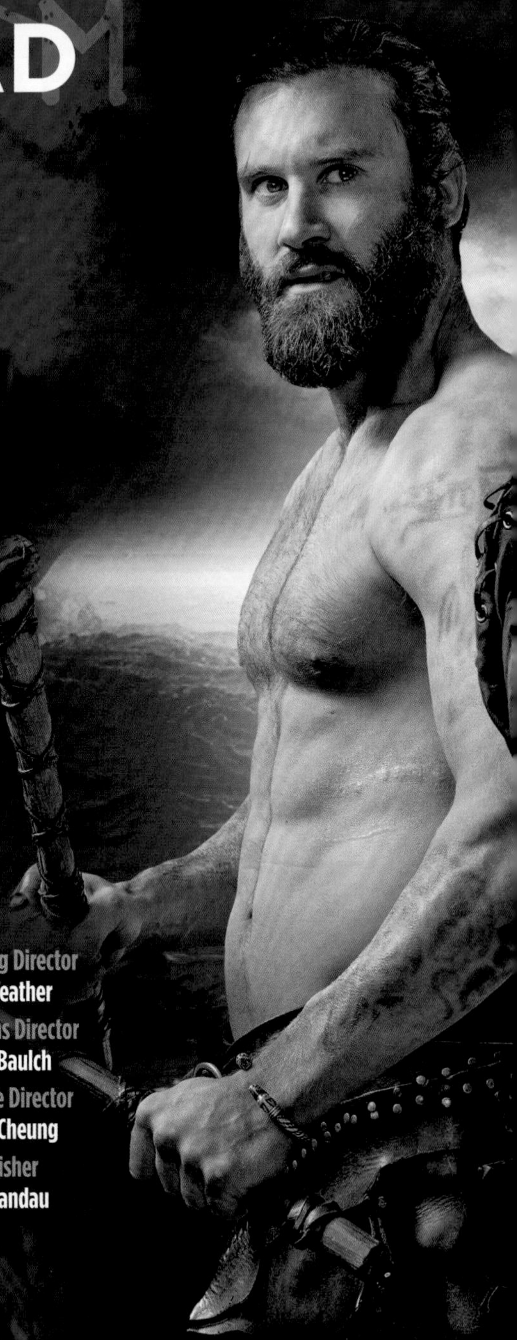

WRITER
CAVAN SCOTT

ARTIST
STAZ JOHNSON

ADDITIONAL ART
RICHARD ELSON
ANDREA MUTTI

COLOURIST
RODRIGO FERNANDES

LETTERER
ROB STEEN

EDITOR
NEIL D. EDWARDS

TITAN COMICS

Senior Editor
Martin Eden

Collection Designer
Wilfried Tshikana-Ekutshu

Production Manager
Obi Onuora

Production Supervisors
Jackie Flook, Maria Pearson

Production Assistant
Peter James

Art Director
Oz Browne

Publishing Manager
Darryl Tothill

Senior Sales Manager
Steve Tothill

Publishing Director
Chris Teather

Operations Director
Leigh Baulch

Executive Director
Vivian Cheung

Publisher
Nick Landau

WWW.TITAN-COMICS.COM

Become a fan on
Facebook.com/comicstitan

Follow us on Twitter
@comicstitan

ISBN: 9781785853579

10 9 8 7 6 5 4 3 2 1
A CIP catalogue record for this title is available from the British Library.
First edition: First published January 2017

MGM

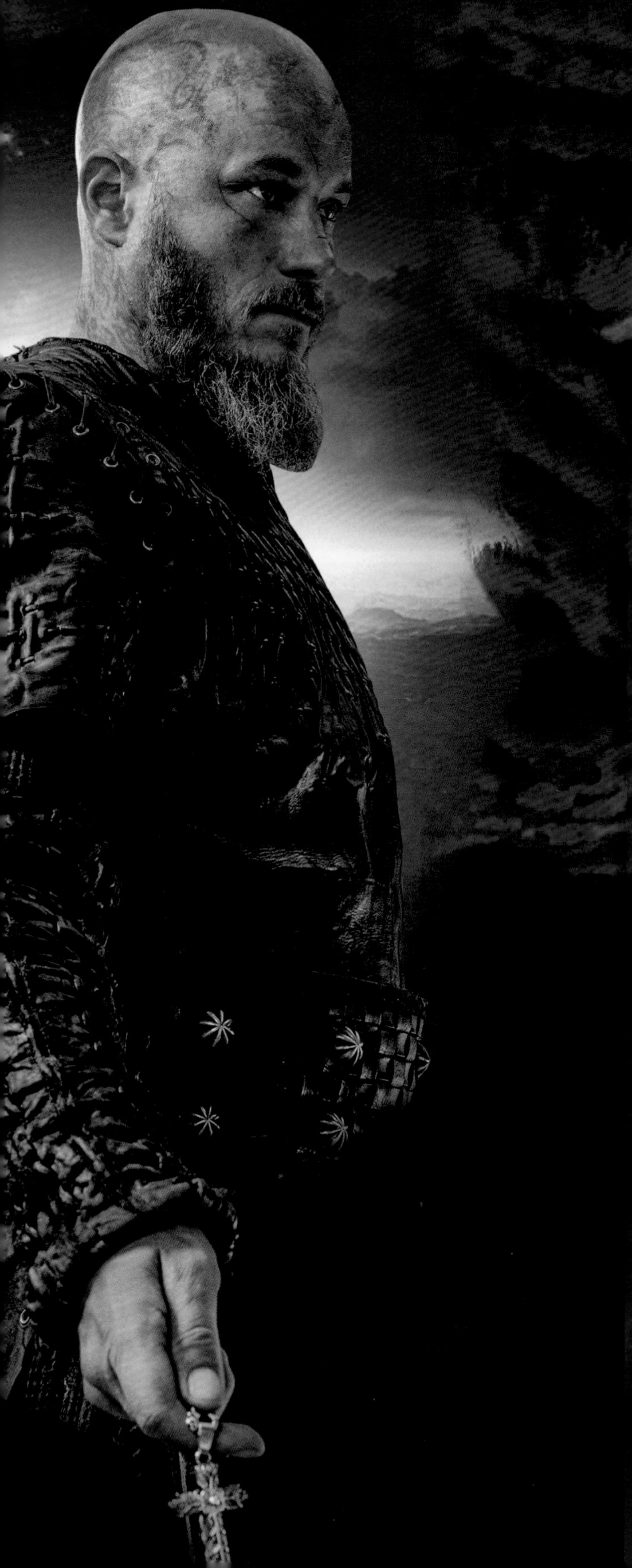

THE PANTHEON OF CHARACTERS

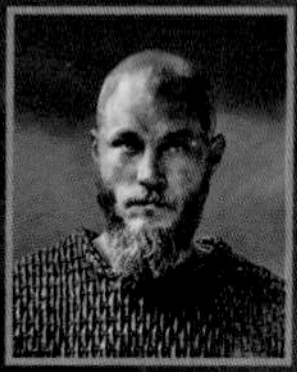

RAGNAR

Ragnar Lothbrok has risen from being a simple farmer to a King and one of the most feared of Viking raiders. Ragnar's plans now extend beyond pillage; he has sought an alliance with King Ecbert of Wessex, much to the displeasure of some of his crew.

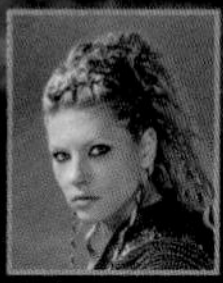

LAGERTHA

Once the wife of Ragnar, the two were estranged, during which time she became an Earl in her own right and remains a powerful shield maiden.

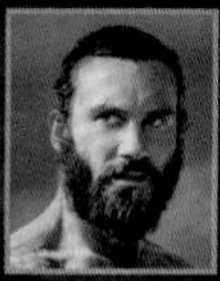

ROLLO

Ragnar's brother. He is a powerful warrior, but has a troubled relationship with Ragnar, his feelings of envy leading him to betray him.

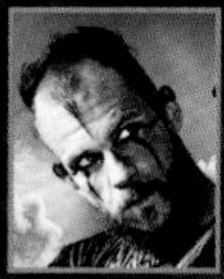

FLOKI

A skilled shipwright, Floki's genius borders on madness. Yet he is a close advisor to Ragnar, although tormented by his leader's closeness to the English king and his acceptance of Christianity.

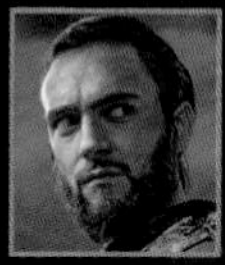

ATHELSTAN

A monk seized by Ragnar during a raid and enslaved, Athelstan has developed Ragnar's trust and become a close confidant, much to Floki's chagrin …

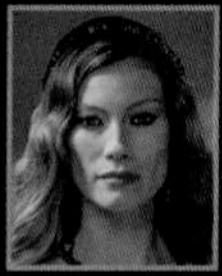

QUEEN ASLAUG

Ragnar's second wife, she is the mother of Ragnar's crippled son, Ivar, who is prophesied to become a powerful Viking leader.

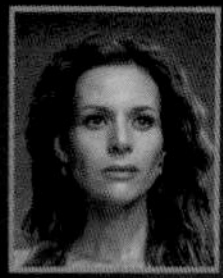

SIGGY

Once married to the Earl of Kattegat, Siggy has fallen from grace and is now a servant and friend to Aslaug.

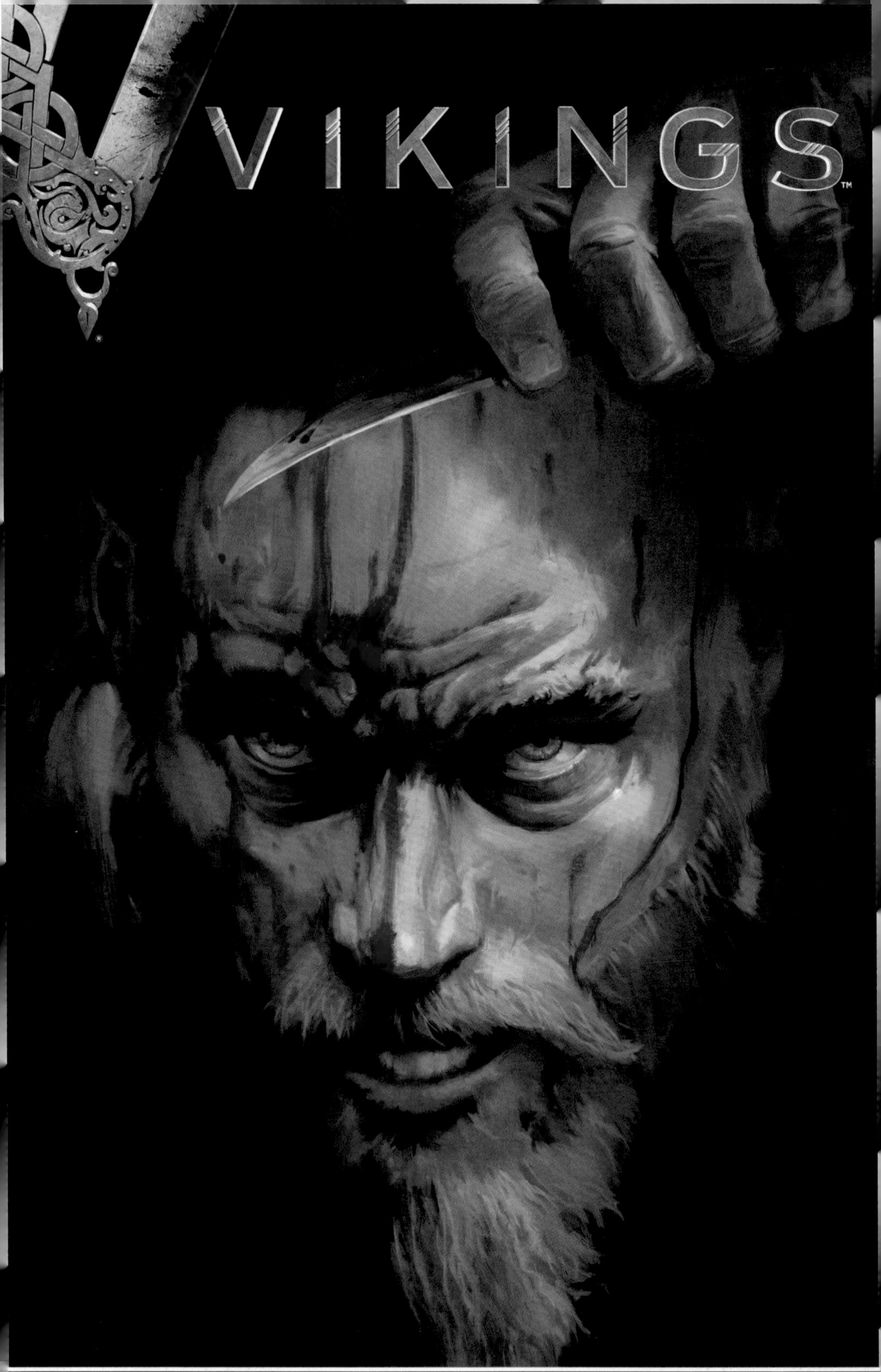
VIKINGS

#1 COVER A
ARTIST SHANE PIERCE

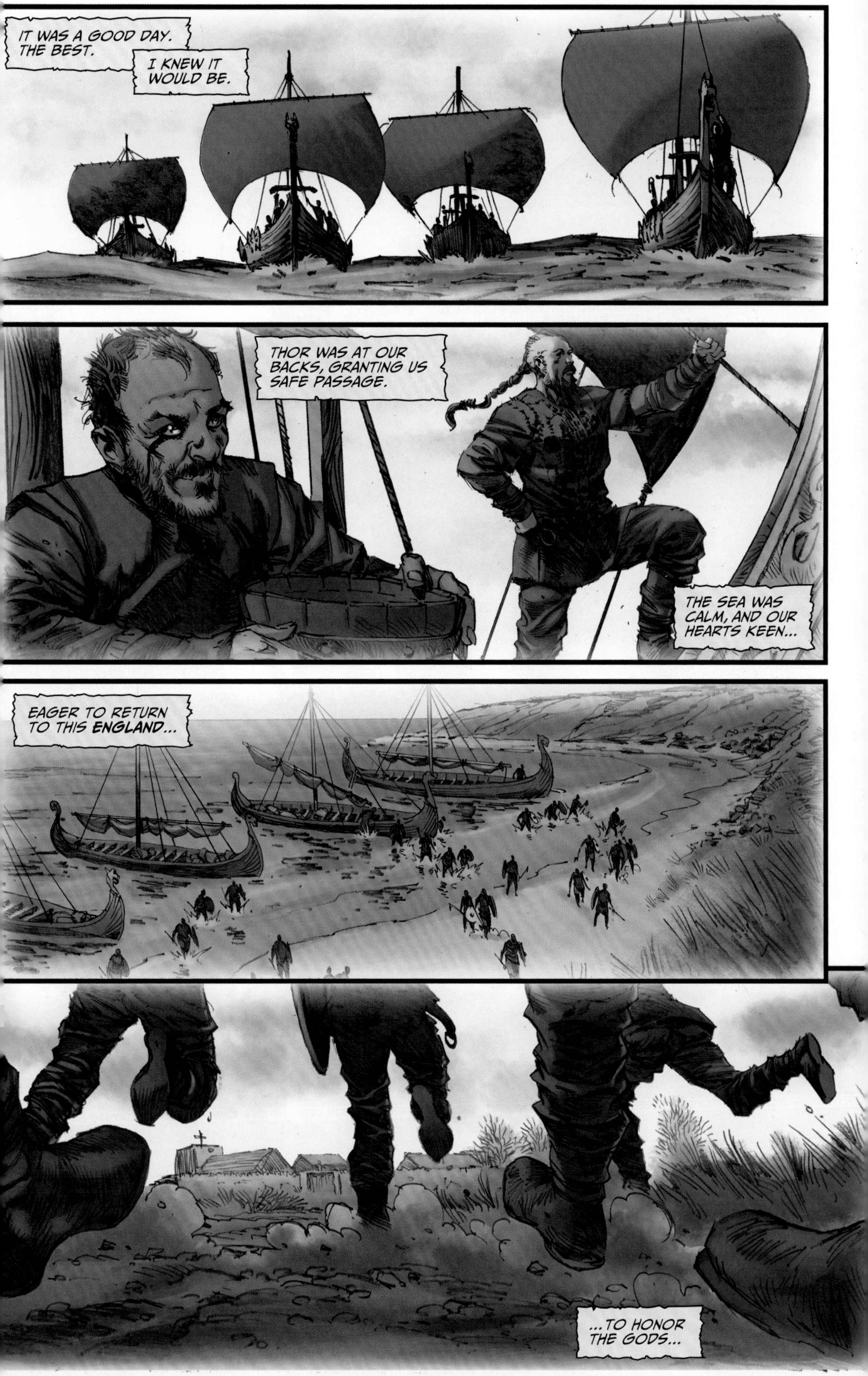
IT WAS A GOOD DAY. THE BEST.
I KNEW IT WOULD BE.
THOR WAS AT OUR BACKS, GRANTING US SAFE PASSAGE.
THE SEA WAS CALM, AND OUR HEARTS KEEN...
EAGER TO RETURN TO THIS **ENGLAND**...
...TO HONOR THE GODS...

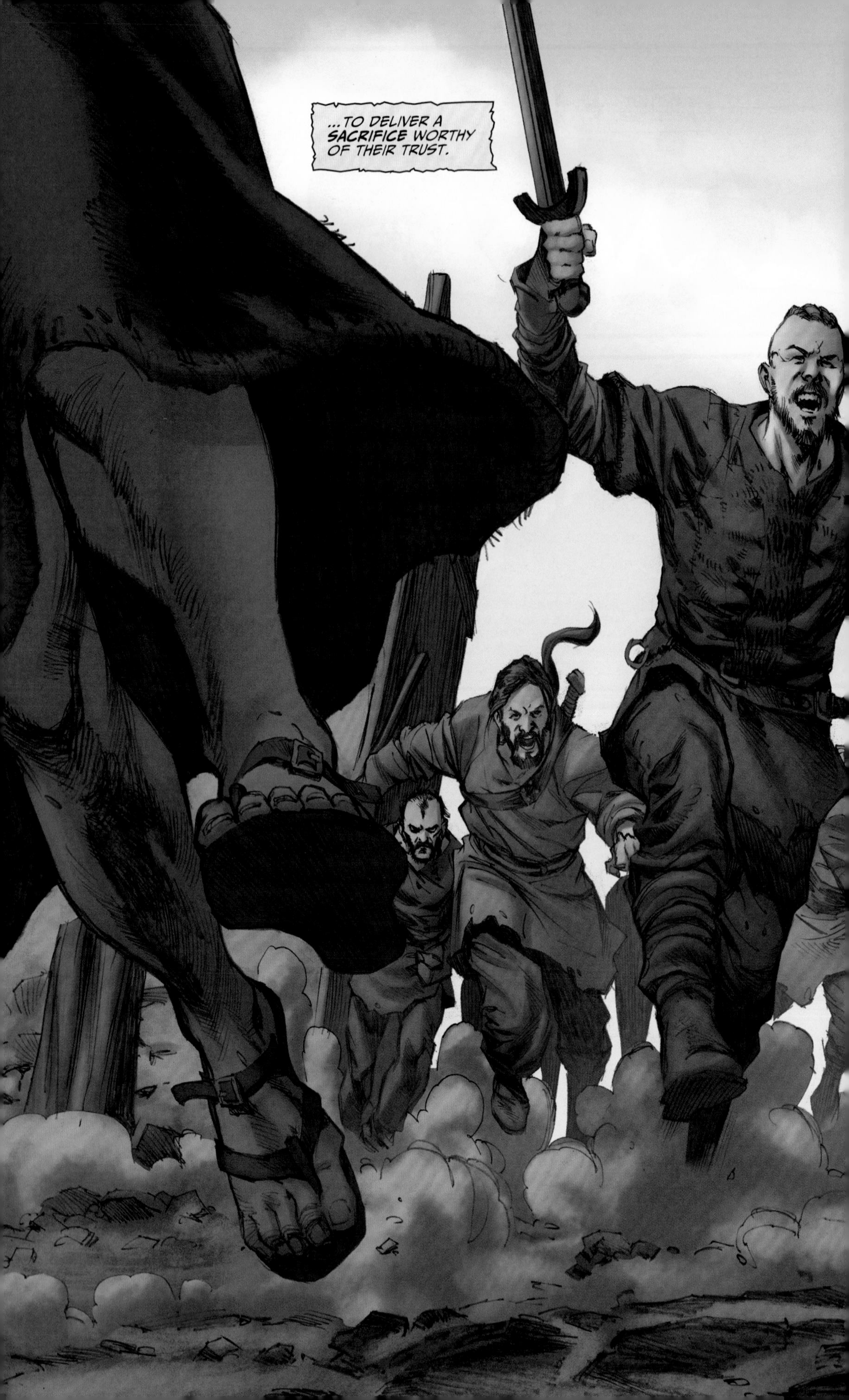
...TO DELIVER A SACRIFICE WORTHY OF THEIR TRUST.

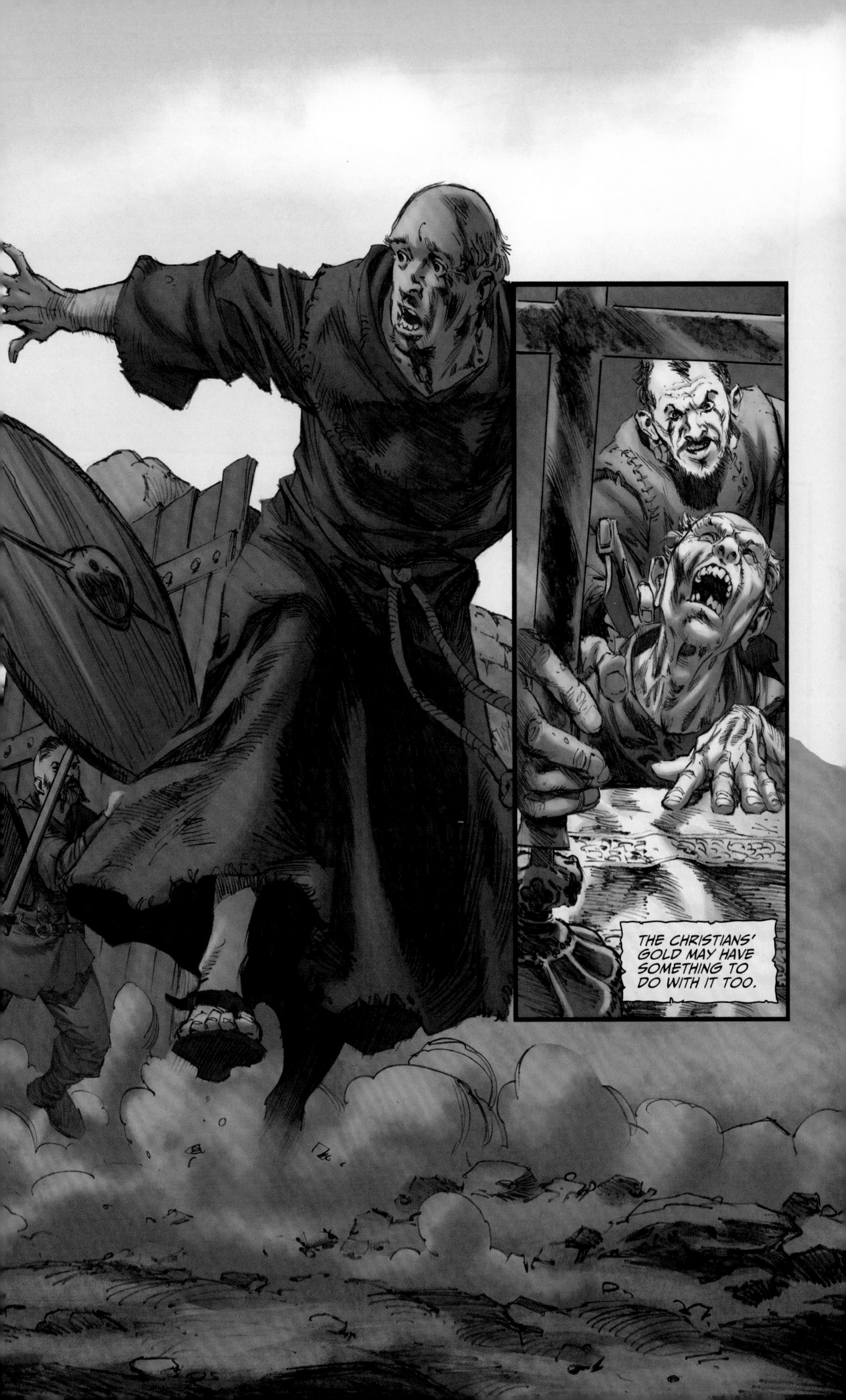
THE CHRISTIANS' GOLD MAY HAVE SOMETHING TO DO WITH IT TOO.

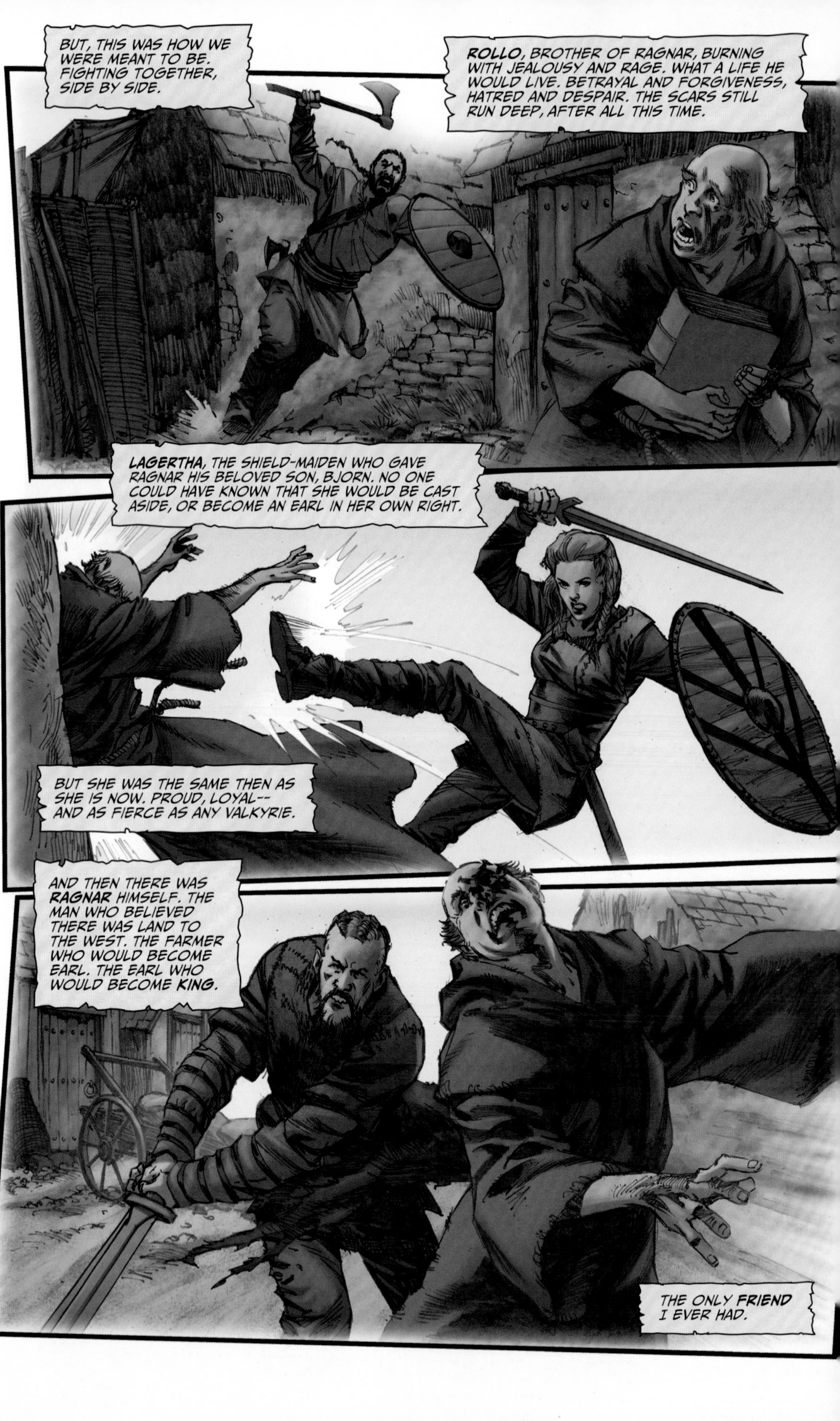
BUT, THIS WAS HOW WE WERE MEANT TO BE. FIGHTING TOGETHER, SIDE BY SIDE.
ROLLO, BROTHER OF RAGNAR, BURNING WITH JEALOUSY AND RAGE. WHAT A LIFE HE WOULD LIVE. BETRAYAL AND FORGIVENESS, HATRED AND DESPAIR. THE SCARS STILL RUN DEEP, AFTER ALL THIS TIME.
LAGERTHA, THE SHIELD-MAIDEN WHO GAVE RAGNAR HIS BELOVED SON, BJORN. NO ONE COULD HAVE KNOWN THAT SHE WOULD BE CAST ASIDE, OR BECOME AN EARL IN HER OWN RIGHT.
BUT SHE WAS THE SAME THEN AS SHE IS NOW. PROUD, LOYAL-- AND AS FIERCE AS ANY VALKYRIE.
AND THEN THERE WAS RAGNAR HIMSELF. THE MAN WHO BELIEVED THERE WAS LAND TO THE WEST. THE FARMER WHO WOULD BECOME EARL. THE EARL WHO WOULD BECOME KING.
THE ONLY FRIEND I EVER HAD.

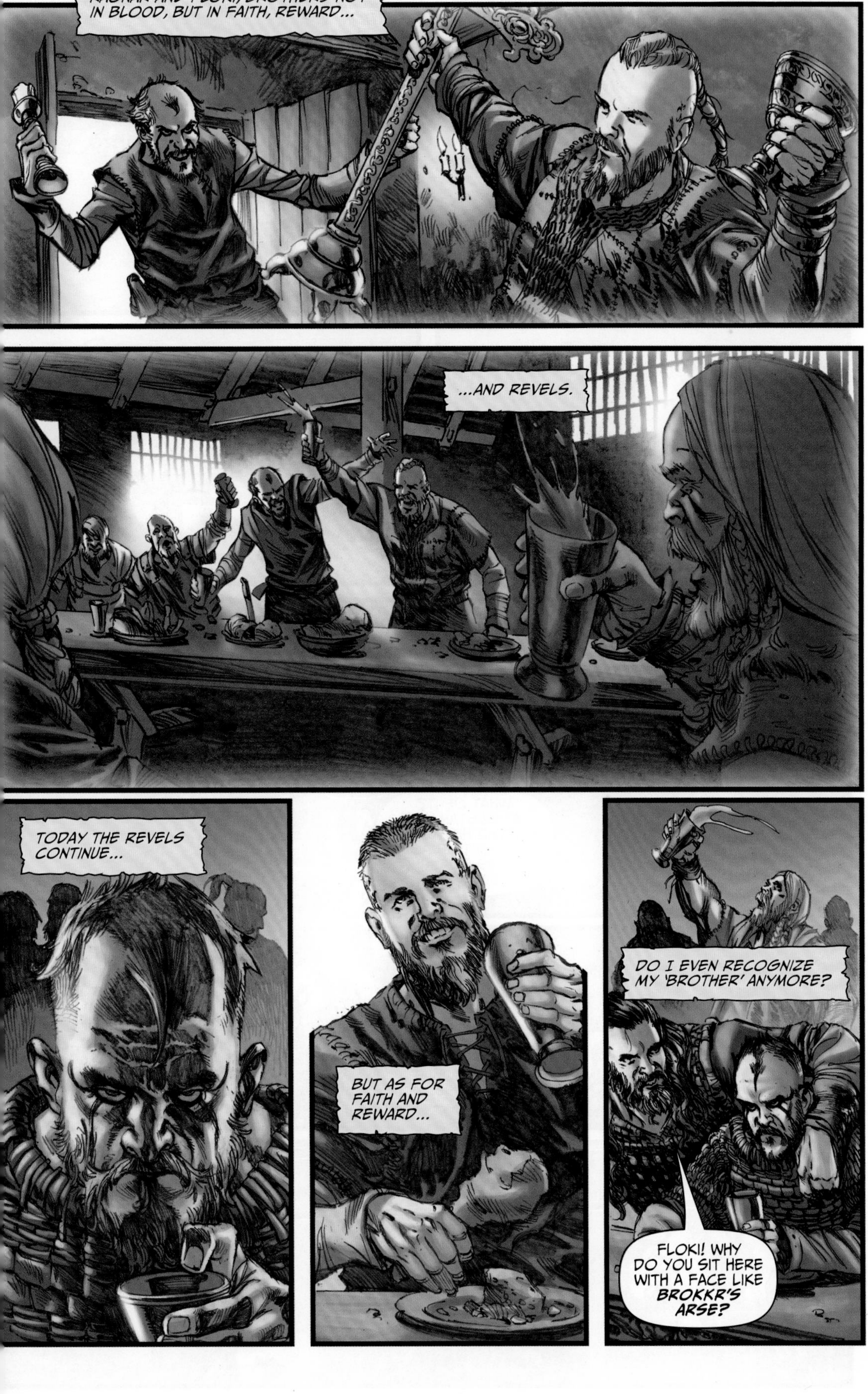
IT WAS US AGAINST THE WORLD. RAGNAR AND FLOKI, BROTHERS NOT IN BLOOD, BUT IN FAITH, REWARD...
...AND REVELS.
TODAY THE REVELS CONTINUE...
BUT AS FOR FAITH AND REWARD...
DO I EVEN RECOGNIZE MY 'BROTHER' ANYMORE?
FLOKI! WHY DO YOU SIT HERE WITH A FACE LIKE BROKKR'S ARSE?

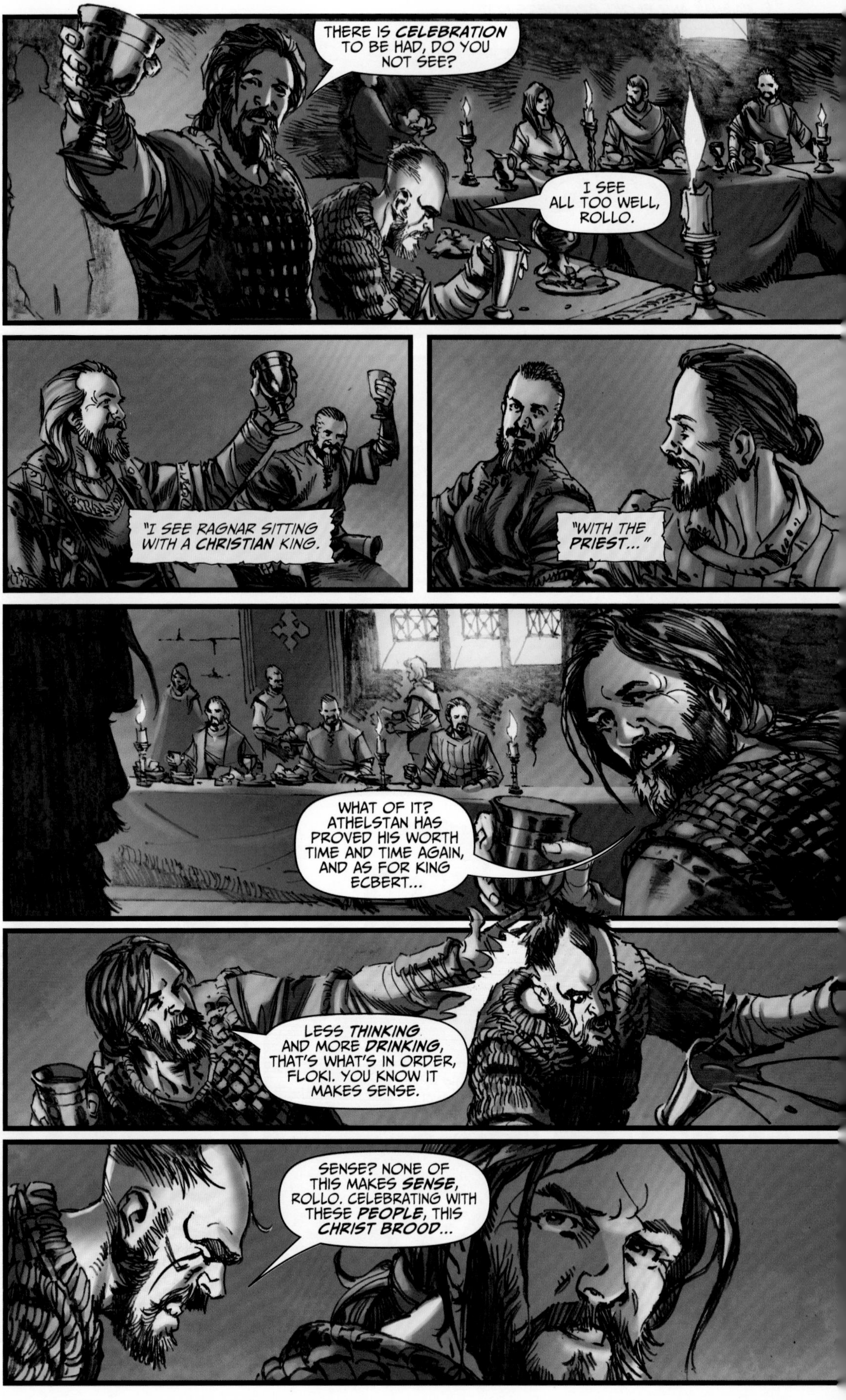
THERE IS *CELEBRATION* TO BE HAD, DO YOU NOT SEE?
I SEE ALL TOO WELL, ROLLO.
"I SEE RAGNAR SITTING WITH A **CHRISTIAN** KING.
"WITH THE *PRIEST*..."
WHAT OF IT? ATHELSTAN HAS PROVED HIS WORTH TIME AND TIME AGAIN, AND AS FOR KING ECBERT...
LESS *THINKING* AND MORE *DRINKING*, THAT'S WHAT'S IN ORDER, FLOKI. YOU KNOW IT MAKES SENSE.
SENSE? NONE OF THIS MAKES *SENSE*, ROLLO. CELEBRATING WITH THESE *PEOPLE*, THIS *CHRIST BROOD*...

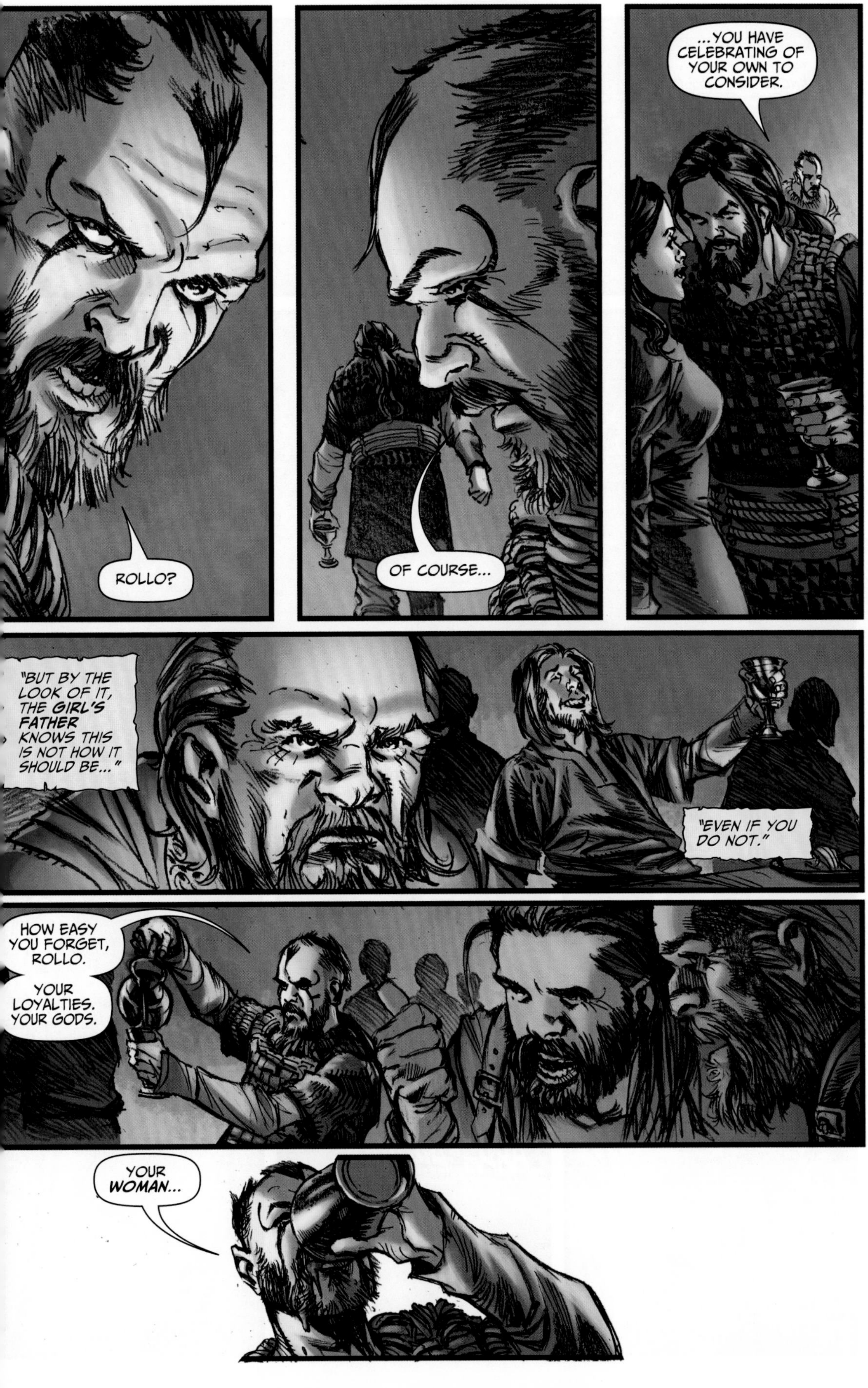
ROLLO?
OF COURSE...
...YOU HAVE CELEBRATING OF YOUR OWN TO CONSIDER.
"BUT BY THE LOOK OF IT, THE **GIRL'S FATHER** KNOWS THIS IS NOT HOW IT SHOULD BE..."
"EVEN IF YOU DO NOT."
HOW EASY YOU FORGET, ROLLO.
YOUR LOYALTIES. YOUR GODS.
YOUR **WOMAN**...

"SIGGY WOULD KNOW WHY THIS IS WRONG. SIGGY UNDERSTANDS THE WAY OF THINGS..."

SIGGY!

S-SORRY ASLAUG...

IT IS ALMOST TIME FOR THE AUDIENCE, I CAN'T SETTLE IVAR AND THE BOYS–

WAAAH

OW!

WILL YOU NOT HELP WITH THEM?

OF COURSE. COME ON BOYS, YOUR MOTHER NEEDS TO GET TO THE ASSEMBLY. QUIET NOW.

IF ONLY YOU WOULD BE QUIET, MY SON.

AAAA-AAAAAH

I CANNOT WAIT. HELGA, YOU WILL HAVE TO TAKE HIM....

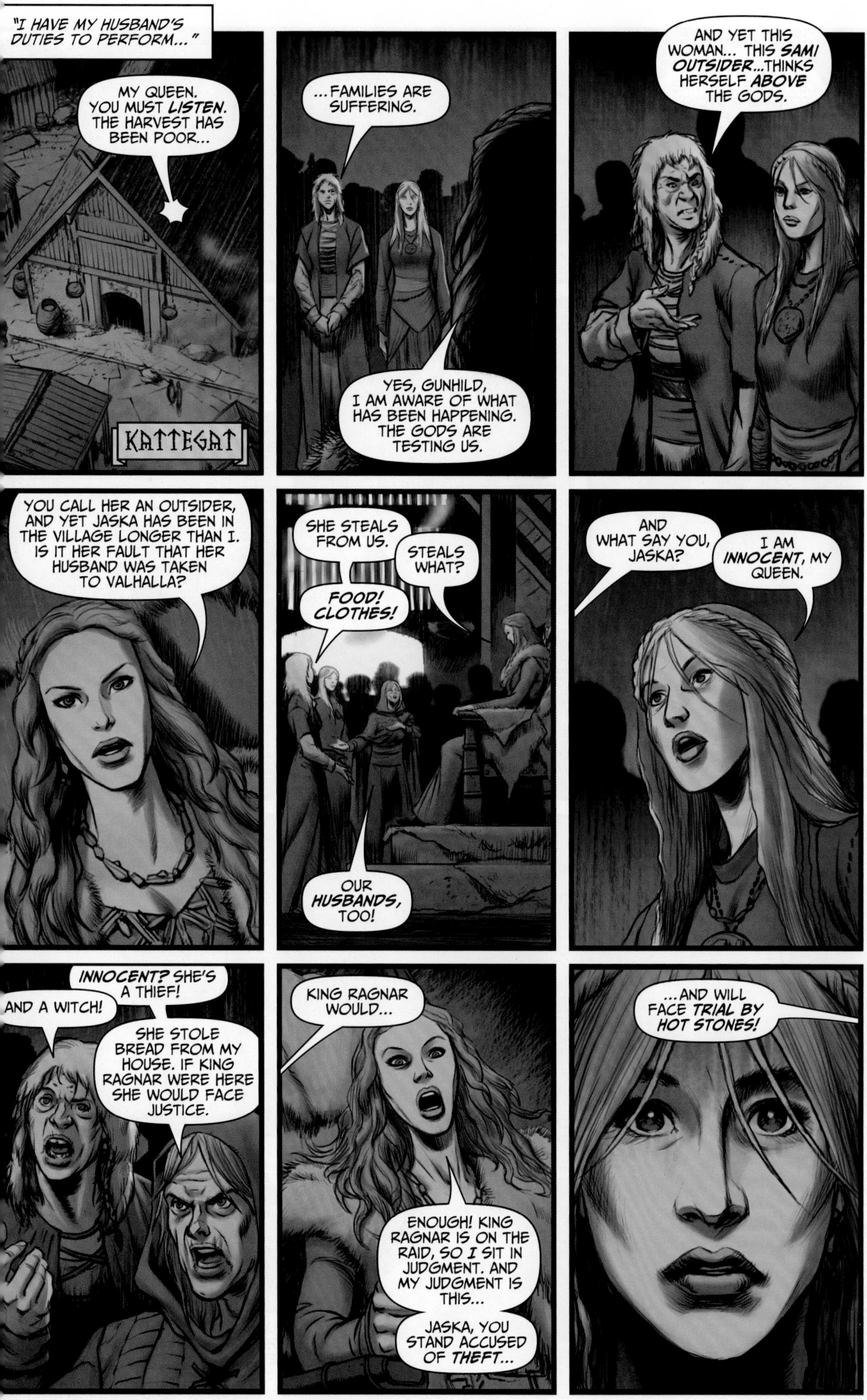
"I HAVE MY HUSBAND'S DUTIES TO PERFORM..."
MY QUEEN. YOU MUST LISTEN. THE HARVEST HAS BEEN POOR...
KATTEGAT
...FAMILIES ARE SUFFERING.
YES, GUNHILD, I AM AWARE OF WHAT HAS BEEN HAPPENING. THE GODS ARE TESTING US.
AND YET THIS WOMAN... THIS SAMI OUTSIDER...THINKS HERSELF ABOVE THE GODS.
YOU CALL HER AN OUTSIDER, AND YET JASKA HAS BEEN IN THE VILLAGE LONGER THAN I. IS IT HER FAULT THAT HER HUSBAND WAS TAKEN TO VALHALLA?
SHE STEALS FROM US.
STEALS WHAT?
FOOD! CLOTHES!
OUR HUSBANDS, TOO!
AND WHAT SAY YOU, JASKA?
I AM INNOCENT, MY QUEEN.
INNOCENT? SHE'S A THIEF!
AND A WITCH!
SHE STOLE BREAD FROM MY HOUSE. IF KING RAGNAR WERE HERE SHE WOULD FACE JUSTICE.
KING RAGNAR WOULD...
ENOUGH! KING RAGNAR IS ON THE RAID, SO I SIT IN JUDGMENT. AND MY JUDGMENT IS THIS...
JASKA, YOU STAND ACCUSED OF THEFT...
...AND WILL FACE TRIAL BY HOT STONES!

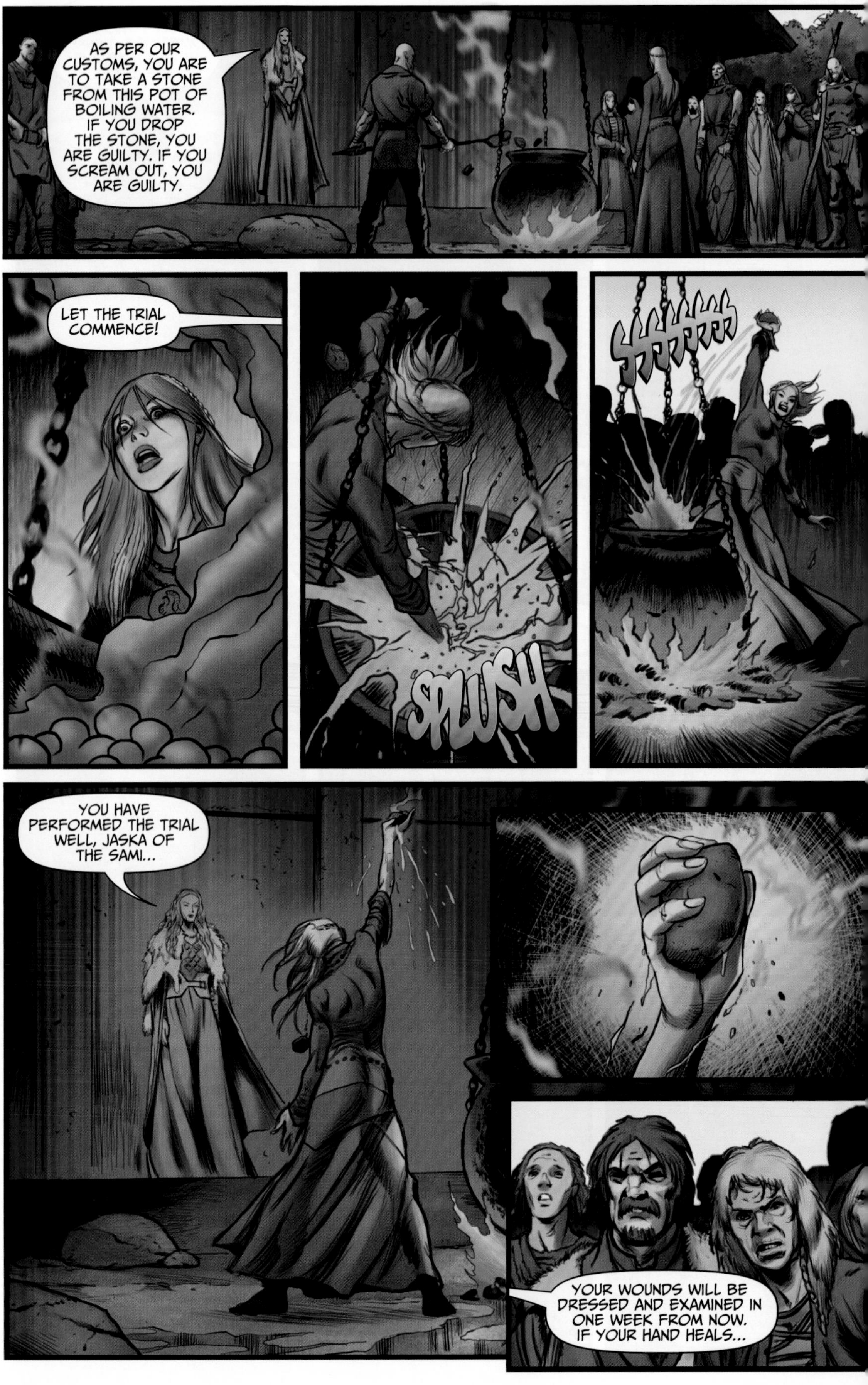
AS PER OUR CUSTOMS, YOU ARE TO TAKE A STONE FROM THIS POT OF BOILING WATER. IF YOU DROP THE STONE, YOU ARE GUILTY. IF YOU SCREAM OUT, YOU ARE GUILTY.
LET THE TRIAL COMMENCE!
SPLUSH
SSSHHHHSSS
YOU HAVE PERFORMED THE TRIAL WELL, JASKA OF THE SAMI...
YOUR WOUNDS WILL BE DRESSED AND EXAMINED IN ONE WEEK FROM NOW. IF YOUR HAND HEALS...

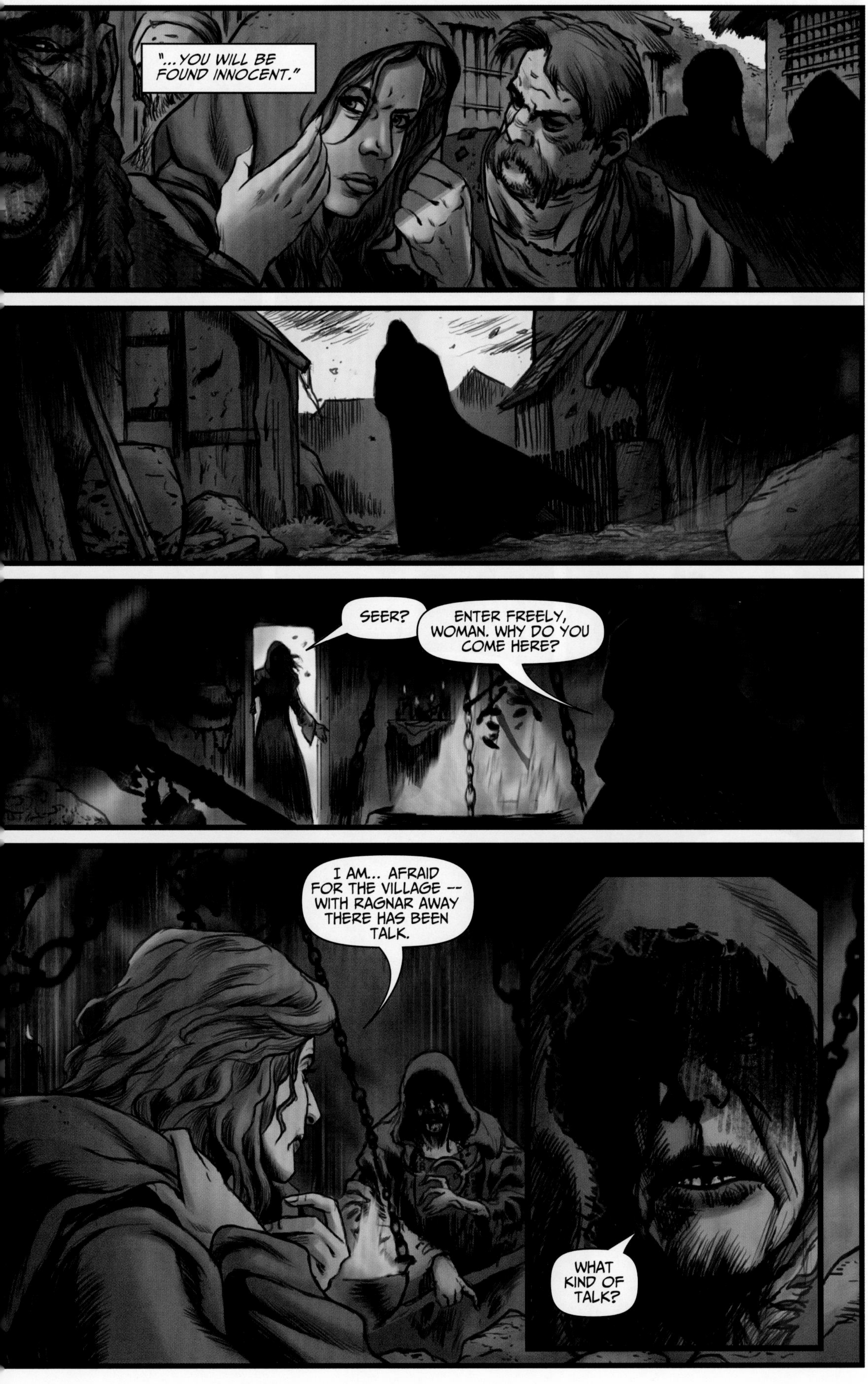
"...YOU WILL BE FOUND INNOCENT."
SEER?
ENTER FREELY, WOMAN. WHY DO YOU COME HERE?
I AM... AFRAID FOR THE VILLAGE -- WITH RAGNAR AWAY THERE HAS BEEN TALK.
WHAT KIND OF TALK?

"THE PEOPLE... THEY BLAME ASLAUG.

"FOR THE HARVEST. FOR EVERYTHING..."

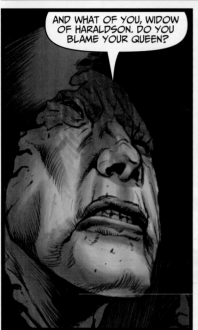

AND WHAT OF YOU, WIDOW OF HARALDSON. DO YOU BLAME YOUR QUEEN?

OF COURSE NOT, BUT--

BUT YOU WISH TO KNOW WHEN RAGNAR WILL RETURN. WHEN *ROLLO* WILL RETURN...

AS I SAID, I WORRY--

FOR THE VILLAGE, YES. AND WORRY YOU SHOULD -- FOR THE WOLVES WILL TURN ON THEIR OWN TO ATONE THE SINS OF THE BEAR.

I DON'T UNDERSTAND. WHAT DOES THAT MEAN?

HAHAHAHAHA

ANSWER ME. PLEASE.

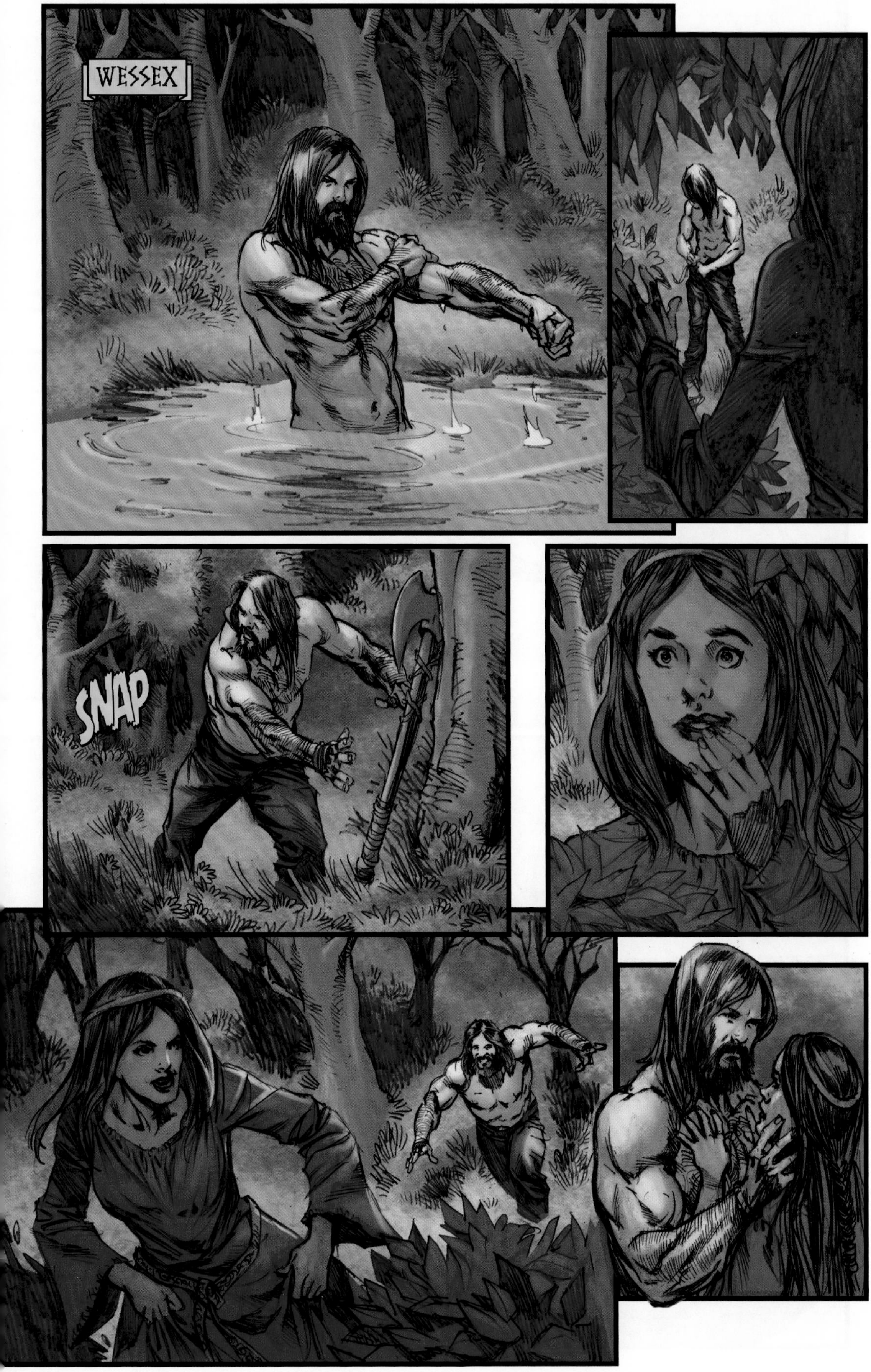
WESSEX
SNAP

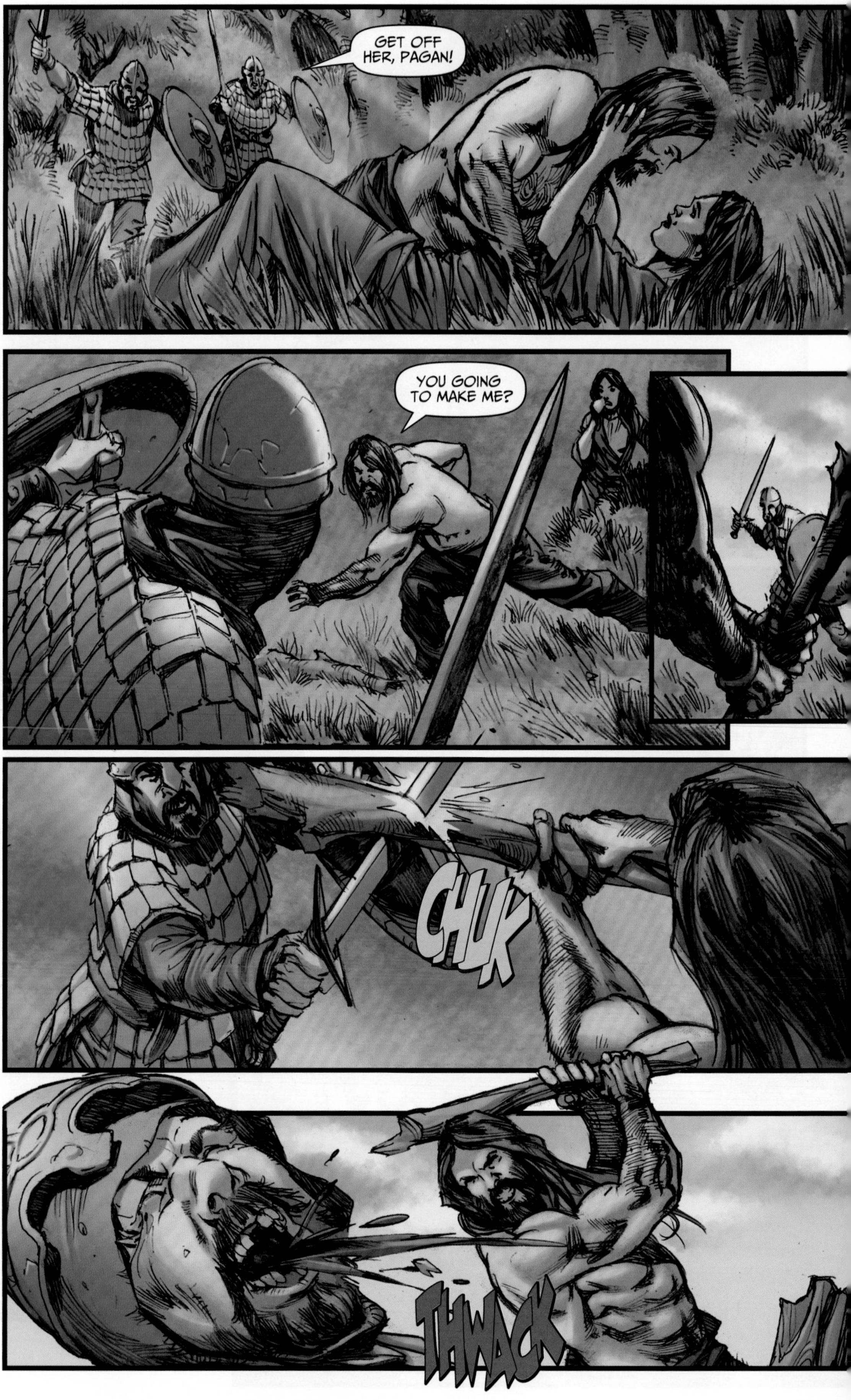
GET OFF HER, PAGAN!
YOU GOING TO MAKE ME?
CHUK
THWACK

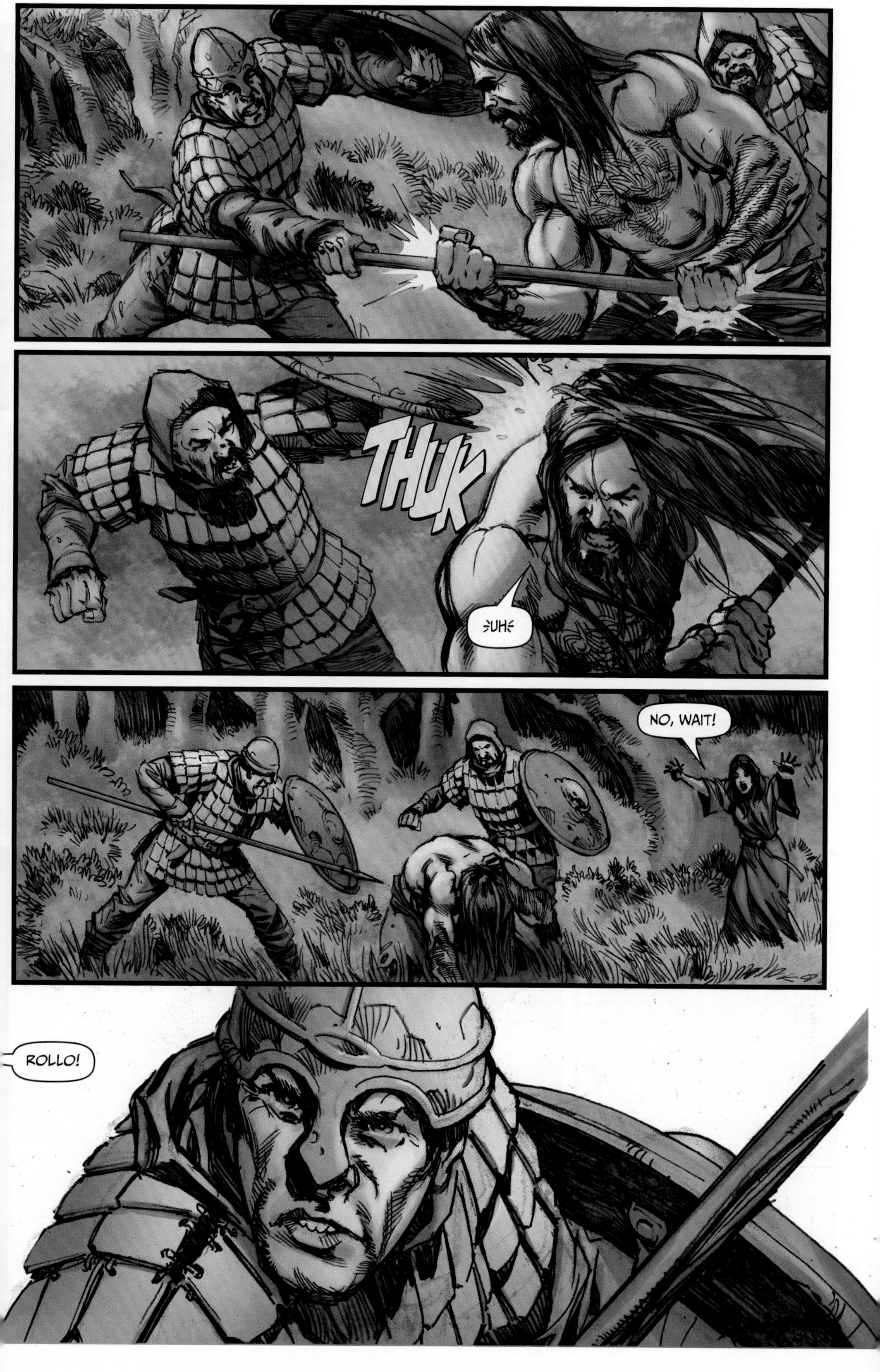
THUK
UH
NO, WAIT!
ROLLO!

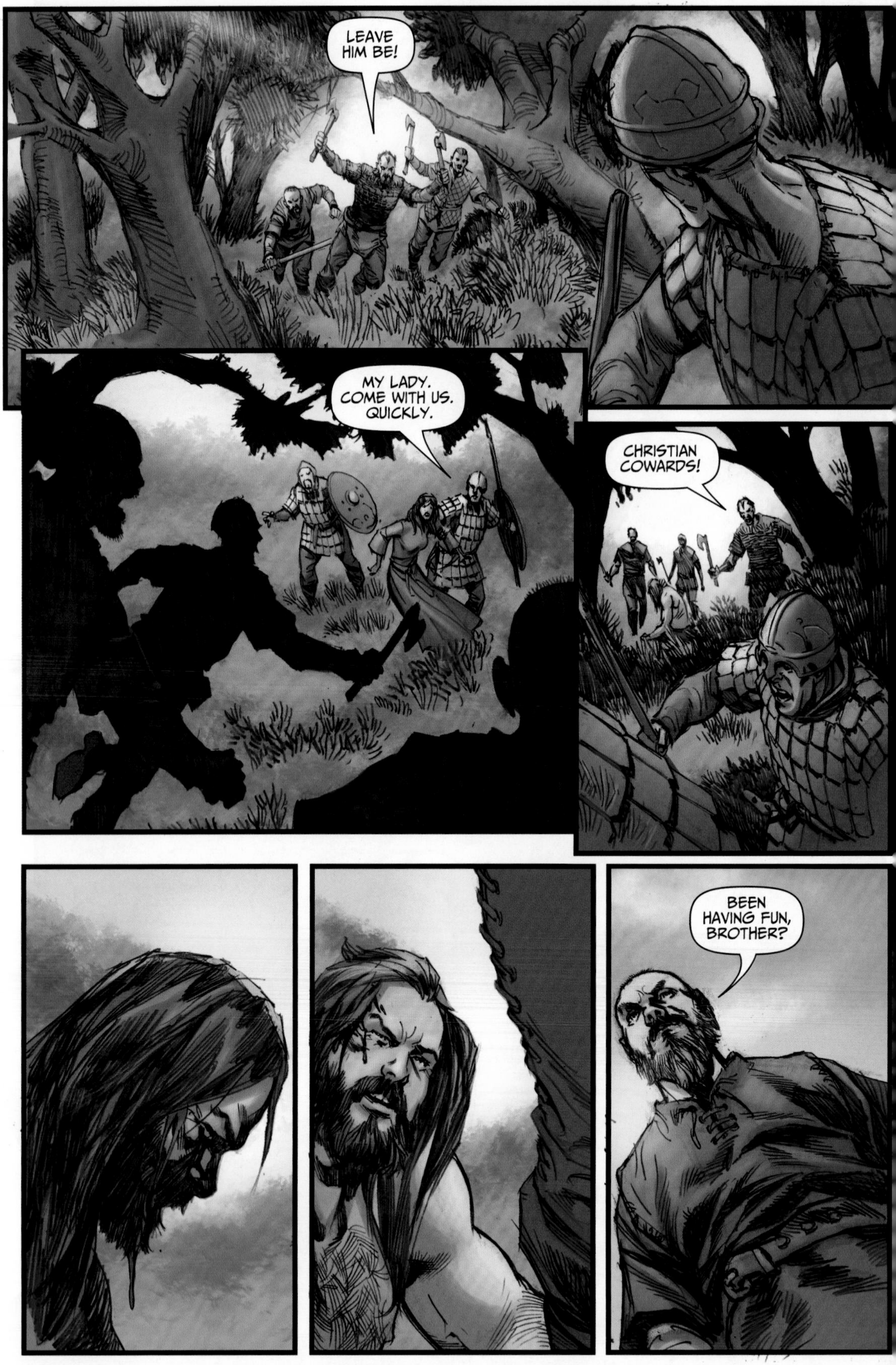
LEAVE HIM BE!
MY LADY. COME WITH US. QUICKLY.
CHRISTIAN COWARDS!
BEEN HAVING FUN, BROTHER?

YOUR MAJESTY, I IMPLORE YOU -- WILL YOU NOT DEAL WITH THESE NORTHMEN ONCE AND FOR ALL?

AND WHAT WOULD YOU HAVE ME DO, ETHELWOLD?

DRIVE THEM OUT!

THEY HAVE NO PLACE HERE. THEY CLAIM TO BE OUR ALLIES, AND YET STEAL LAND FROM BENEATH OUR NOSES AND ATTACK OUR WOMEN.

AND THAT IS WHAT HAPPENED TO YOUR DAUGHTER? THE LADY QUAN WAS ATTACKED?

VICIOUSLY. I DREAD TO THINK WHAT WOULD HAVE HAPPENED IF MY MEN HADN'T FOUND HER WHEN THEY DID!

YOUR MAJESTY. KING RAGNAR WOULD NEVER COUNTENANCE SUCH A THING. HE IS A MAN OF HONOR, OF PRINCIPLES--

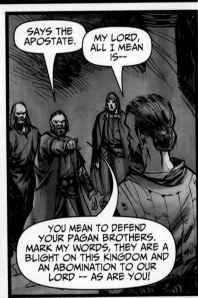

SAYS THE APOSTATE.

MY LORD, ALL I MEAN IS--

YOU MEAN TO DEFEND YOUR PAGAN BROTHERS. MARK MY WORDS, THEY ARE A BLIGHT ON THIS KINGDOM AND AN ABOMINATION TO OUR LORD -- AS ARE YOU!

SILENCE!

YOU FORGET YOURSELF, ETHELWOLD. YOU THINK I SHOULD DRIVE THE NORTHMEN FROM OUR LAND. SHOULD I ALSO ALLOW FOR MY NOBLES TO QUESTION THEIR KING SO OPENLY IN HIS OWN COURT?

NO, YOU SHOULD NOT!

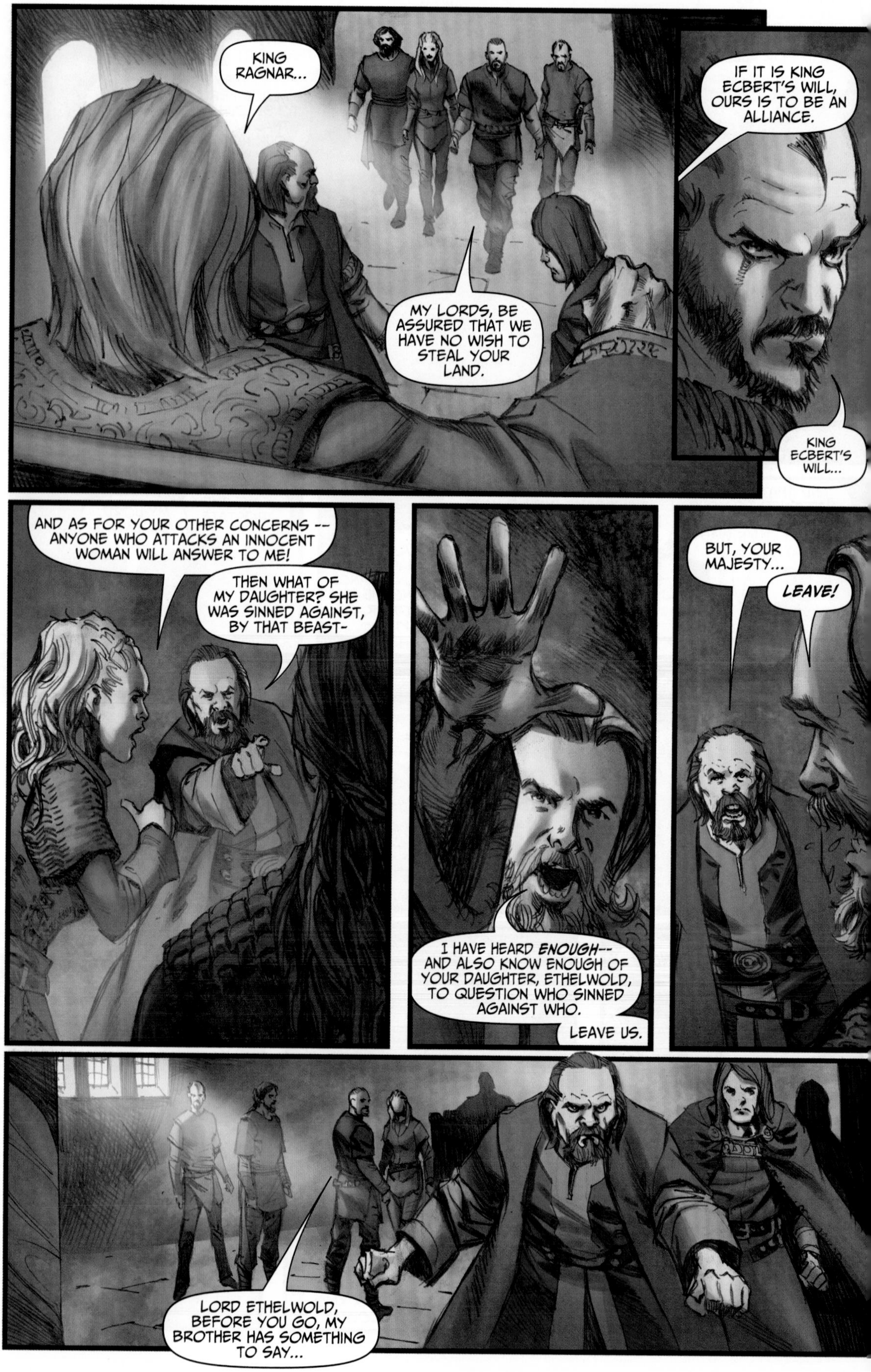
KING RAGNAR...
MY LORDS, BE ASSURED THAT WE HAVE NO WISH TO STEAL YOUR LAND.
IF IT IS KING ECBERT'S WILL, OURS IS TO BE AN ALLIANCE.
KING ECBERT'S WILL...
AND AS FOR YOUR OTHER CONCERNS -- ANYONE WHO ATTACKS AN INNOCENT WOMAN WILL ANSWER TO ME!
THEN WHAT OF MY DAUGHTER? SHE WAS SINNED AGAINST, BY THAT BEAST-
I HAVE HEARD *ENOUGH*-- AND ALSO KNOW ENOUGH OF YOUR DAUGHTER, ETHELWOLD, TO QUESTION WHO SINNED AGAINST WHO.
LEAVE US.
BUT, YOUR MAJESTY...
LEAVE!
LORD ETHELWOLD, BEFORE YOU GO, MY BROTHER HAS SOMETHING TO SAY...

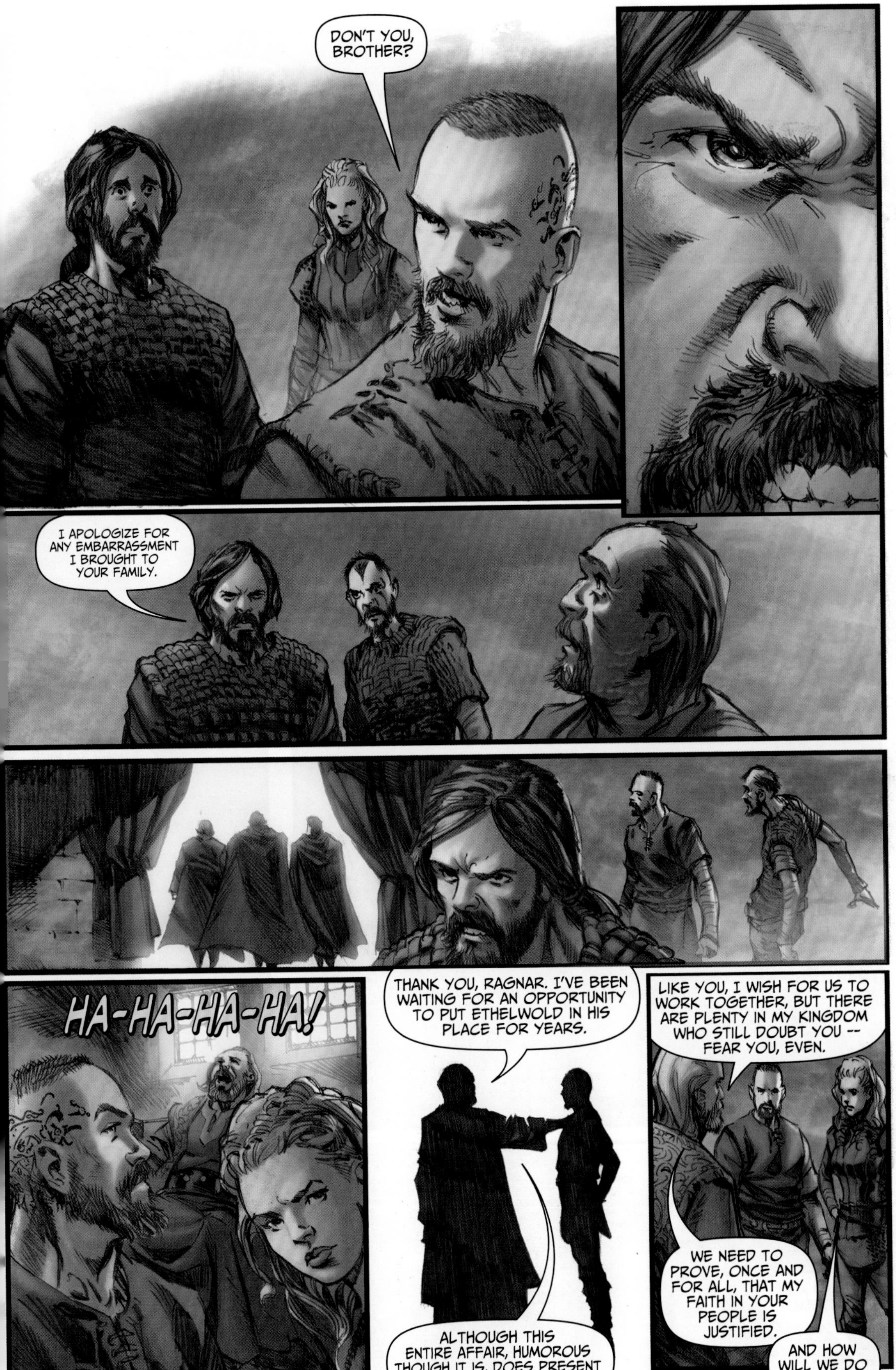
DON'T YOU, BROTHER?
I APOLOGIZE FOR ANY EMBARRASSMENT I BROUGHT TO YOUR FAMILY.
HA-HA-HA-HA!
THANK YOU, RAGNAR. I'VE BEEN WAITING FOR AN OPPORTUNITY TO PUT ETHELWOLD IN HIS PLACE FOR YEARS.
ALTHOUGH THIS ENTIRE AFFAIR, HUMOROUS THOUGH IT IS, DOES PRESENT ME WITH A PROBLEM.
LIKE YOU, I WISH FOR US TO WORK TOGETHER, BUT THERE ARE PLENTY IN MY KINGDOM WHO STILL DOUBT YOU -- FEAR YOU, EVEN.
WE NEED TO PROVE, ONCE AND FOR ALL, THAT MY FAITH IN YOUR PEOPLE IS JUSTIFIED.
AND HOW WILL WE DO THAT?

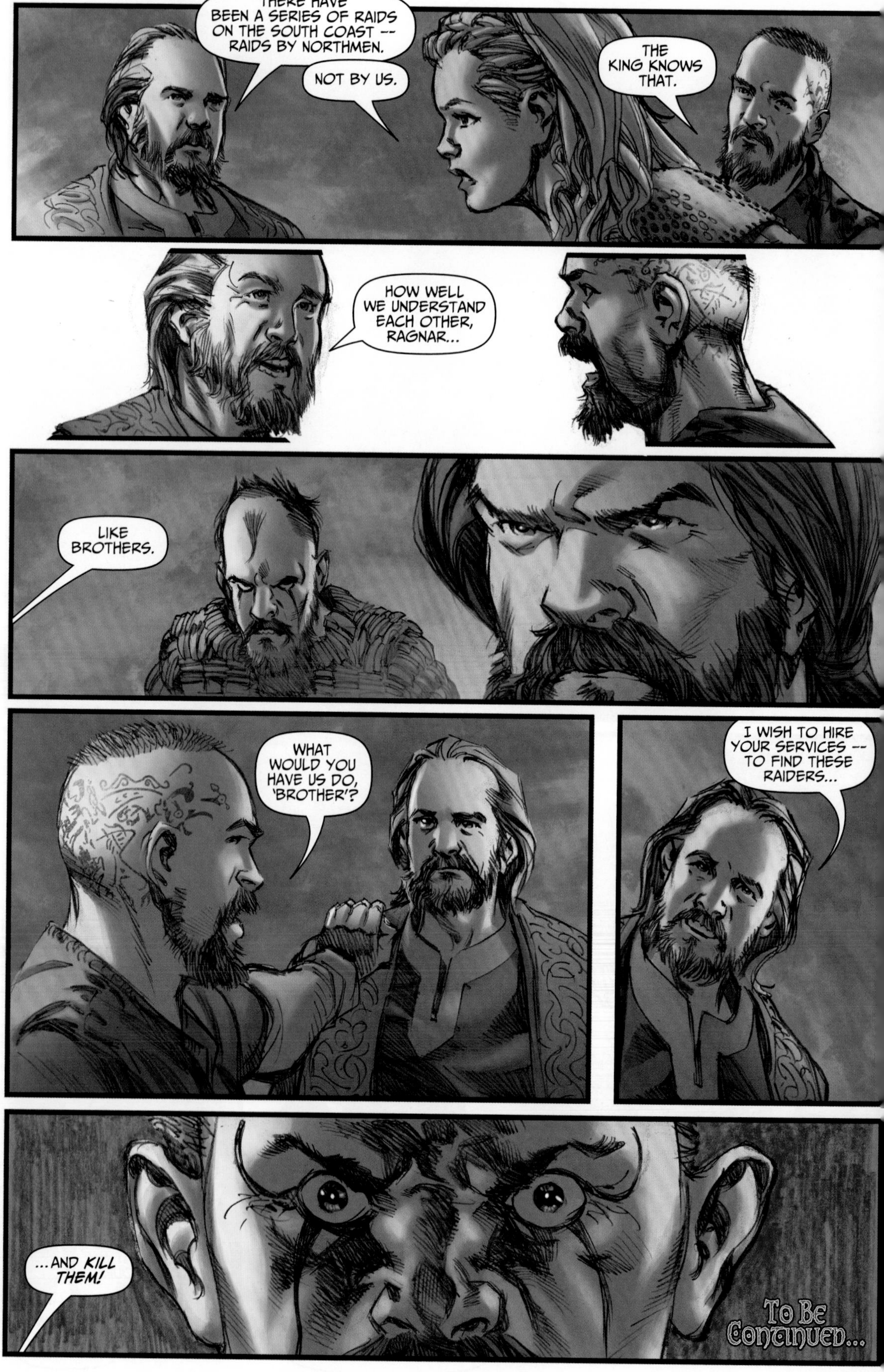
THERE HAVE BEEN A SERIES OF RAIDS ON THE SOUTH COAST -- RAIDS BY NORTHMEN.
NOT BY US.
THE KING KNOWS THAT.
HOW WELL WE UNDERSTAND EACH OTHER, RAGNAR...
LIKE BROTHERS.
WHAT WOULD YOU HAVE US DO, 'BROTHER'?
I WISH TO HIRE YOUR SERVICES -- TO FIND THESE RAIDERS...
...AND KILL THEM!
To Be Continued...

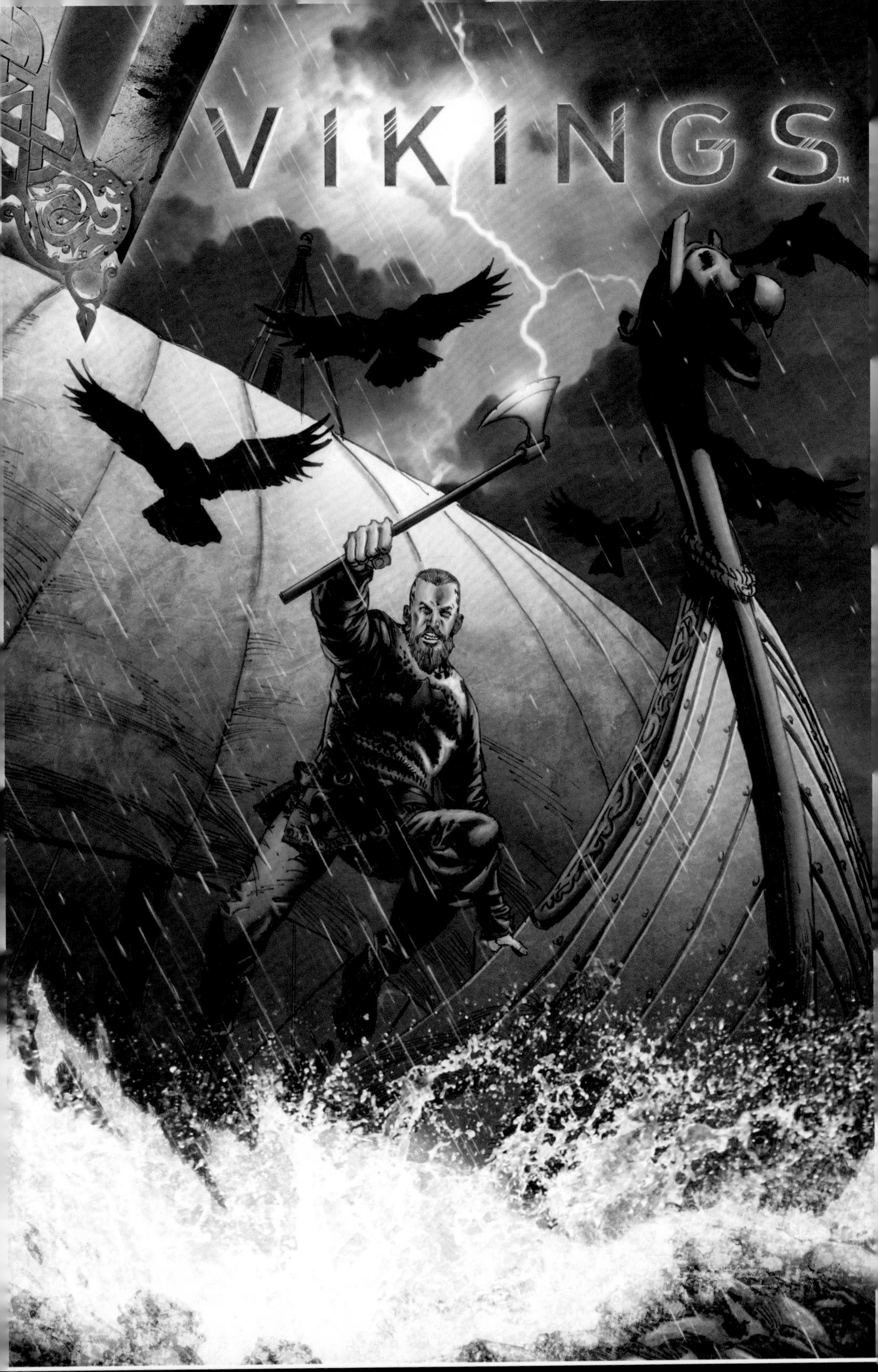
VIKINGS™

#2 COVER A
ARTIST STAZ JOHNSON

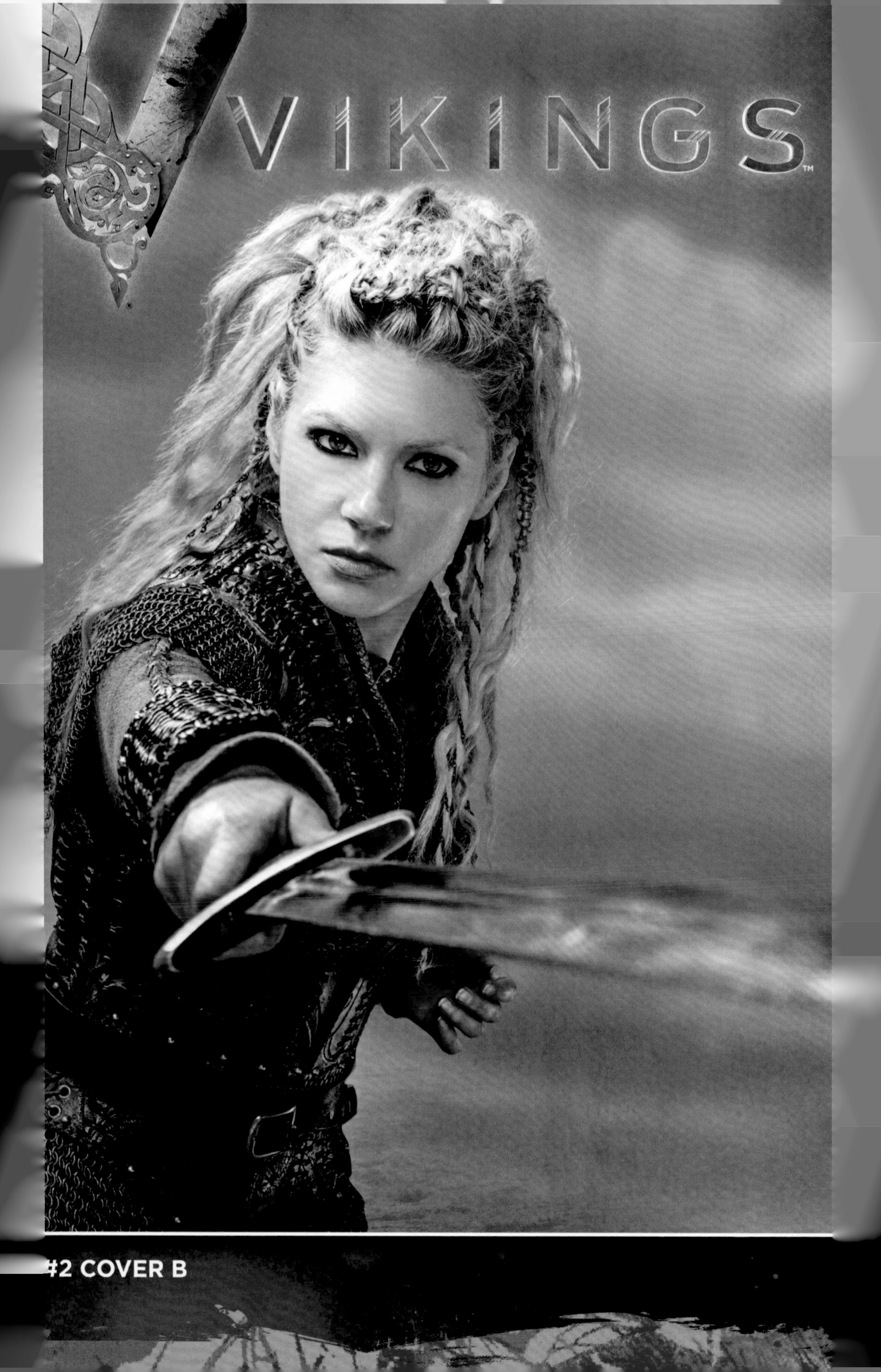
VIKINGS

#2 COVER B

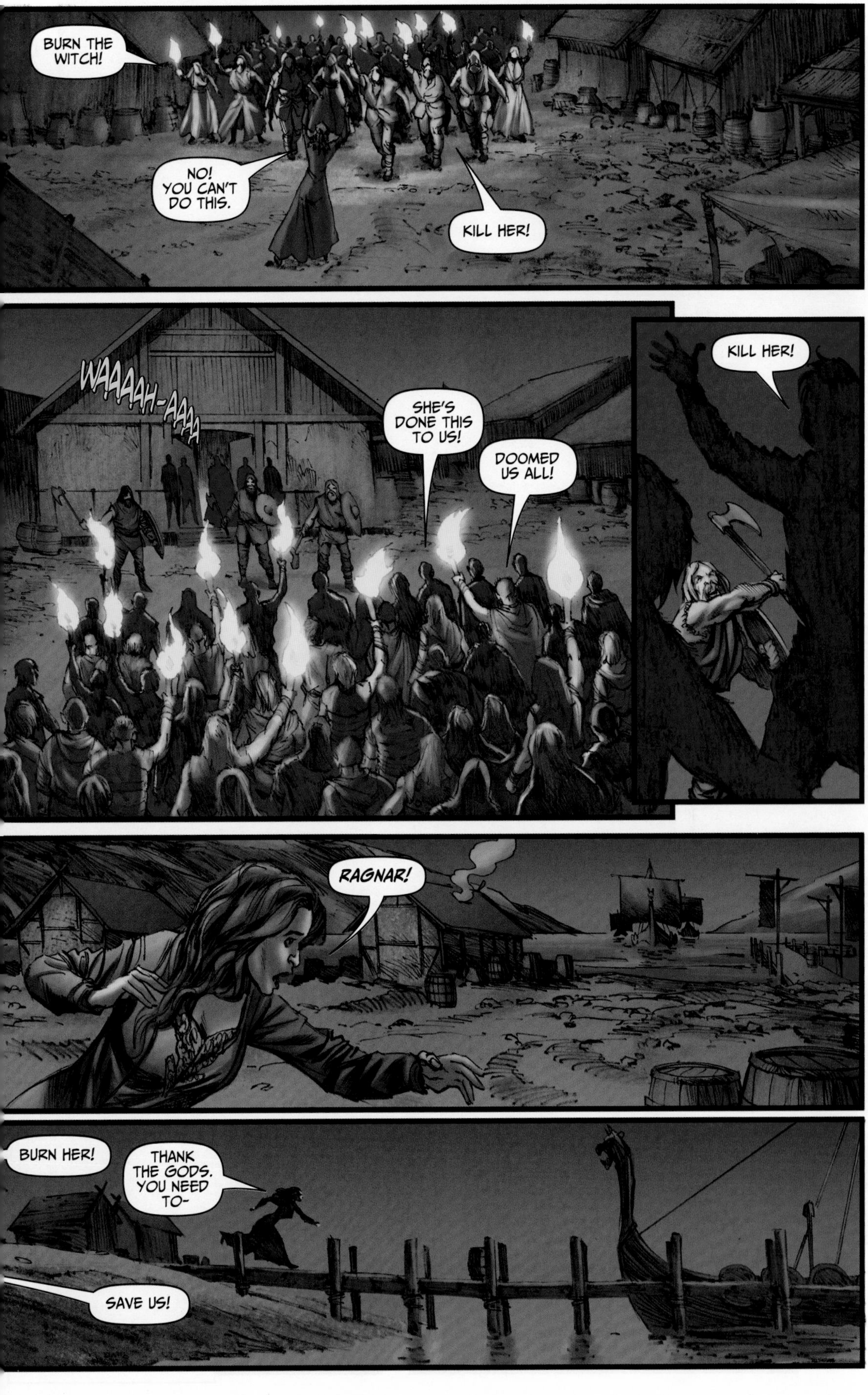
BURN THE WITCH!
NO! YOU CAN'T DO THIS.
KILL HER!
WAAAAH-AAAA
SHE'S DONE THIS TO US!
DOOMED US ALL!
KILL HER!
RAGNAR!
BURN HER!
THANK THE GODS. YOU NEED TO-
SAVE US!

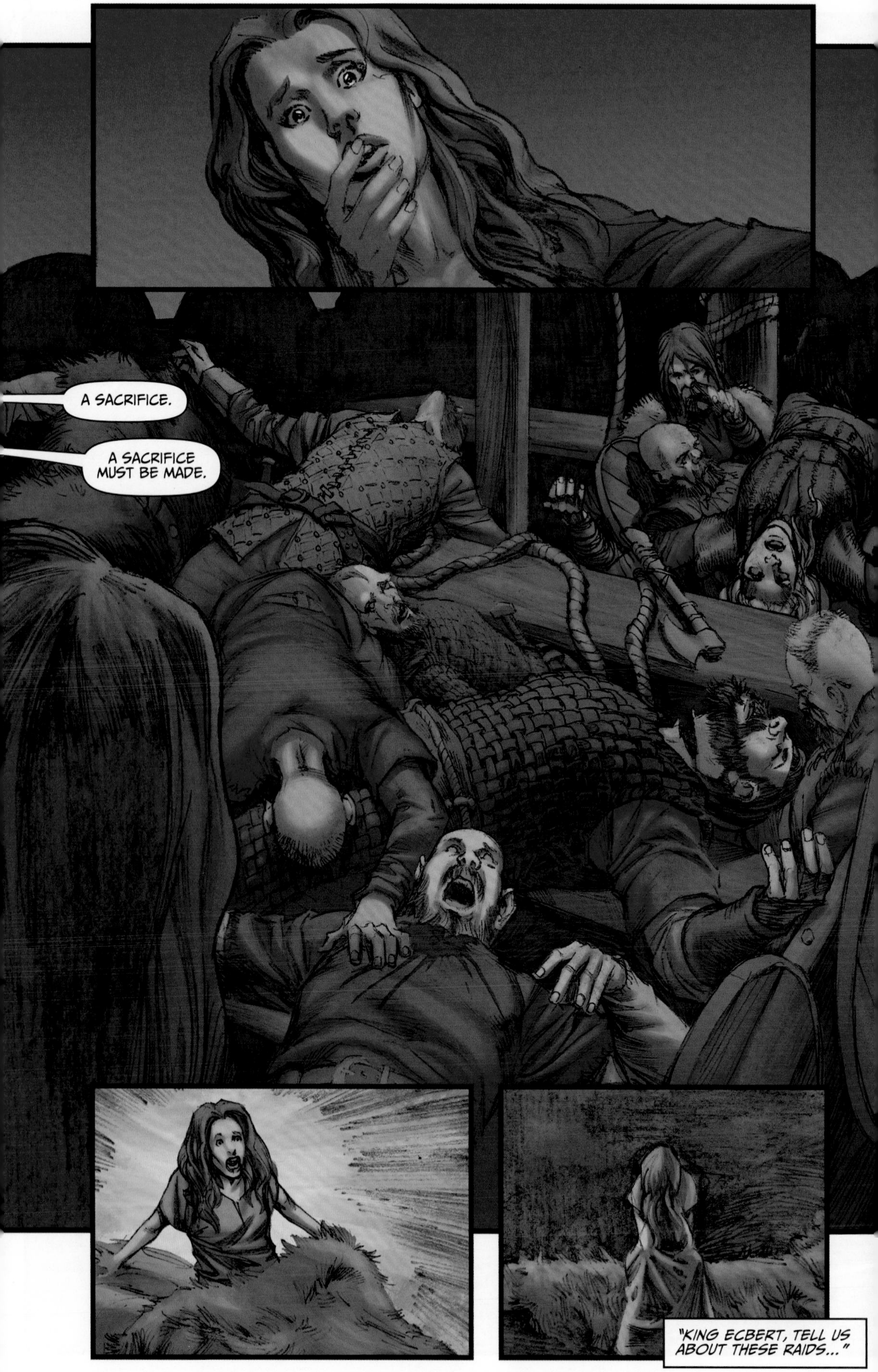
A SACRIFICE.
A SACRIFICE MUST BE MADE.
"KING ECBERT, TELL US ABOUT THESE RAIDS..."

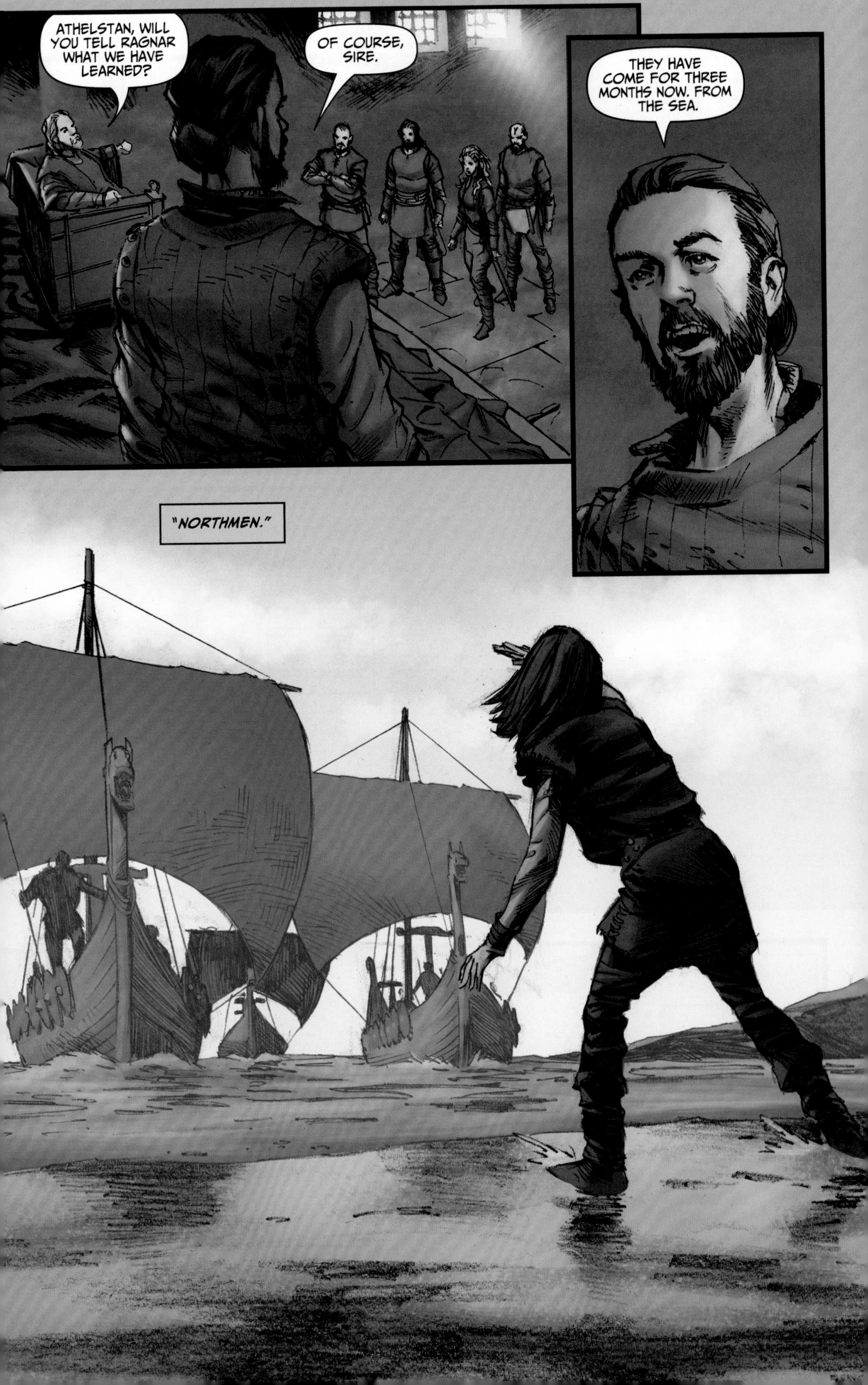
ATHELSTAN, WILL YOU TELL RAGNAR WHAT WE HAVE LEARNED?
OF COURSE, SIRE.
THEY HAVE COME FOR THREE MONTHS NOW. FROM THE SEA.
"NORTHMEN."

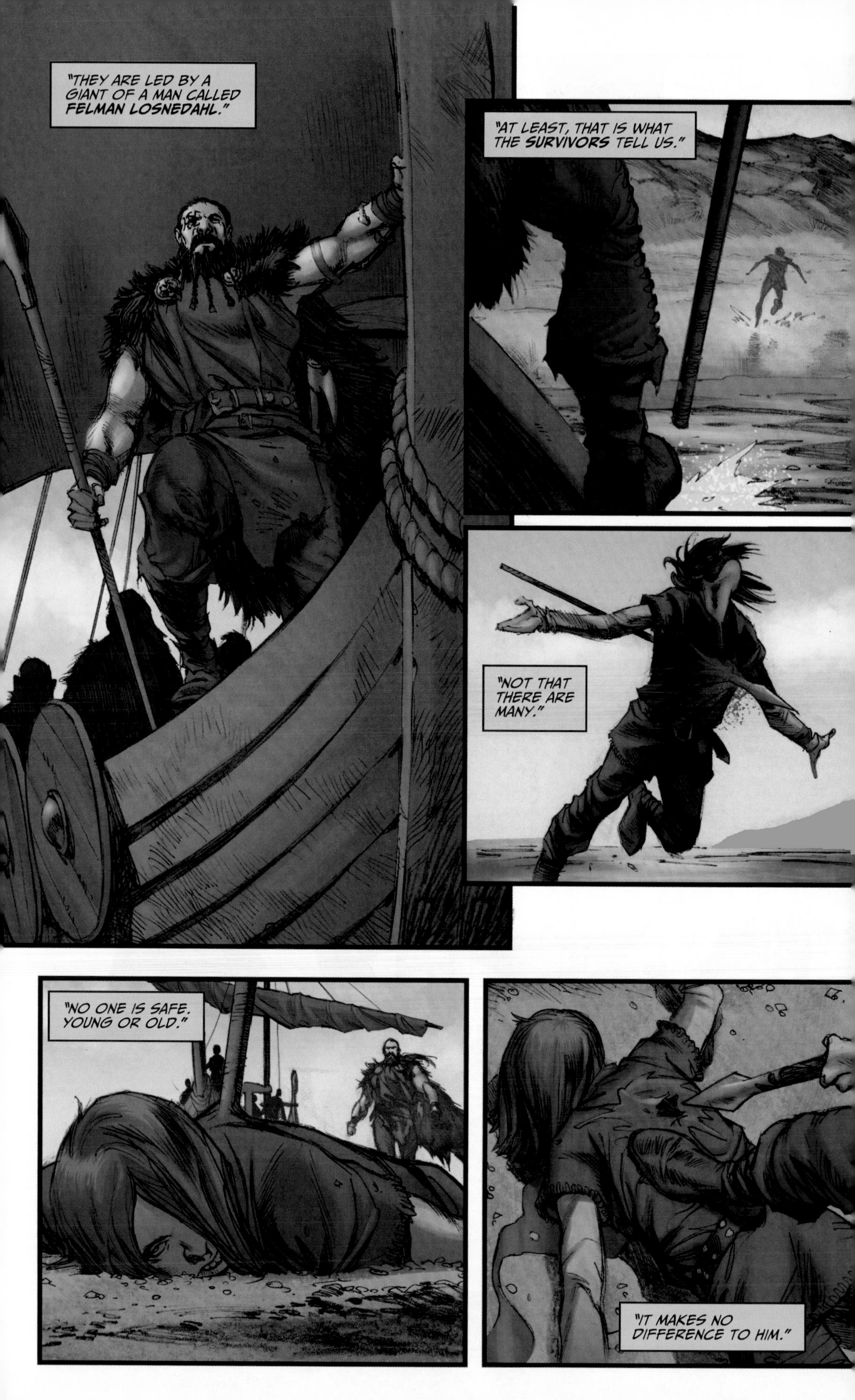
"THEY ARE LED BY A GIANT OF A MAN CALLED FELMAN LOSNEDAHL."
"AT LEAST, THAT IS WHAT THE SURVIVORS TELL US."
"NOT THAT THERE ARE MANY."
"NO ONE IS SAFE. YOUNG OR OLD."
"IT MAKES NO DIFFERENCE TO HIM."

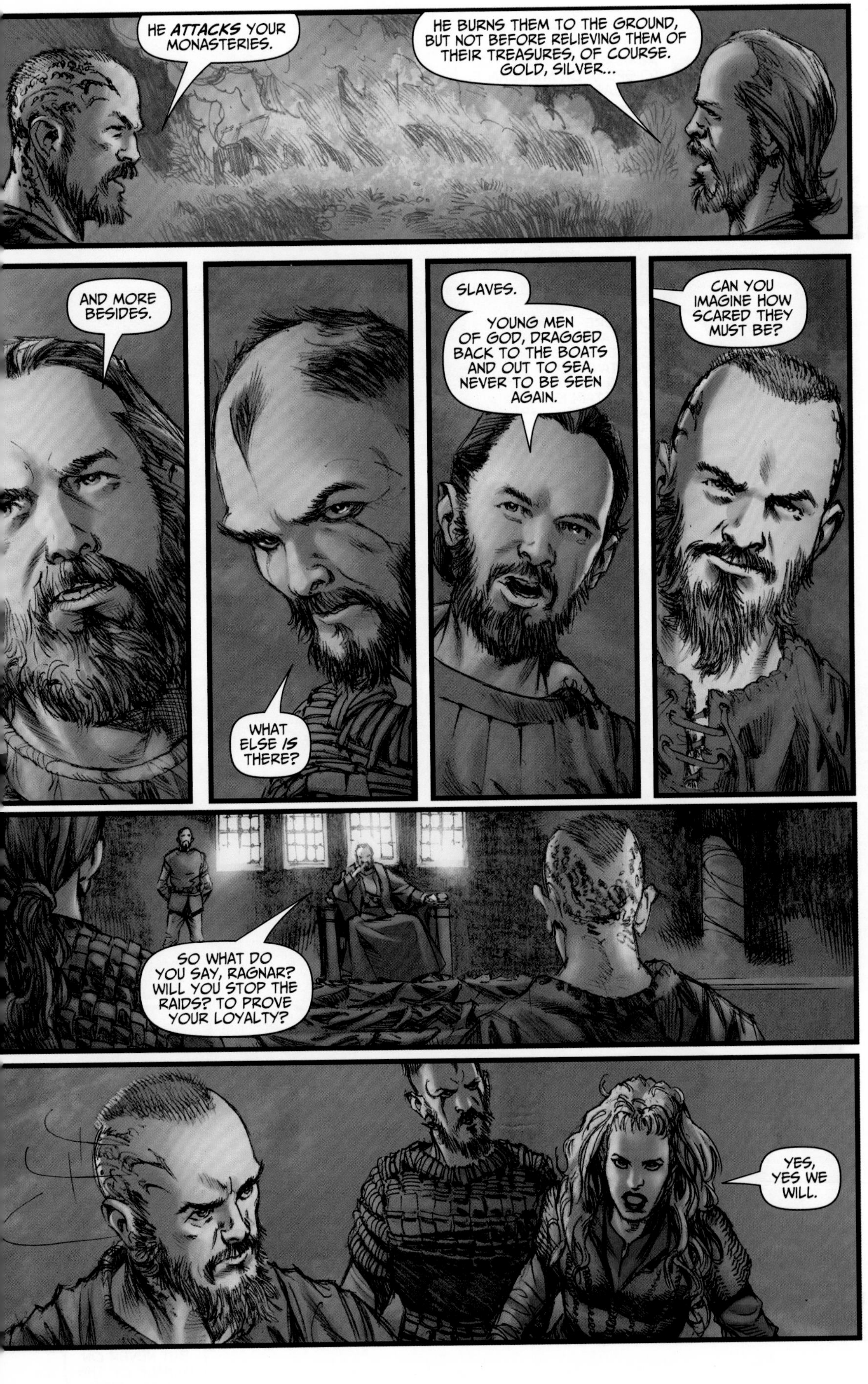
HE *ATTACKS* YOUR MONASTERIES.
HE BURNS THEM TO THE GROUND, BUT NOT BEFORE RELIEVING THEM OF THEIR TREASURES, OF COURSE. GOLD, SILVER...
AND MORE BESIDES.
WHAT ELSE *IS* THERE?
SLAVES.
YOUNG MEN OF GOD, DRAGGED BACK TO THE BOATS AND OUT TO SEA, NEVER TO BE SEEN AGAIN.
CAN YOU IMAGINE HOW SCARED THEY MUST BE?
SO WHAT DO YOU SAY, RAGNAR? WILL YOU STOP THE RAIDS? TO PROVE YOUR LOYALTY?
YES, YES WE WILL.

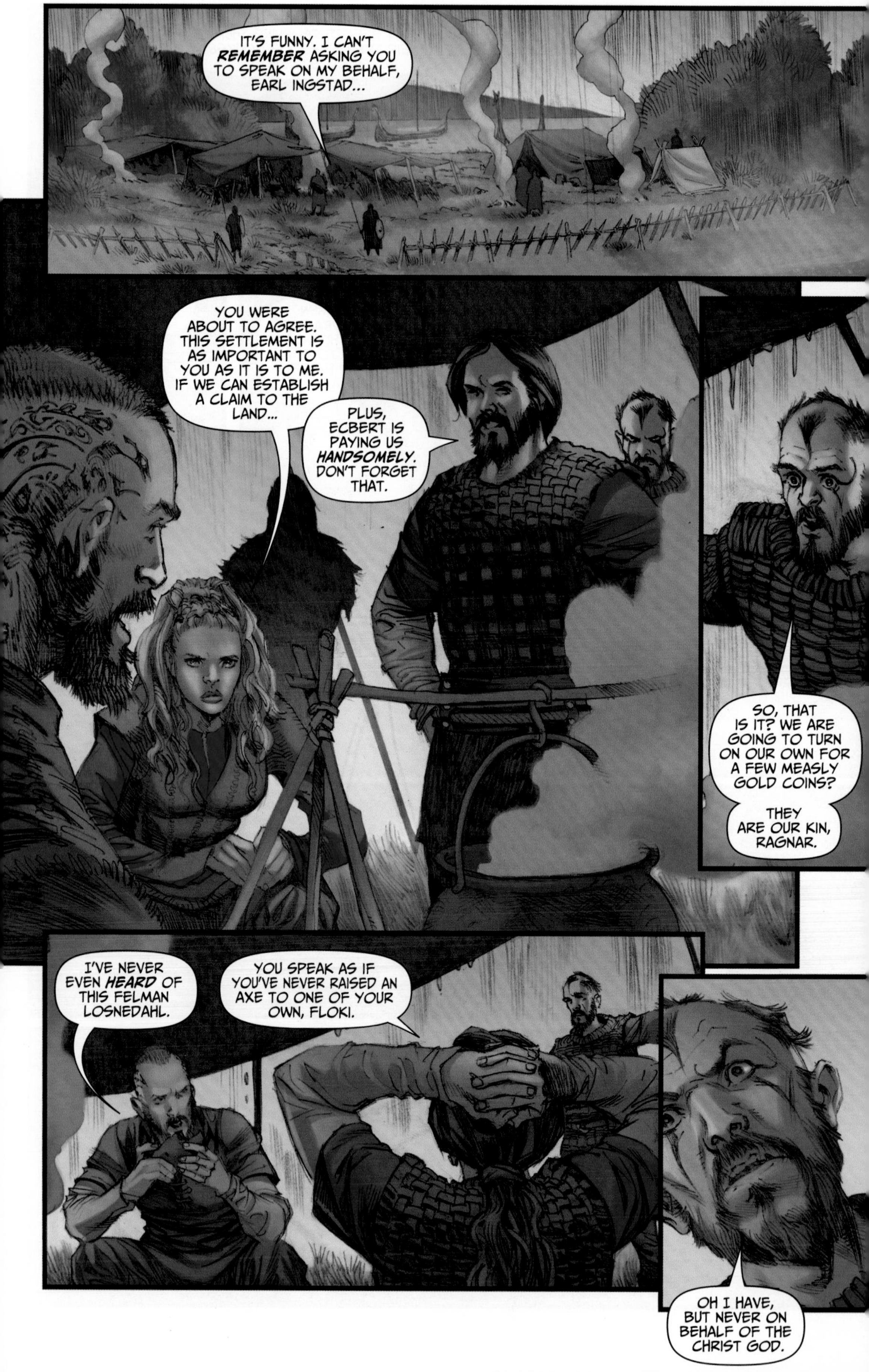
IT'S FUNNY. I CAN'T *REMEMBER* ASKING YOU TO SPEAK ON MY BEHALF, EARL INGSTAD...
YOU WERE ABOUT TO AGREE. THIS SETTLEMENT IS AS IMPORTANT TO YOU AS IT IS TO ME. IF WE CAN ESTABLISH A CLAIM TO THE LAND...
PLUS, ECBERT IS PAYING US *HANDSOMELY*. DON'T FORGET THAT.
SO, THAT IS IT? WE ARE GOING TO TURN ON OUR OWN FOR A FEW MEASLY GOLD COINS?
THEY ARE OUR KIN, RAGNAR.
I'VE NEVER EVEN *HEARD* OF THIS FELMAN LOSNEDAHL.
YOU SPEAK AS IF YOU'VE NEVER RAISED AN AXE TO ONE OF YOUR OWN, FLOKI.
OH I HAVE, BUT NEVER ON BEHALF OF THE CHRIST GOD.

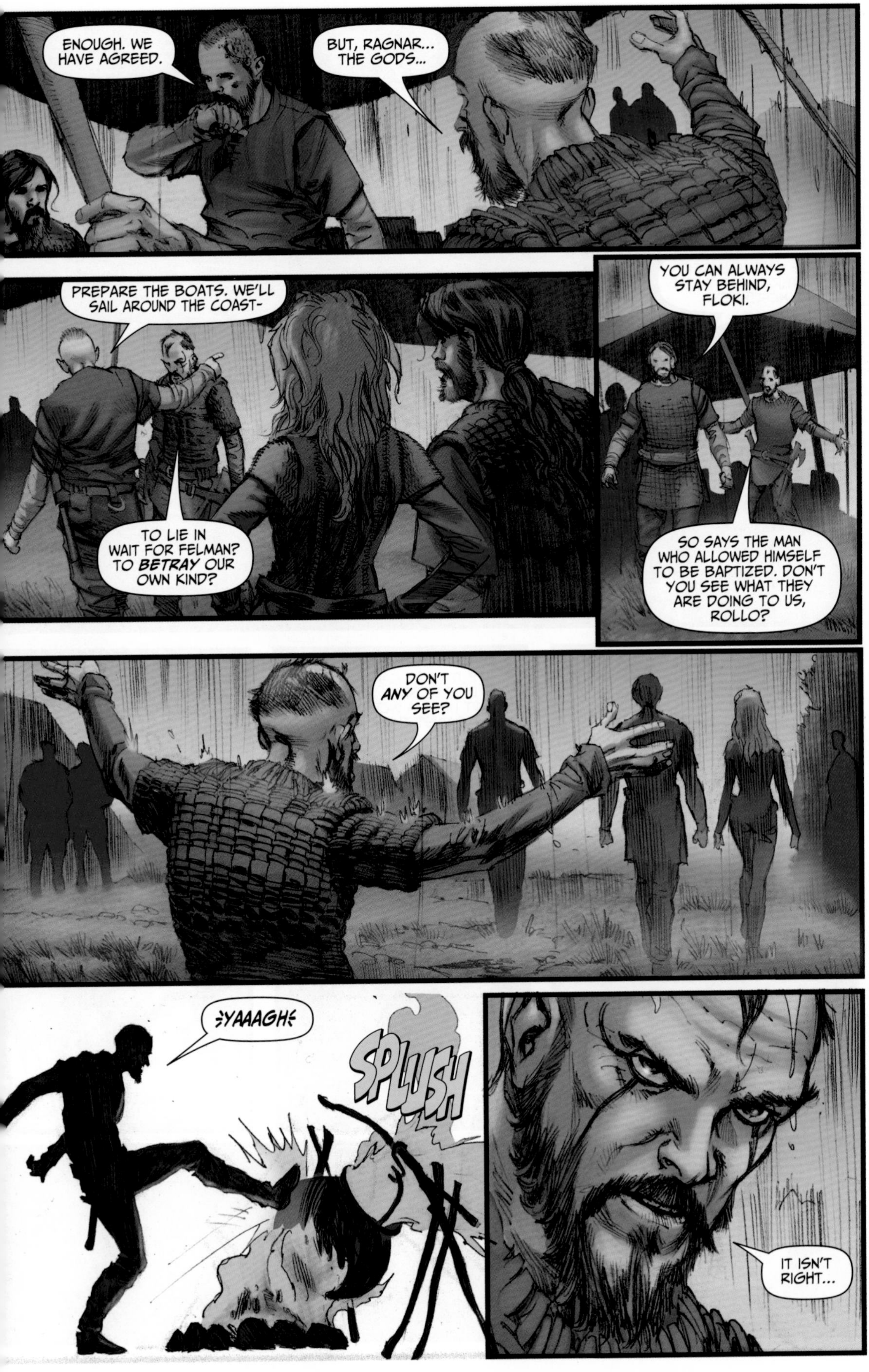
ENOUGH. WE HAVE AGREED.
BUT, RAGNAR... THE GODS...
PREPARE THE BOATS. WE'LL SAIL AROUND THE COAST-
TO LIE IN WAIT FOR FELMAN? TO *BETRAY* OUR OWN KIND?
YOU CAN ALWAYS STAY BEHIND, FLOKI.
SO SAYS THE MAN WHO ALLOWED HIMSELF TO BE BAPTIZED. DON'T YOU SEE WHAT THEY ARE DOING TO US, ROLLO?
DON'T *ANY* OF YOU SEE?
YAAAGH
SPLUSH
IT ISN'T RIGHT...

IT ISN'T RIGHT, I TELL YOU.

THE KING IS UNDER THE THRALL OF THESE NORTHMEN.

IT'S THAT PAGAN WITCH, LAGERTHA! YOU'VE SEEN THE WAY HE LOOKS AT HER.

SHE'S BEWITCHED HIM!

BUT WHAT CAN WE DO? ECBERT WILL NOT HEAR A WORD AGAINST THEM.

WHAT CAN WE DO? WE CAN *ACT!* THE ENTIRE KINGDOM IS THREATENED BY THEIR PRESENCE.

SLAM

WE WILL DELIVER KING ECBERT FROM THESE PAGANS AND THEIR BALEFUL INFLUENCE, ONCE AND FOR ALL.

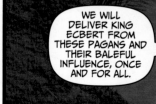

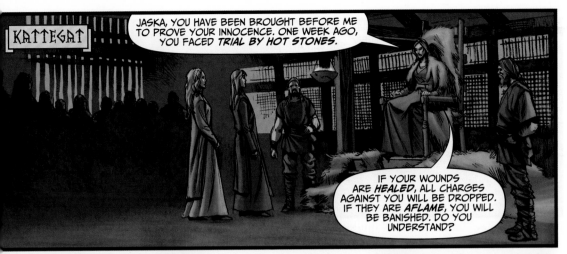

KATTEGAT

JASKA, YOU HAVE BEEN BROUGHT BEFORE ME TO PROVE YOUR INNOCENCE. ONE WEEK AGO, YOU FACED *TRIAL BY HOT STONES.*

IF YOUR WOUNDS ARE *HEALED,* ALL CHARGES AGAINST YOU WILL BE DROPPED. IF THEY ARE *AFLAME,* YOU WILL BE BANISHED. DO YOU UNDERSTAND?

I DO, MY LADY.

THEN LET US SEE. REMOVE THE BANDAGES.

THEY ARE HEALED.

THEN WE WILL *HONOR* THE JUDGMENT OF THE GODS. YOU ARE FREE TO GO, JASKA.

MY QUEEN, SHE IS *GUILTY!* SHE STOLE FOOD FROM HER NEIGHBORS. SHE MUST BE PUNISHED!

I HAVE MADE MY DECISION. THE ASSEMBLY IS AT AN END.

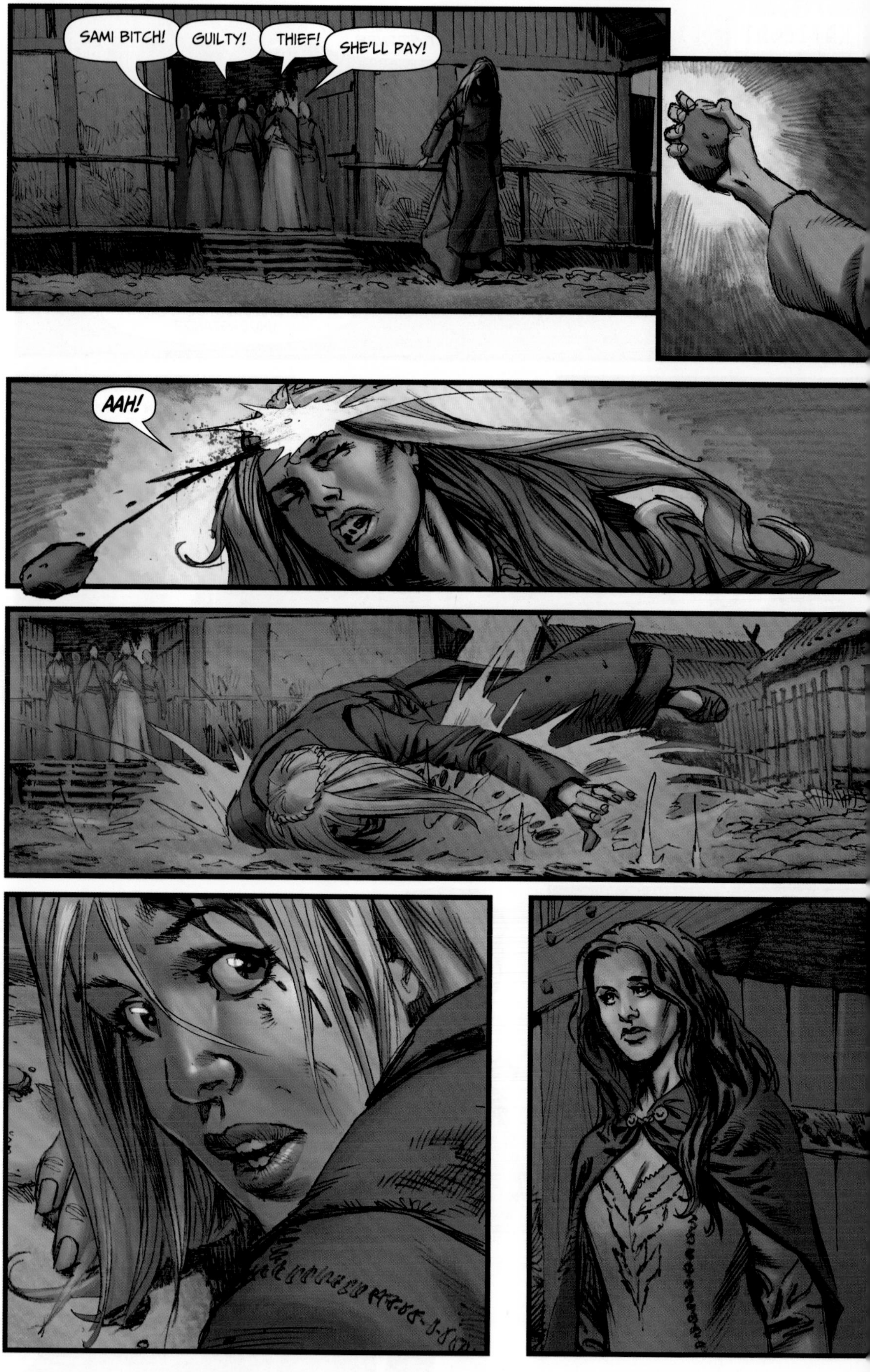
SAMI BITCH!
GUILTY!
THIEF!
SHE'LL PAY!
AAH!

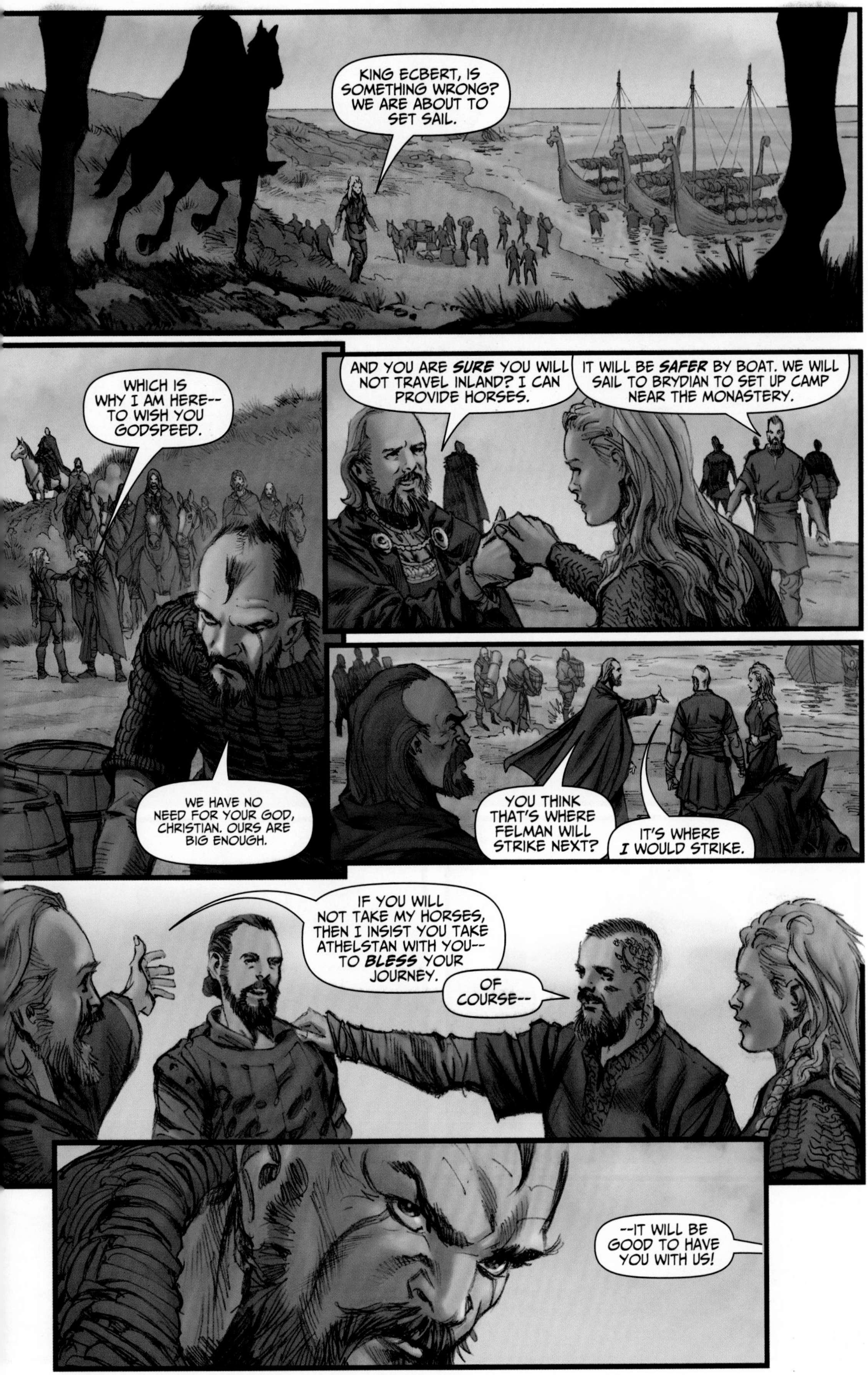

KING ECBERT, IS SOMETHING WRONG? WE ARE ABOUT TO SET SAIL.
WHICH IS WHY I AM HERE-- TO WISH YOU GODSPEED.
WE HAVE NO NEED FOR YOUR GOD, CHRISTIAN. OURS ARE BIG ENOUGH.
AND YOU ARE **SURE** YOU WILL NOT TRAVEL INLAND? I CAN PROVIDE HORSES.
IT WILL BE **SAFER** BY BOAT. WE WILL SAIL TO BRYDIAN TO SET UP CAMP NEAR THE MONASTERY.
YOU THINK THAT'S WHERE FELMAN WILL STRIKE NEXT?
IT'S WHERE *I* WOULD STRIKE.
IF YOU WILL NOT TAKE MY HORSES, THEN I INSIST YOU TAKE ATHELSTAN WITH YOU-- TO **BLESS** YOUR JOURNEY.
OF COURSE--
--IT WILL BE GOOD TO HAVE YOU WITH US!

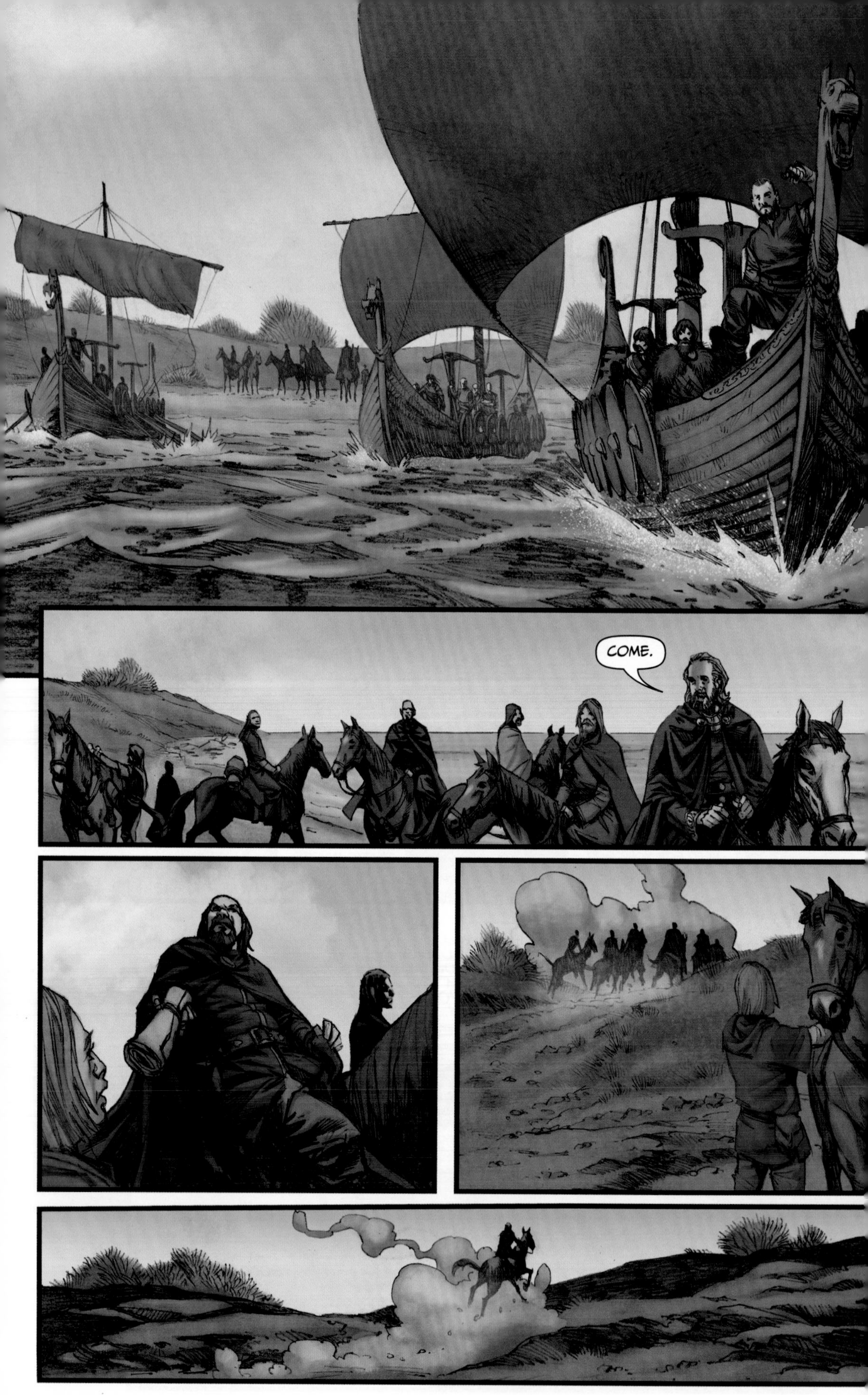
COME.

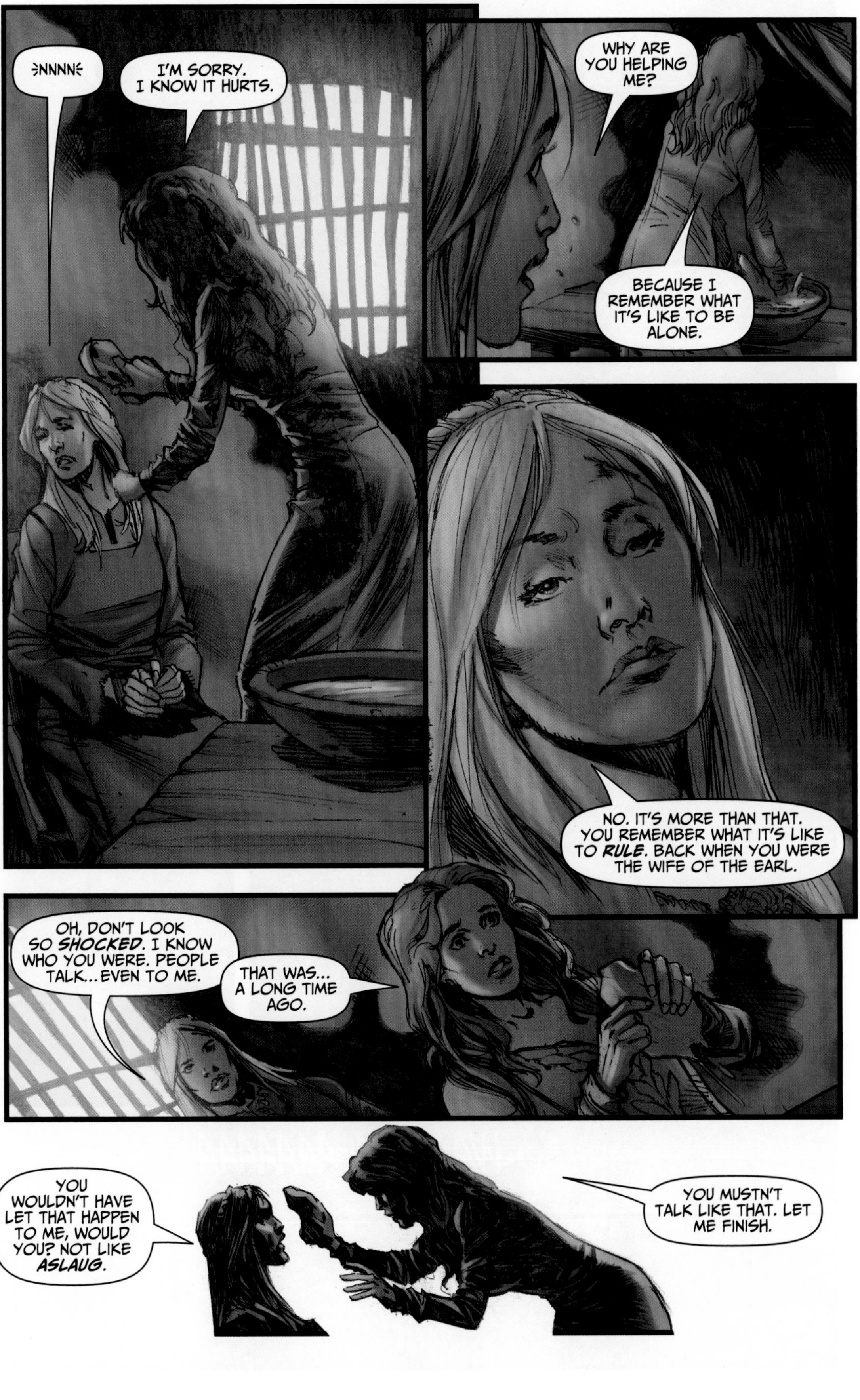

NNNN
I'M SORRY. I KNOW IT HURTS.
WHY ARE YOU HELPING ME?
BECAUSE I REMEMBER WHAT IT'S LIKE TO BE ALONE.
NO. IT'S MORE THAN THAT. YOU REMEMBER WHAT IT'S LIKE TO RULE. BACK WHEN YOU WERE THE WIFE OF THE EARL.
OH, DON'T LOOK SO SHOCKED. I KNOW WHO YOU WERE. PEOPLE TALK... EVEN TO ME.
THAT WAS... A LONG TIME AGO.
YOU WOULDN'T HAVE LET THAT HAPPEN TO ME, WOULD YOU? NOT LIKE ASLAUG.
YOU MUSTN'T TALK LIKE THAT. LET ME FINISH.

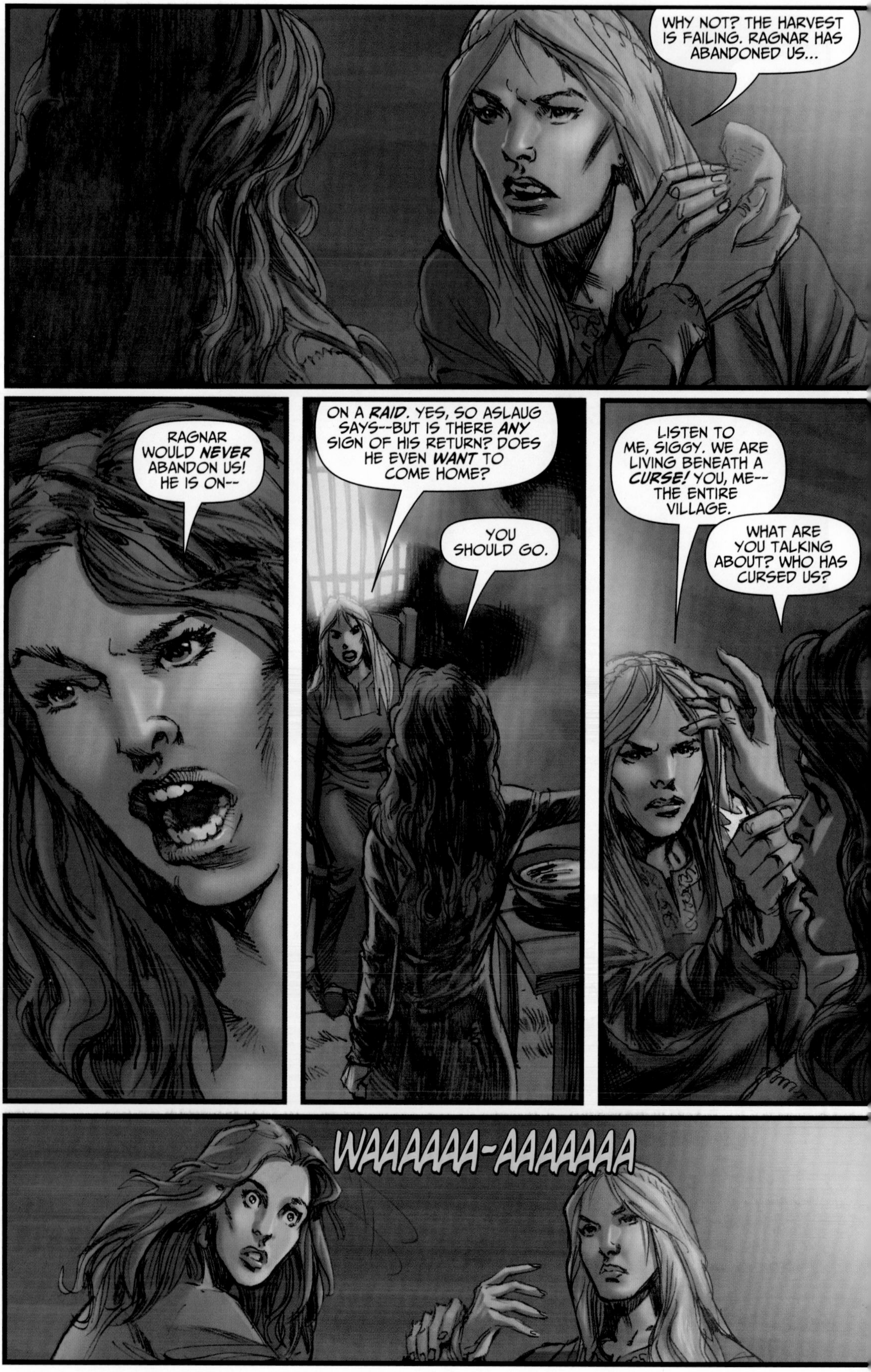
WHY NOT? THE HARVEST IS FAILING. RAGNAR HAS ABANDONED US...
RAGNAR WOULD NEVER ABANDON US! HE IS ON--
ON A RAID. YES, SO ASLAUG SAYS--BUT IS THERE ANY SIGN OF HIS RETURN? DOES HE EVEN WANT TO COME HOME?
YOU SHOULD GO.
LISTEN TO ME, SIGGY. WE ARE LIVING BENEATH A CURSE! YOU, ME--THE ENTIRE VILLAGE.
WHAT ARE YOU TALKING ABOUT? WHO HAS CURSED US?
WAAAAAA-AAAAAAA

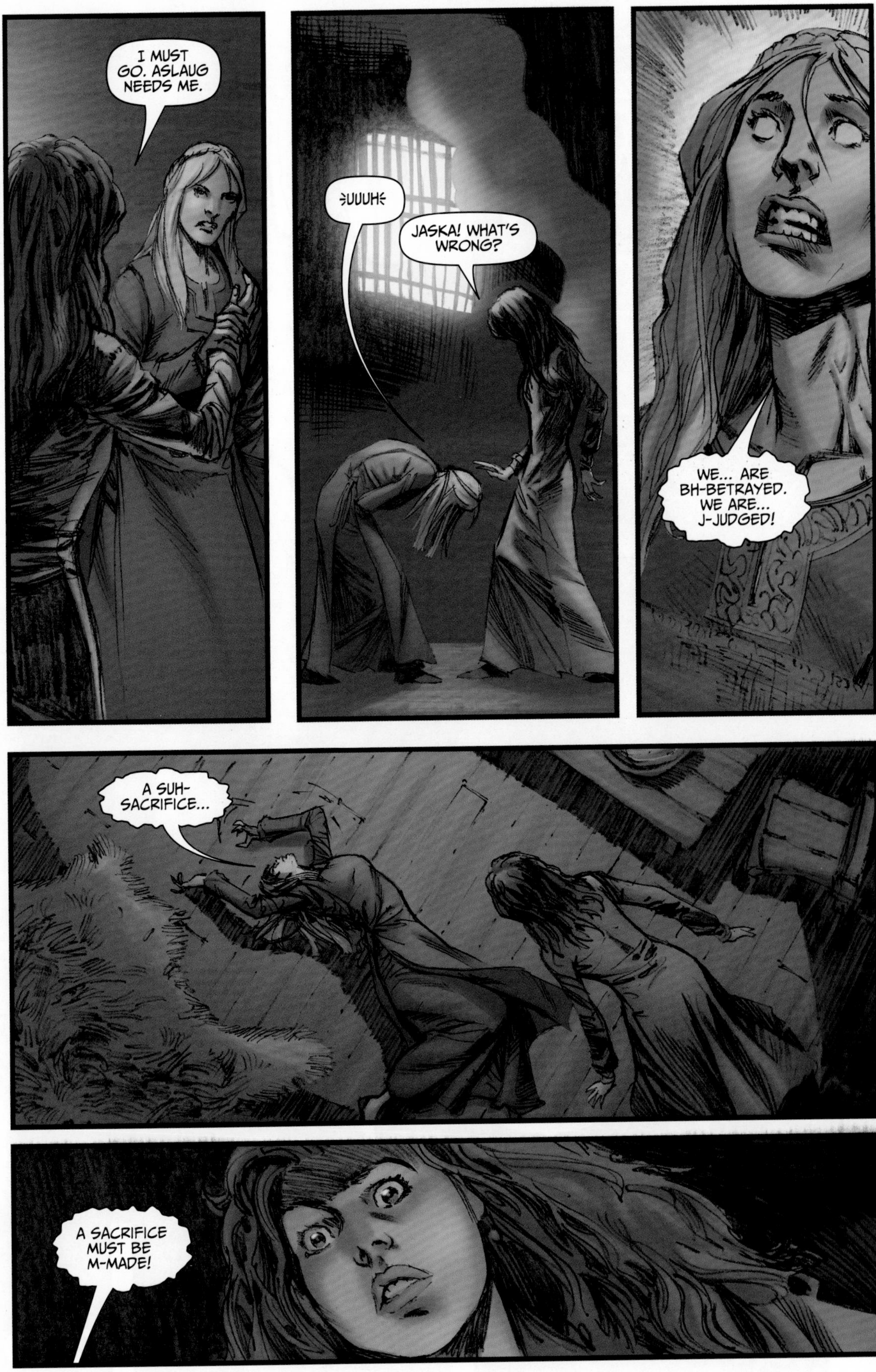
I MUST GO. ASLAUG NEEDS ME.
UUUH
JASKA! WHAT'S WRONG?
WE... ARE BH-BETRAYED. WE ARE... J-JUDGED!
A SUH-SACRIFICE...
A SACRIFICE MUST BE M-MADE!

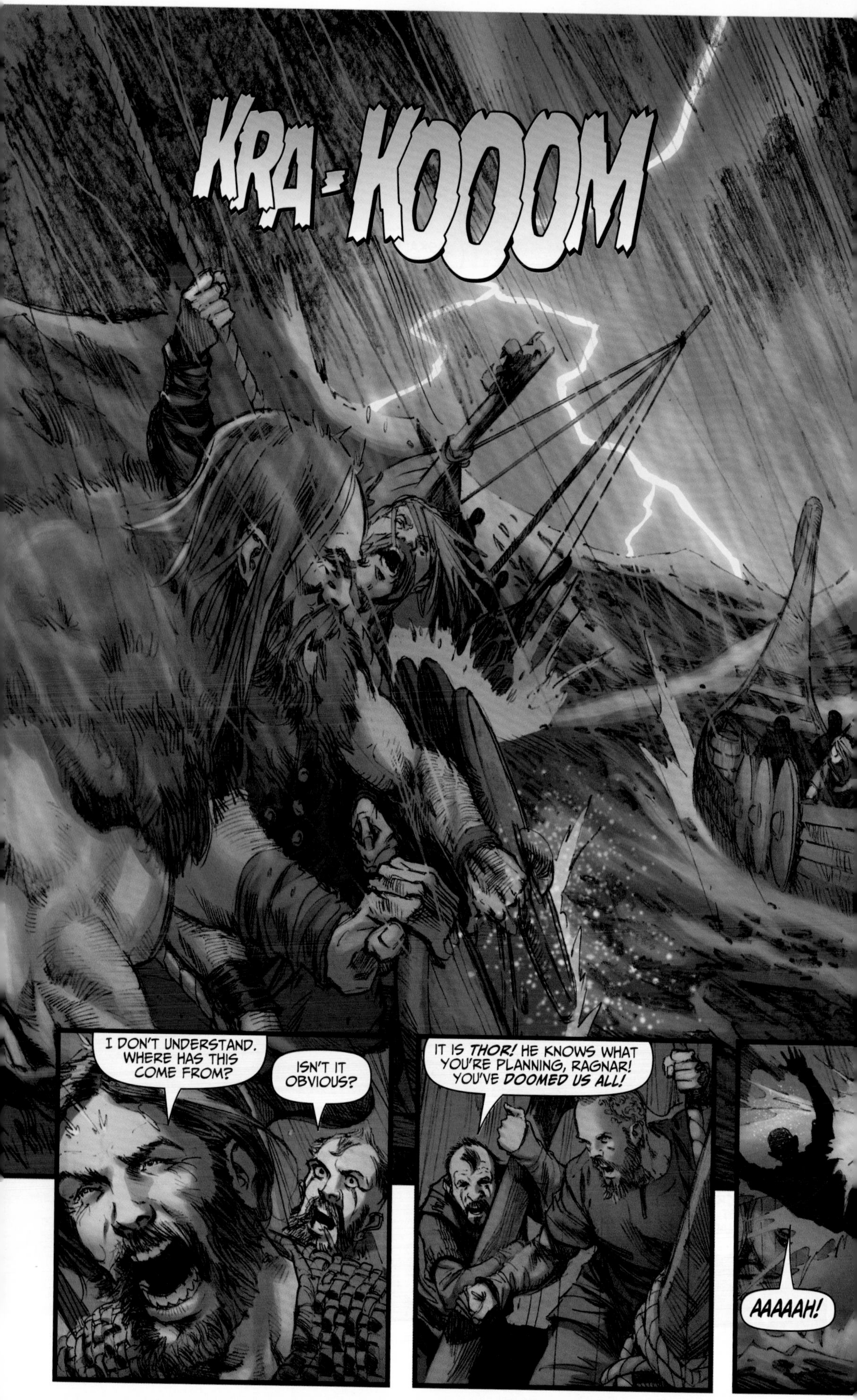
KRA-KOOOM
I DON'T UNDERSTAND. WHERE HAS THIS COME FROM?
ISN'T IT OBVIOUS?
IT IS THOR! HE KNOWS WHAT YOU'RE PLANNING, RAGNAR! YOU'VE DOOMED US ALL!
AAAAAH!

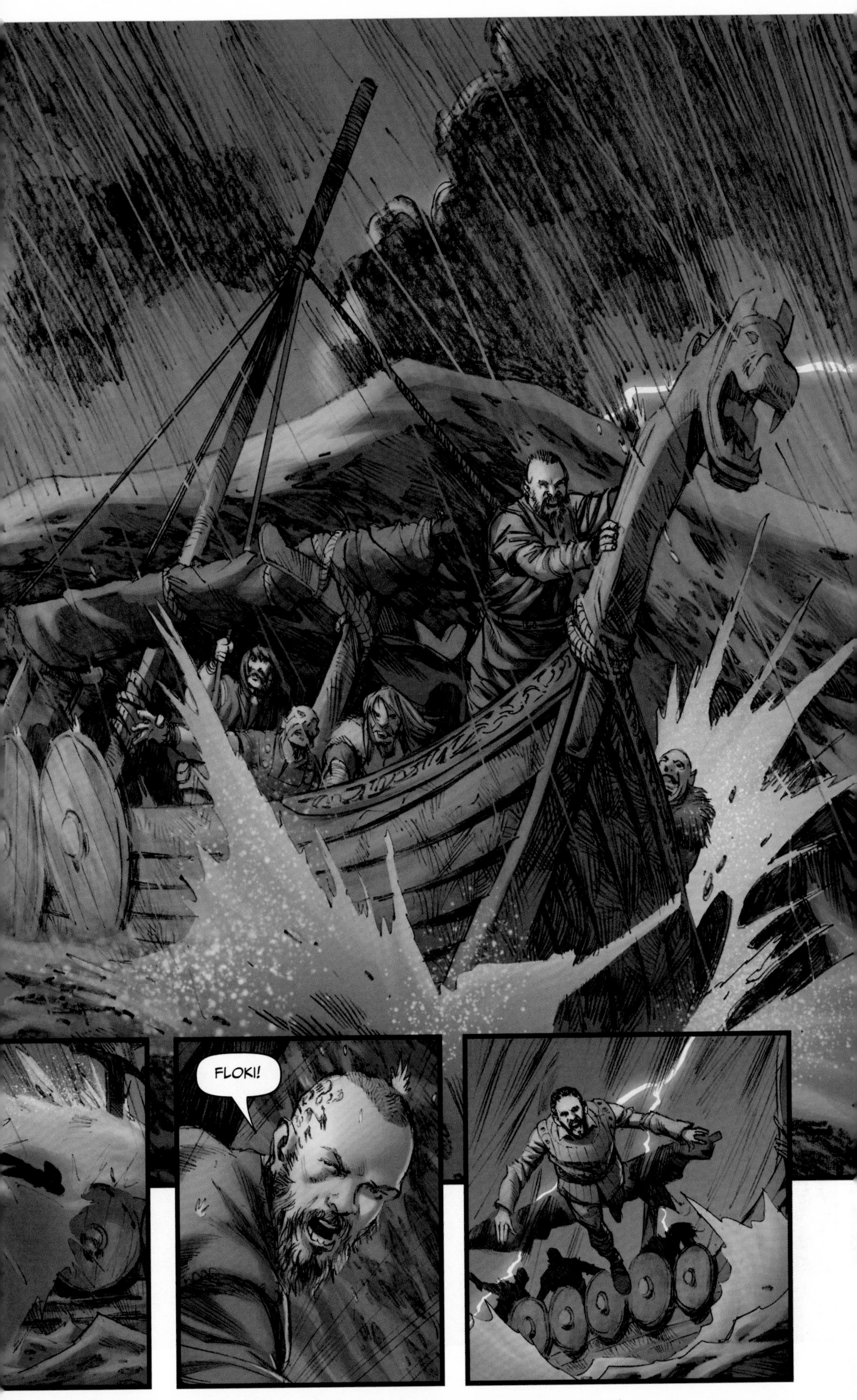
FLOKI!

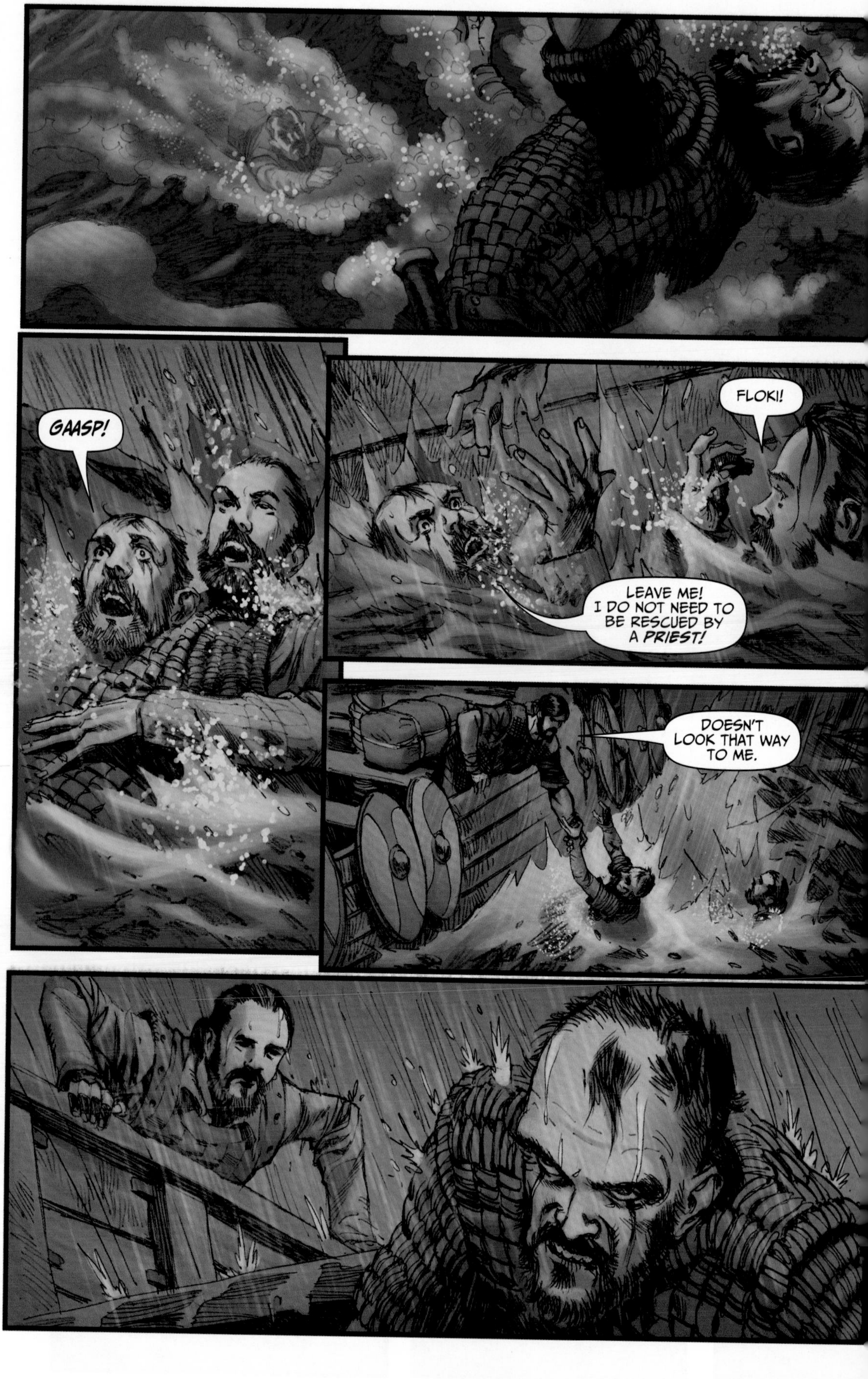
GAASP!
FLOKI!
LEAVE ME! I DO NOT NEED TO BE RESCUED BY A PRIEST!
DOESN'T LOOK THAT WAY TO ME.

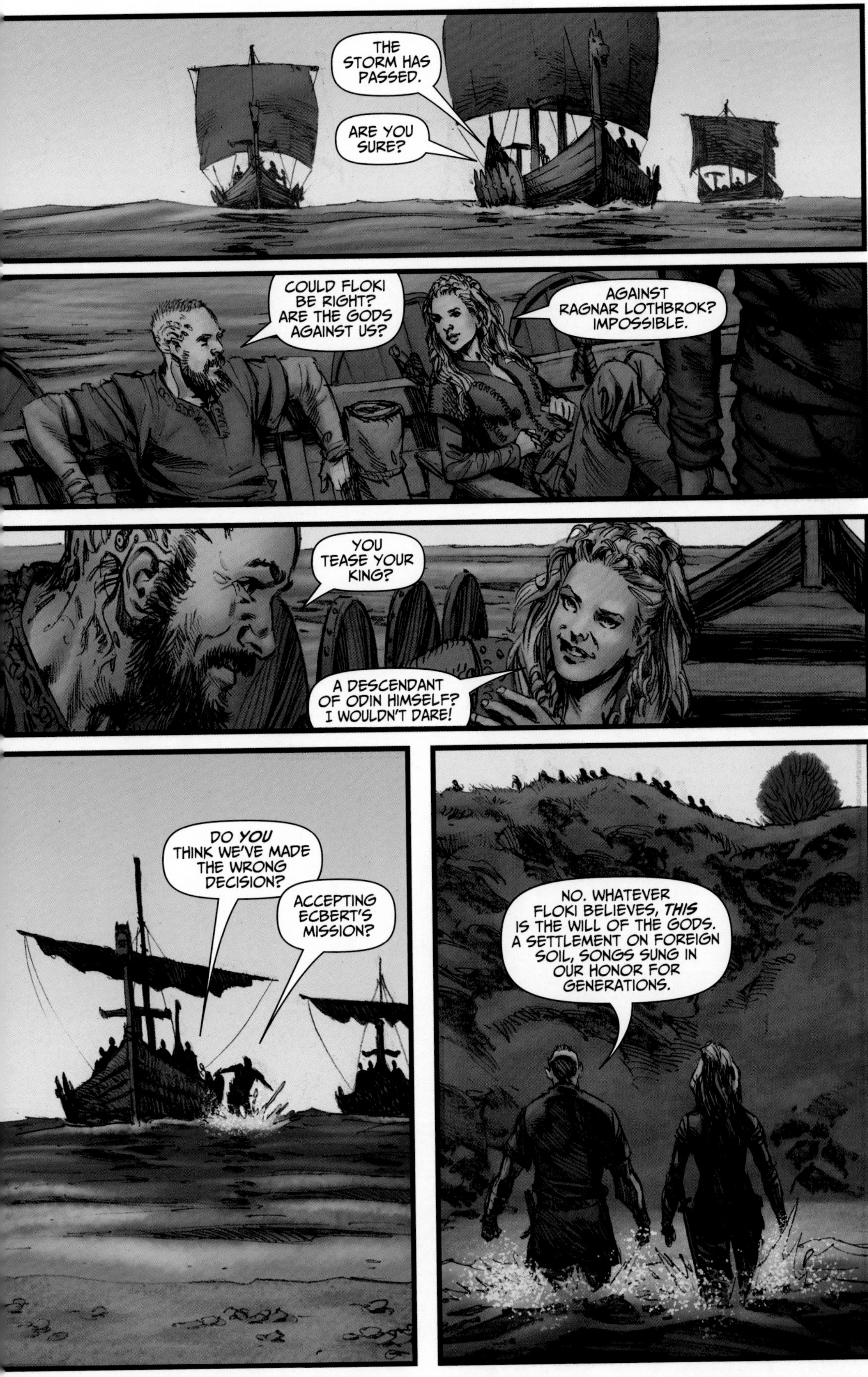
THE STORM HAS PASSED.
ARE YOU SURE?
COULD FLOKI BE RIGHT? ARE THE GODS AGAINST US?
AGAINST RAGNAR LOTHBROK? IMPOSSIBLE.
YOU TEASE YOUR KING?
A DESCENDANT OF ODIN HIMSELF? I WOULDN'T DARE!
DO *YOU* THINK WE'VE MADE THE WRONG DECISION?
ACCEPTING ECBERT'S MISSION?
NO. WHATEVER FLOKI BELIEVES, *THIS* IS THE WILL OF THE GODS. A SETTLEMENT ON FOREIGN SOIL, SONGS SUNG IN OUR HONOR FOR GENERATIONS.

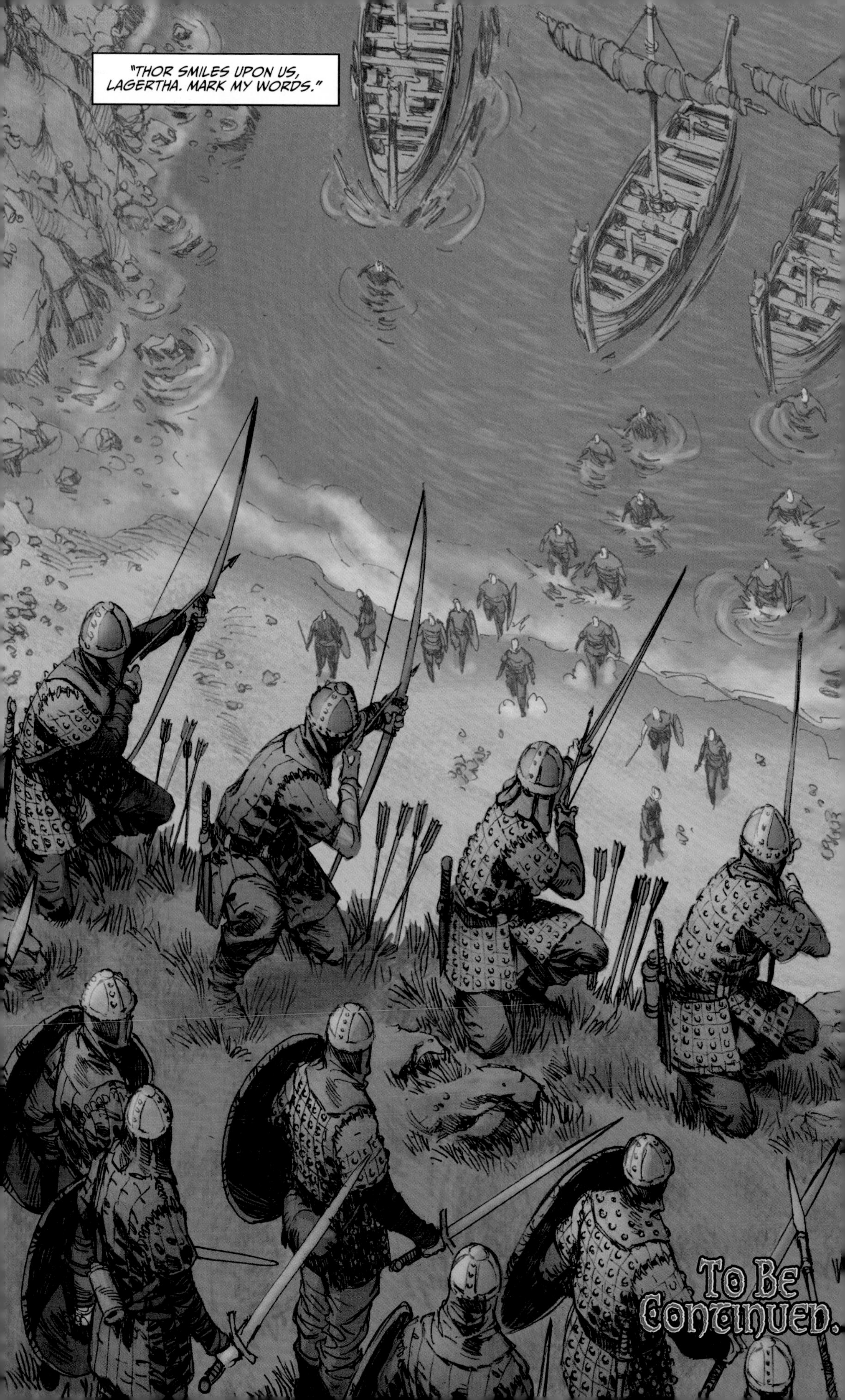
"THOR SMILES UPON US, LAGERTHA. MARK MY WORDS."
To Be Continued.

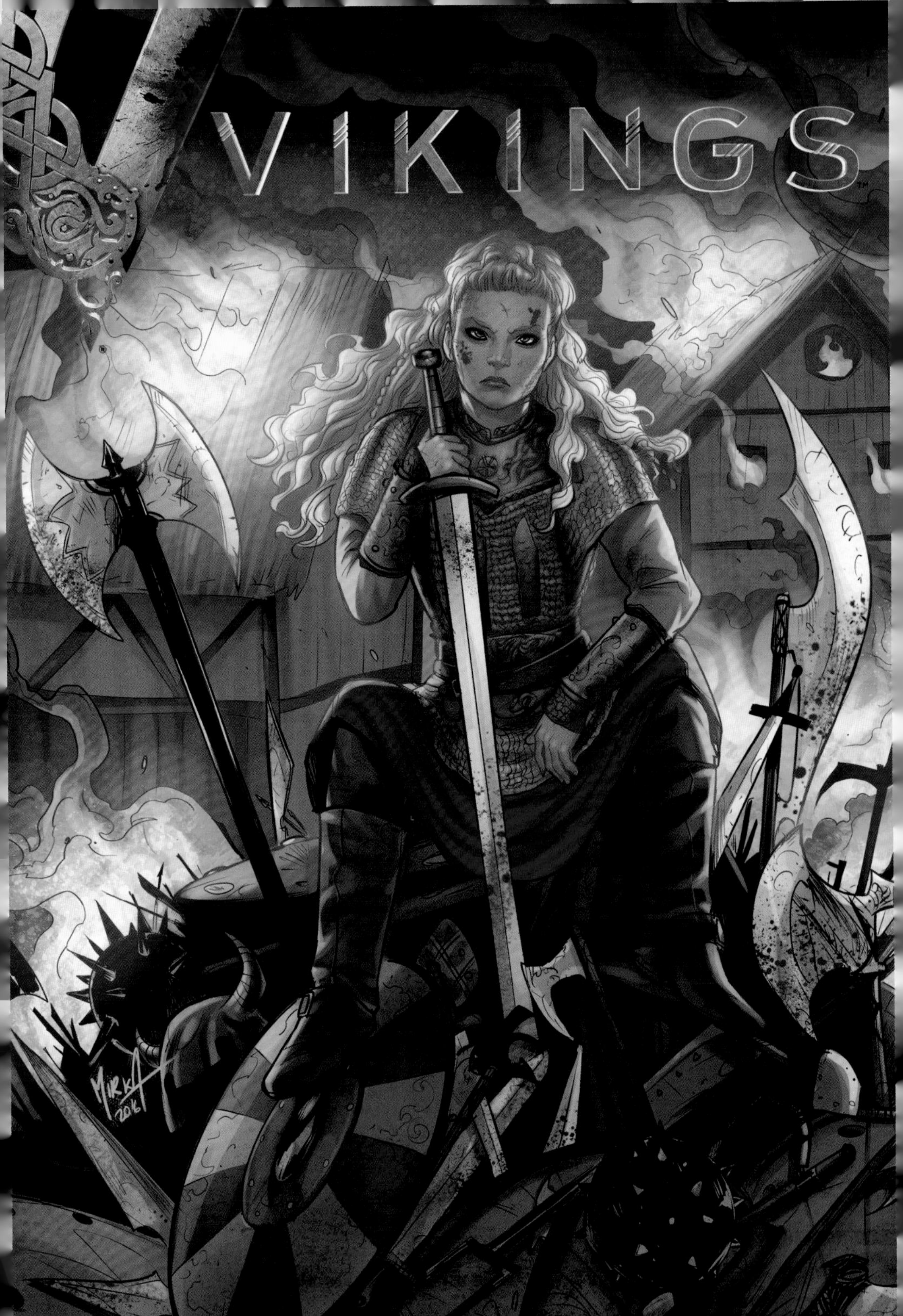
VIKINGS
MIRKA
2016

#3 COVER A
ARTIST MIRKA ANDOLFO

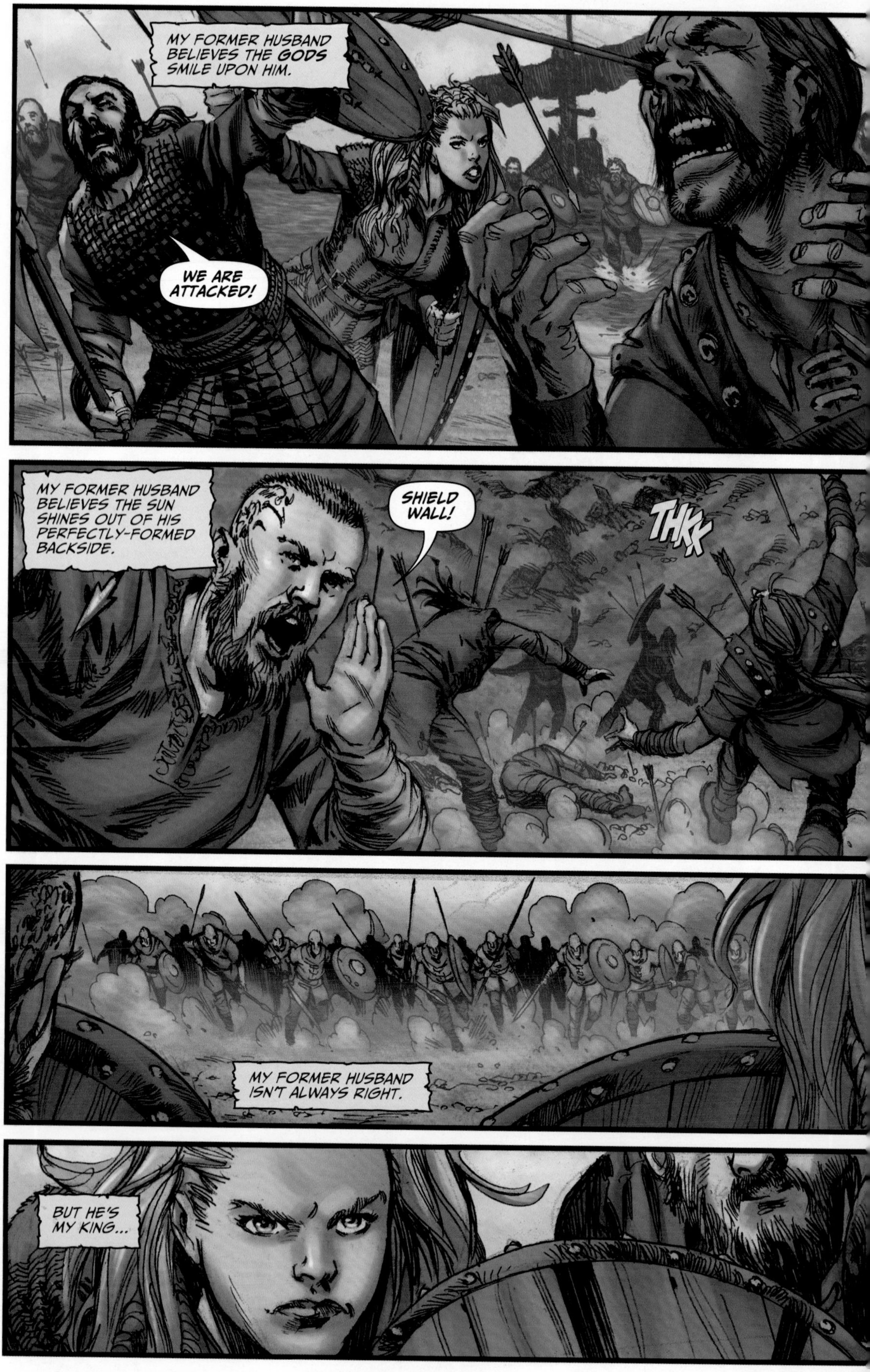
MY FORMER HUSBAND BELIEVES THE GODS SMILE UPON HIM.
WE ARE ATTACKED!
MY FORMER HUSBAND BELIEVES THE SUN SHINES OUT OF HIS PERFECTLY-FORMED BACKSIDE.
SHIELD WALL!
THKK
MY FORMER HUSBAND ISN'T ALWAYS RIGHT.
BUT HE'S MY KING...

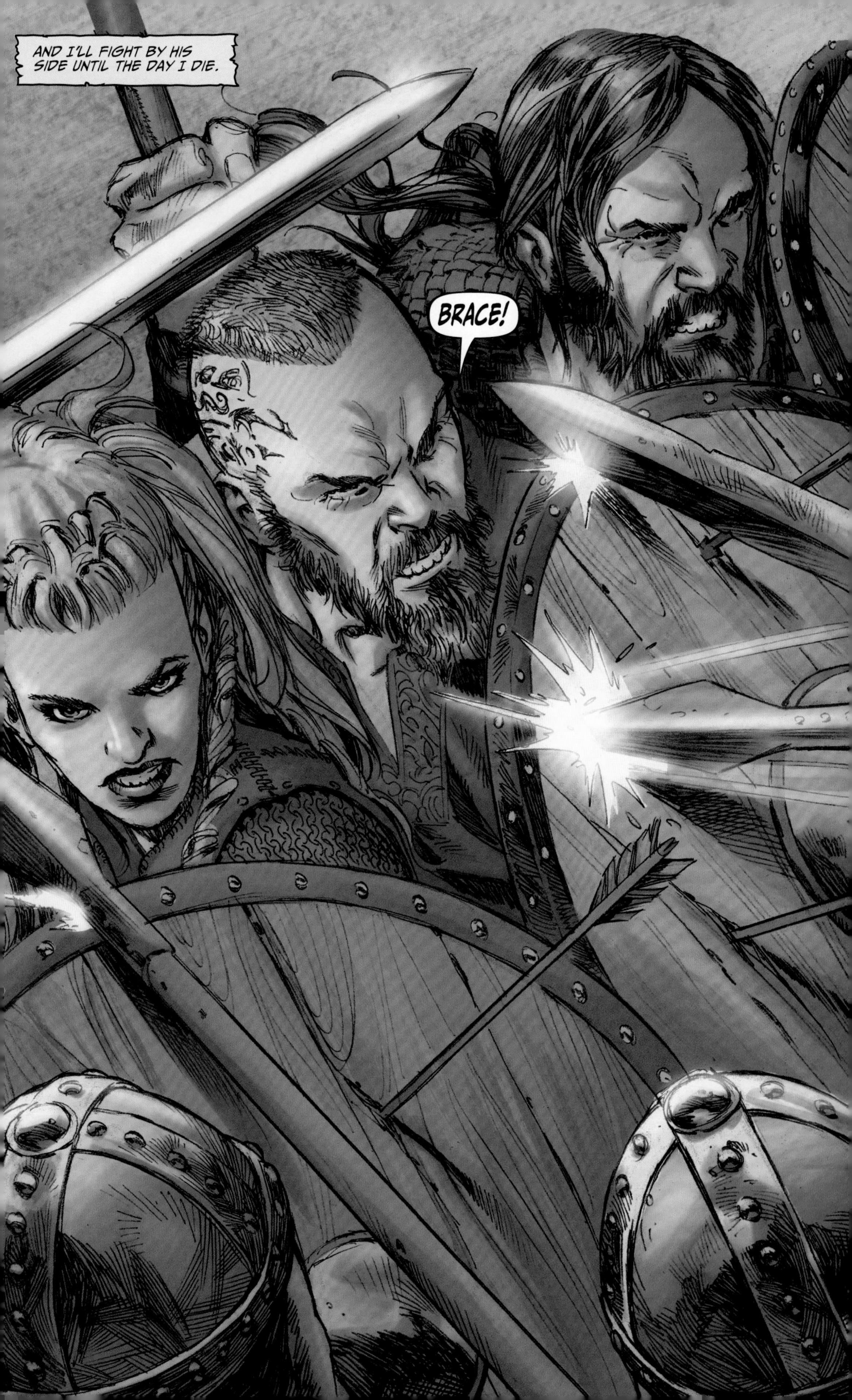
AND I'LL FIGHT BY HIS SIDE UNTIL THE DAY I DIE.
BRACE!

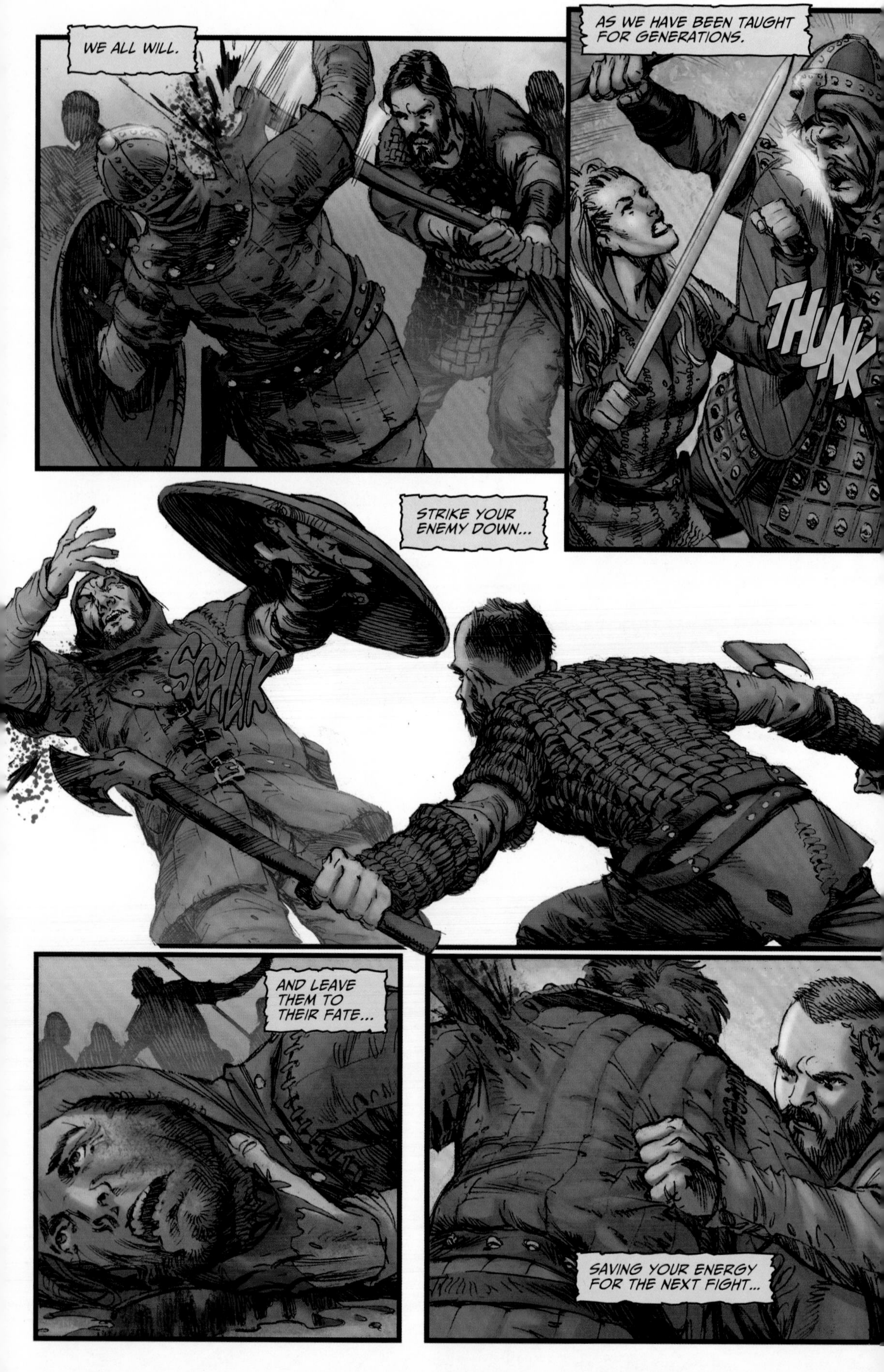
WE ALL WILL.
AS WE HAVE BEEN TAUGHT FOR GENERATIONS.
THUNK
STRIKE YOUR ENEMY DOWN...
SCHLIK
AND LEAVE THEM TO THEIR FATE...
SAVING YOUR ENERGY FOR THE NEXT FIGHT...

FOR THE NEXT KILL.

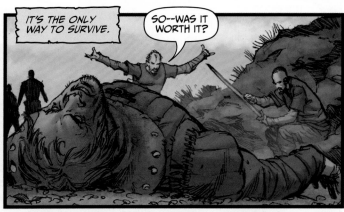

IT'S THE ONLY WAY TO SURVIVE.

SO--WAS IT WORTH IT?

WAS *WHAT* WORTH IT, FLOKI?

SELLING YOUR SOUL, ONLY TO BE *DOUBLE-CROSSED* BY THE CHRISTIAN?

KING ECBERT WOULDN'T BETRAY US.

REALLY, LAGERTHA? THEN WHAT WOULD YOU CALL THIS? A COINCIDENCE?

YOU THINK IT'S A TRAP? WHY WOULD ECBERT SEND US HALFWAY AROUND THE COAST IF HE WANTED US DEAD?

TO WASH HIS HANDS OF US, LIKE THE ROMAN IN THE PRIEST'S FAIRY TALES.

ROMAN?

PONTIUS PILATE.

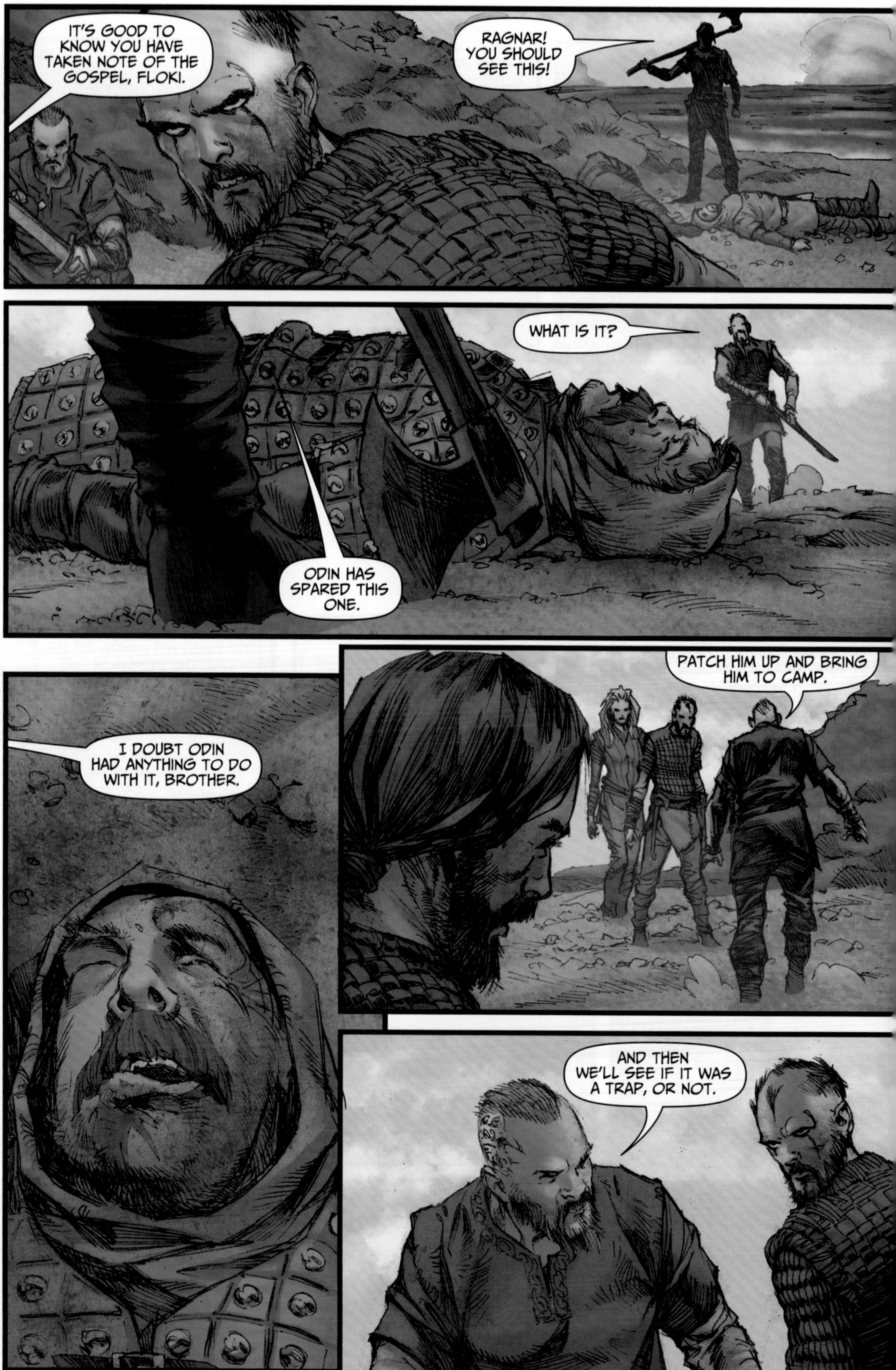
IT'S GOOD TO KNOW YOU HAVE TAKEN NOTE OF THE GOSPEL, FLOKI.
RAGNAR! YOU SHOULD SEE THIS!
WHAT IS IT?
ODIN HAS SPARED THIS ONE.
I DOUBT ODIN HAD ANYTHING TO DO WITH IT, BROTHER.
PATCH HIM UP AND BRING HIM TO CAMP.
AND THEN WE'LL SEE IF IT WAS A TRAP, OR NOT.

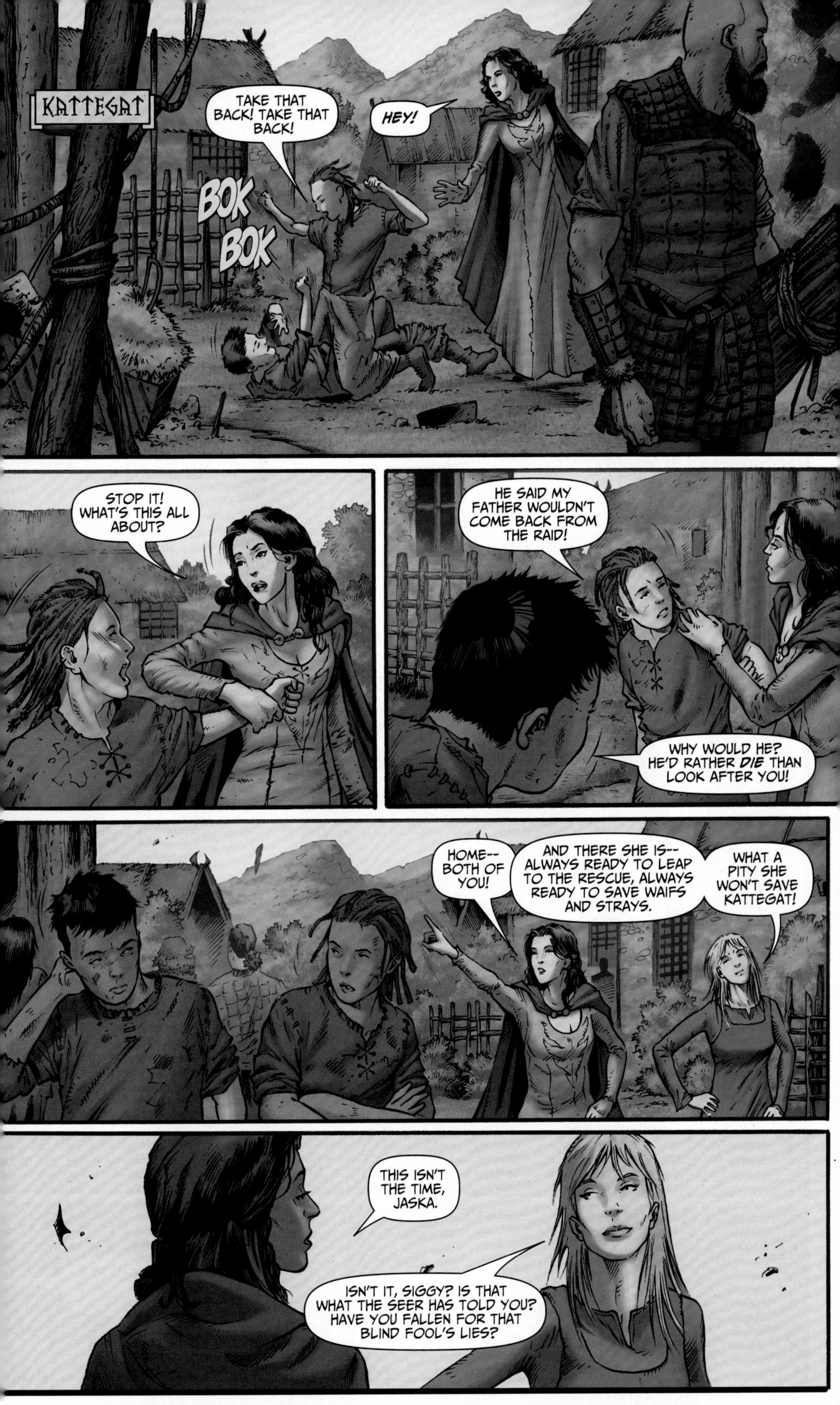
KATTEGAT
TAKE THAT BACK! TAKE THAT BACK!
HEY!
BOK BOK
STOP IT! WHAT'S THIS ALL ABOUT?
HE SAID MY FATHER WOULDN'T COME BACK FROM THE RAID!
WHY WOULD HE? HE'D RATHER DIE THAN LOOK AFTER YOU!
HOME-- BOTH OF YOU!
AND THERE SHE IS-- ALWAYS READY TO LEAP TO THE RESCUE, ALWAYS READY TO SAVE WAIFS AND STRAYS.
WHAT A PITY SHE WON'T SAVE KATTEGAT!
THIS ISN'T THE TIME, JASKA.
ISN'T IT, SIGGY? IS THAT WHAT THE SEER HAS TOLD YOU? HAVE YOU FALLEN FOR THAT BLIND FOOL'S LIES?

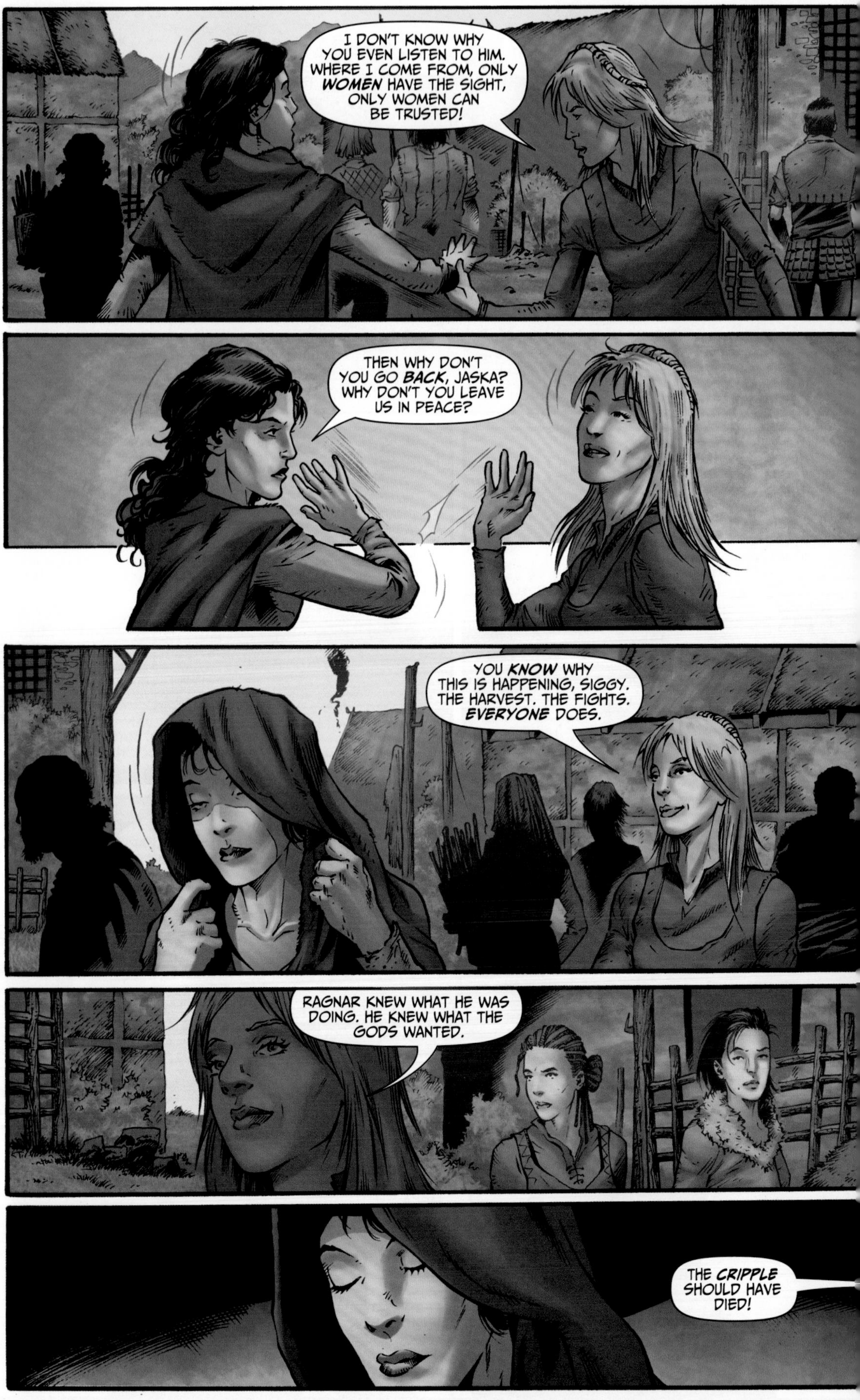
I DON'T KNOW WHY YOU EVEN LISTEN TO HIM. WHERE I COME FROM, ONLY *WOMEN* HAVE THE SIGHT, ONLY WOMEN CAN BE TRUSTED!
THEN WHY DON'T YOU GO *BACK*, JASKA? WHY DON'T YOU LEAVE US IN PEACE?
YOU *KNOW* WHY THIS IS HAPPENING, SIGGY. THE HARVEST. THE FIGHTS. *EVERYONE* DOES.
RAGNAR KNEW WHAT HE WAS DOING. HE KNEW WHAT THE GODS WANTED.
THE *CRIPPLE* SHOULD HAVE DIED!

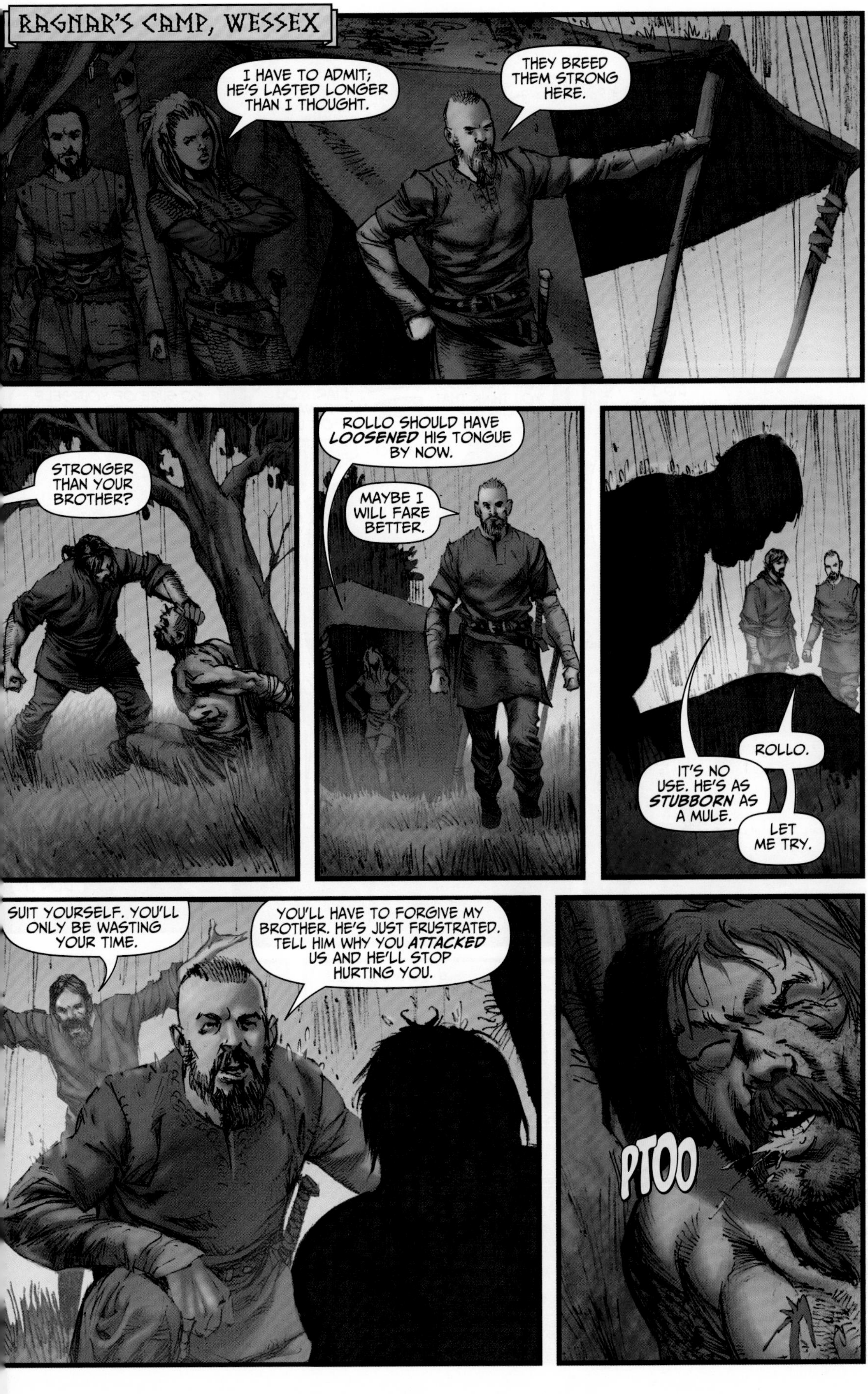
RAGNAR'S CAMP, WESSEX
I HAVE TO ADMIT; HE'S LASTED LONGER THAN I THOUGHT.
THEY BREED THEM STRONG HERE.
STRONGER THAN YOUR BROTHER?
ROLLO SHOULD HAVE LOOSENED HIS TONGUE BY NOW.
MAYBE I WILL FARE BETTER.
ROLLO.
IT'S NO USE. HE'S AS STUBBORN AS A MULE.
LET ME TRY.
SUIT YOURSELF. YOU'LL ONLY BE WASTING YOUR TIME.
YOU'LL HAVE TO FORGIVE MY BROTHER. HE'S JUST FRUSTRATED. TELL HIM WHY YOU ATTACKED US AND HE'LL STOP HURTING YOU.
PTOO

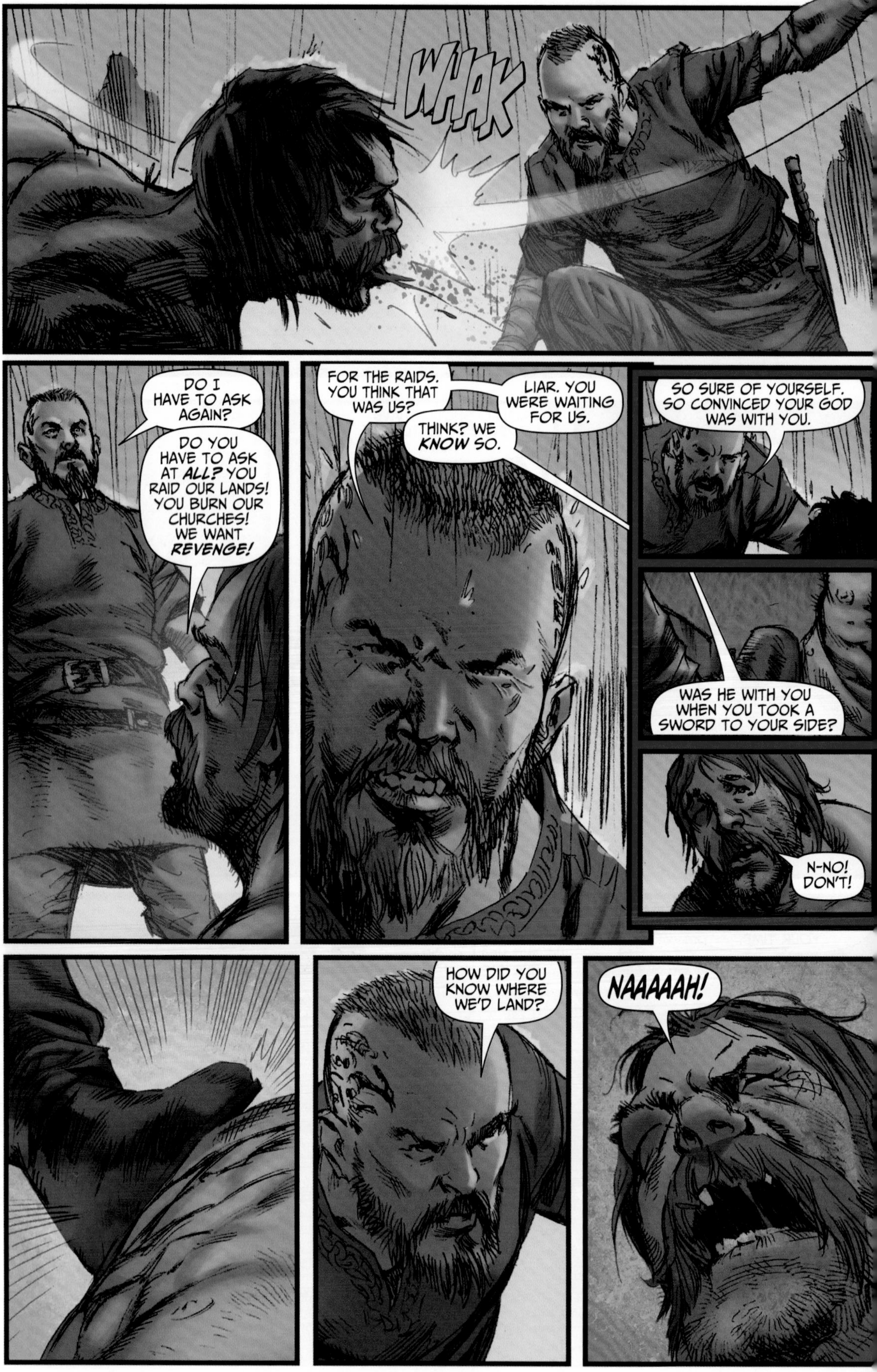
WHAK
DO I HAVE TO ASK AGAIN?
DO YOU HAVE TO ASK AT ALL? YOU RAID OUR LANDS! YOU BURN OUR CHURCHES! WE WANT REVENGE!
FOR THE RAIDS. YOU THINK THAT WAS US?
LIAR. YOU WERE WAITING FOR US.
THINK? WE KNOW SO.
SO SURE OF YOURSELF. SO CONVINCED YOUR GOD WAS WITH YOU.
WAS HE WITH YOU WHEN YOU TOOK A SWORD TO YOUR SIDE?
N-NO! DON'T!
HOW DID YOU KNOW WHERE WE'D LAND?
NAAAAAH!

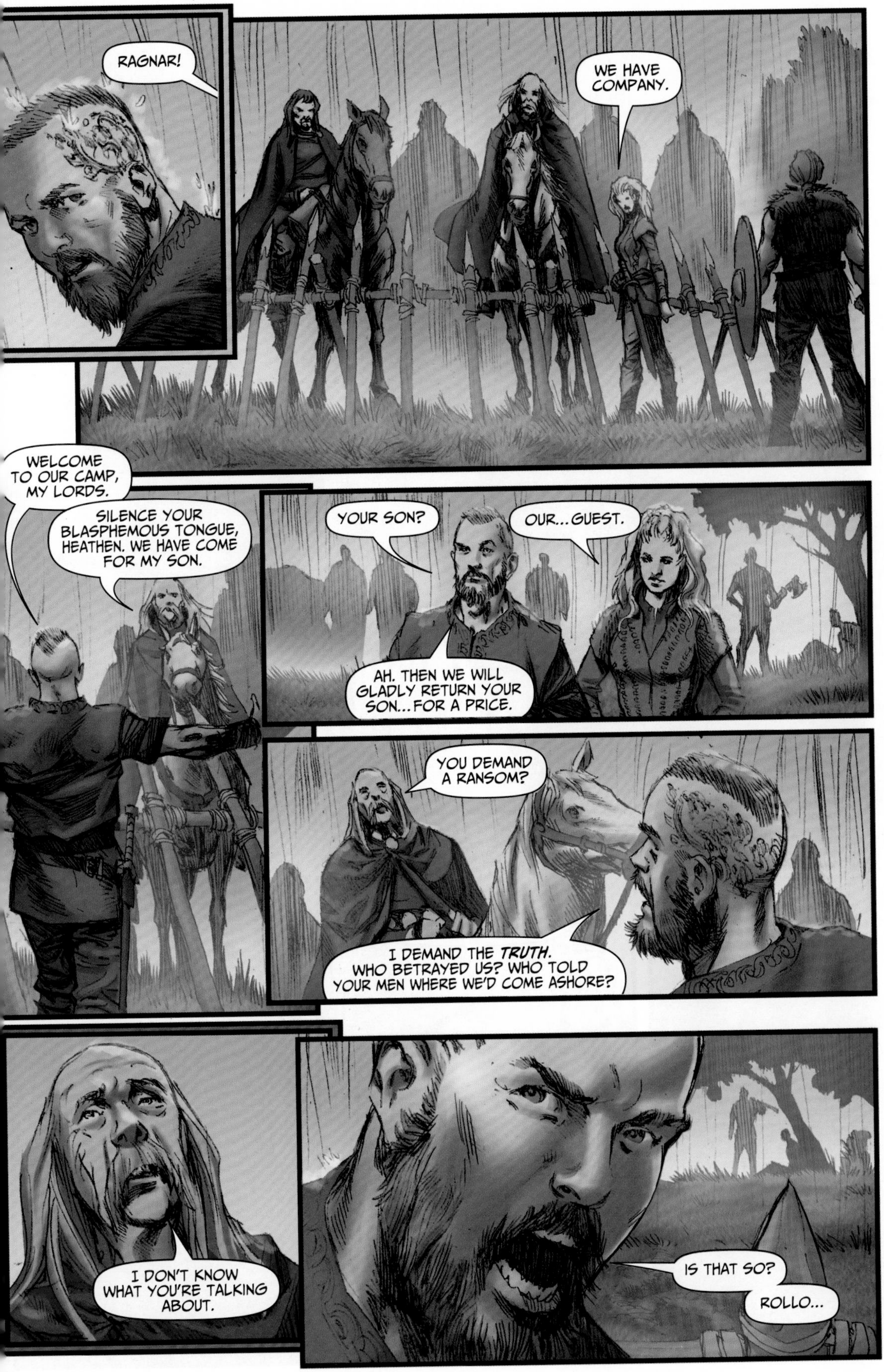

RAGNAR!
WE HAVE COMPANY.
WELCOME TO OUR CAMP, MY LORDS.
SILENCE YOUR BLASPHEMOUS TONGUE, HEATHEN. WE HAVE COME FOR MY SON.
YOUR SON?
OUR... GUEST.
AH. THEN WE WILL GLADLY RETURN YOUR SON... FOR A PRICE.
YOU DEMAND A RANSOM?
I DEMAND THE *TRUTH*. WHO BETRAYED US? WHO TOLD YOUR MEN WHERE WE'D COME ASHORE?
I DON'T KNOW WHAT YOU'RE TALKING ABOUT.
IS THAT SO?
ROLLO...

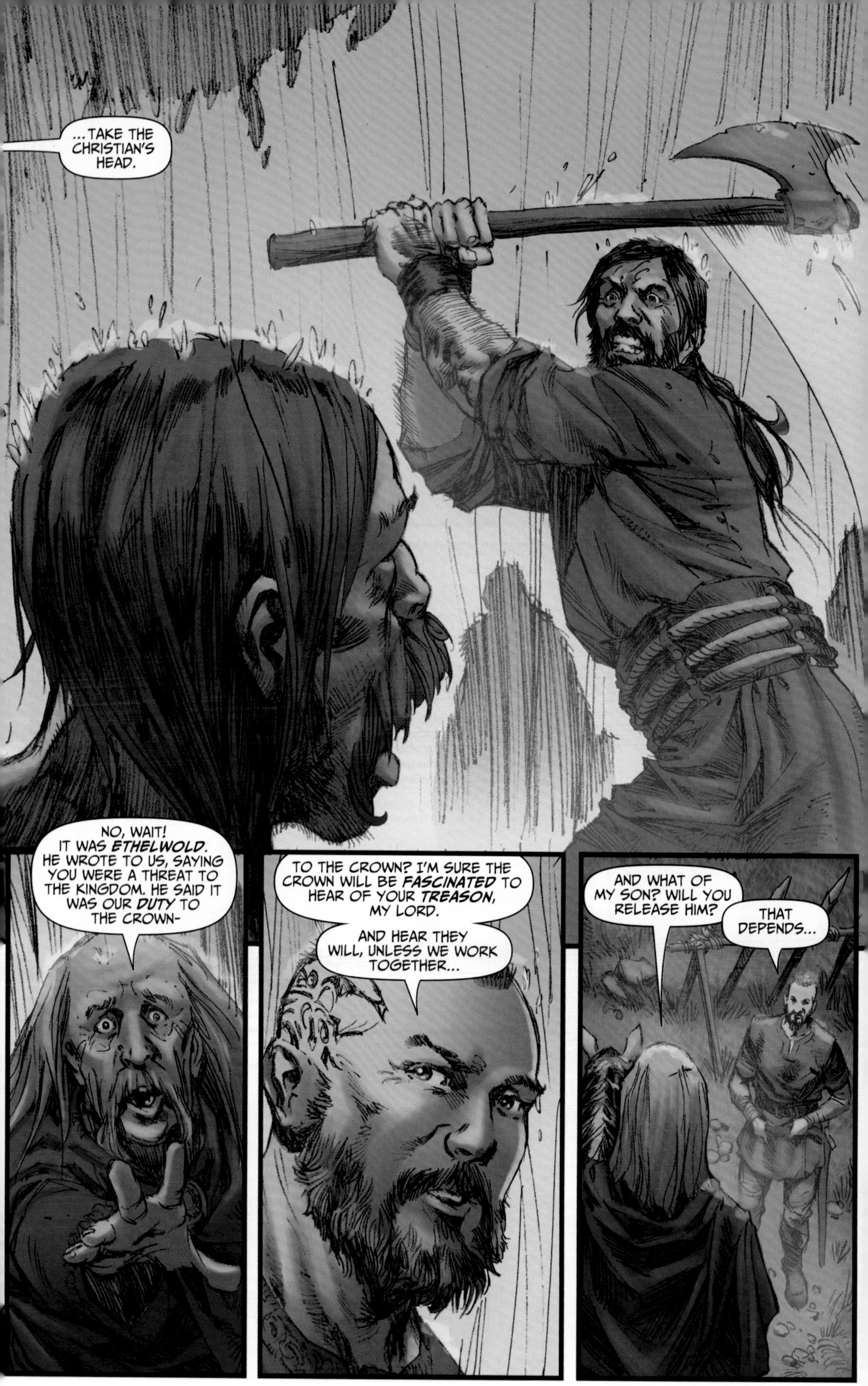
...TAKE THE CHRISTIAN'S HEAD.
NO, WAIT! IT WAS ETHELWOLD. HE WROTE TO US, SAYING YOU WERE A THREAT TO THE KINGDOM. HE SAID IT WAS OUR DUTY TO THE CROWN-
TO THE CROWN? I'M SURE THE CROWN WILL BE FASCINATED TO HEAR OF YOUR TREASON, MY LORD.
AND HEAR THEY WILL, UNLESS WE WORK TOGETHER...
AND WHAT OF MY SON? WILL YOU RELEASE HIM?
THAT DEPENDS...

"...ON WHAT HELP WE RECEIVE."

WAAAAAAAH

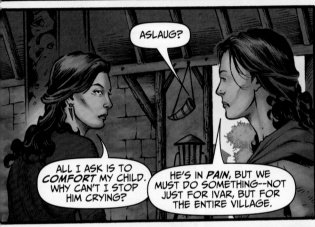

ASLAUG?

ALL I ASK IS TO **COMFORT** MY CHILD. WHY CAN'T I STOP HIM CRYING?

HE'S IN **PAIN**, BUT WE MUST DO SOMETHING--NOT JUST FOR IVAR, BUT FOR THE ENTIRE VILLAGE.

THERE ARE RUMORS THAT THE HARVEST IS IVAR'S FAULT, THAT HE IS **CURSED**. THAT WE **ALL** ARE.

RUMORS?

SPREAD BY THE SAMI WOMAN, **JASKA**. SHE CLAIMS THAT IT'S A MESSAGE FROM THE GODS. IF YOU HAD NOT SPARED HER--

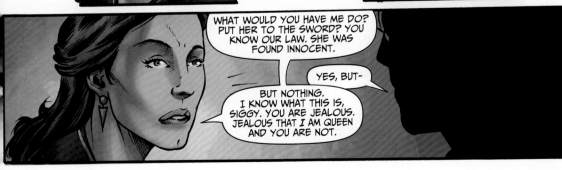

WHAT WOULD YOU HAVE ME DO? PUT HER TO THE SWORD? YOU KNOW OUR LAW. SHE WAS FOUND INNOCENT.

YES, BUT--

BUT NOTHING. I KNOW WHAT THIS IS, SIGGY. YOU ARE JEALOUS. JEALOUS THAT **I** AM QUEEN AND YOU ARE NOT.

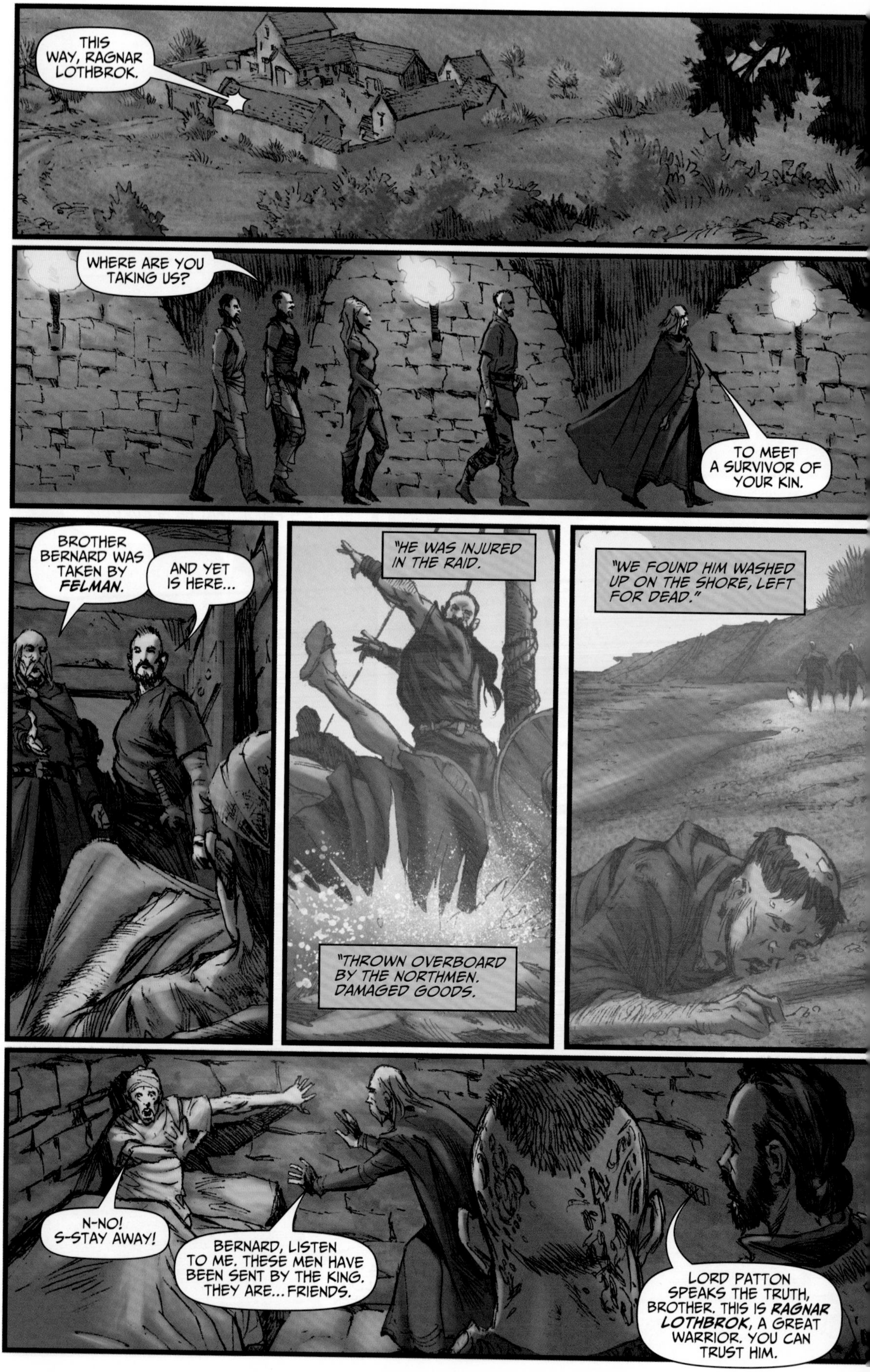
THIS WAY, RAGNAR LOTHBROK.
WHERE ARE YOU TAKING US?
TO MEET A SURVIVOR OF YOUR KIN.
BROTHER BERNARD WAS TAKEN BY FELMAN.
AND YET IS HERE...
"HE WAS INJURED IN THE RAID.
"THROWN OVERBOARD BY THE NORTHMEN. DAMAGED GOODS.
"WE FOUND HIM WASHED UP ON THE SHORE, LEFT FOR DEAD."
N-NO! S-STAY AWAY!
BERNARD, LISTEN TO ME. THESE MEN HAVE BEEN SENT BY THE KING. THEY ARE... FRIENDS.
LORD PATTON SPEAKS THE TRUTH, BROTHER. THIS IS RAGNAR LOTHBROK, A GREAT WARRIOR. YOU CAN TRUST HIM.

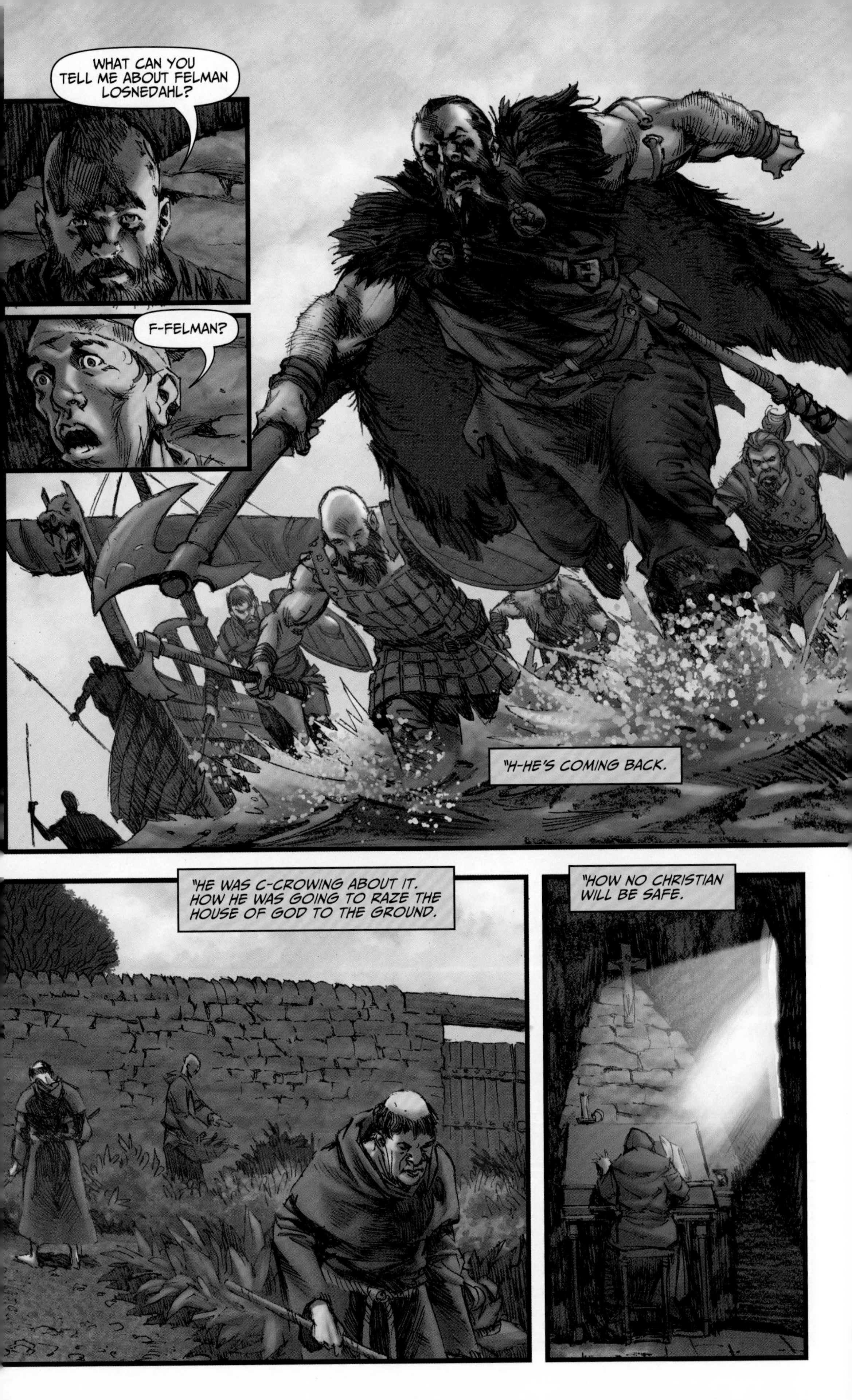
WHAT CAN YOU TELL ME ABOUT FELMAN LOSNEDAHL?
F-FELMAN?
"H-HE'S COMING BACK.
"HE WAS C-CROWING ABOUT IT. HOW HE WAS GOING TO RAZE THE HOUSE OF GOD TO THE GROUND.
"HOW NO CHRISTIAN WILL BE SAFE.

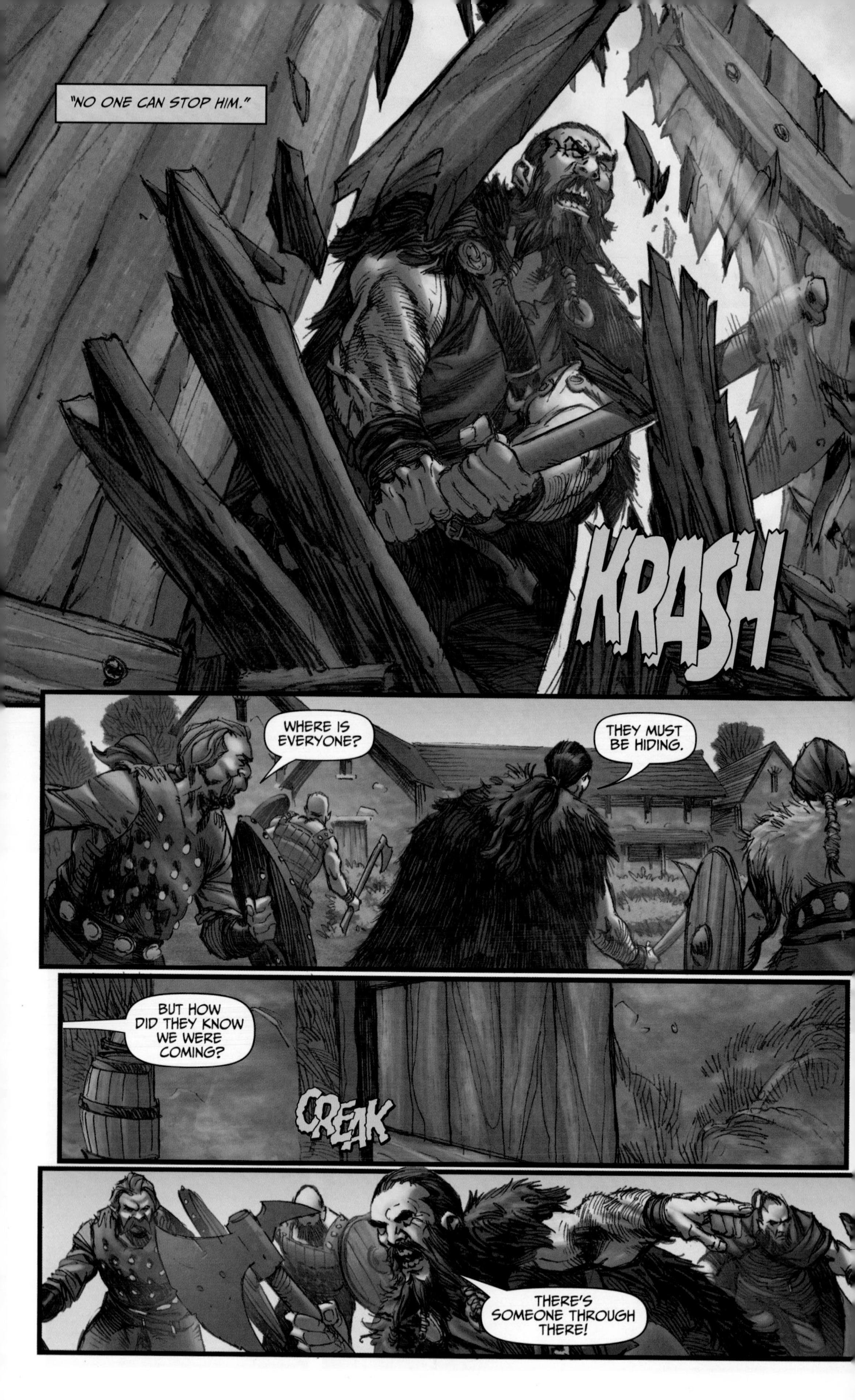
"NO ONE CAN STOP HIM."
KRASH
WHERE IS EVERYONE?
THEY MUST BE HIDING.
BUT HOW DID THEY KNOW WE WERE COMING?
CREAK
THERE'S SOMEONE THROUGH THERE!

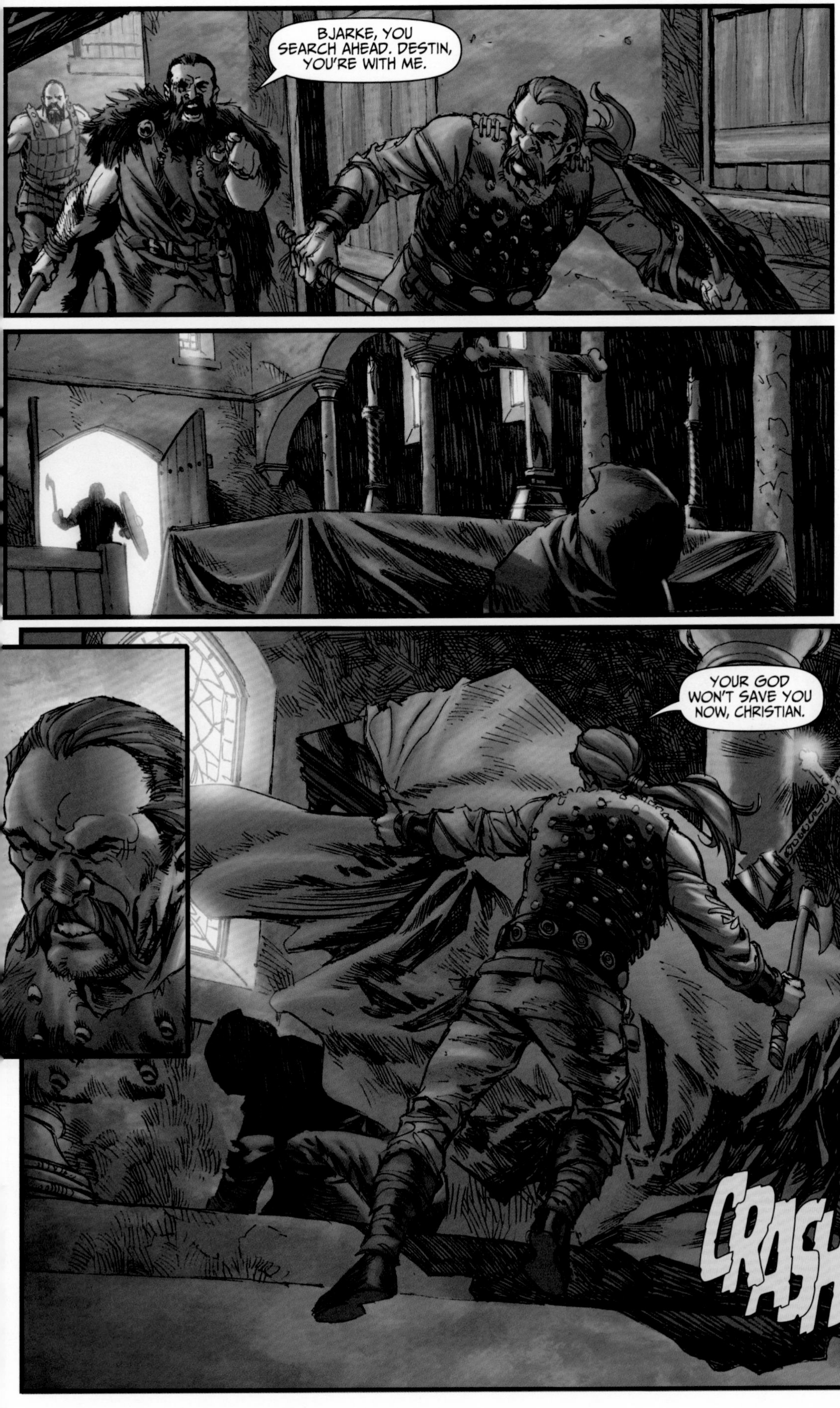
BJARKE, YOU SEARCH AHEAD. DESTIN, YOU'RE WITH ME.
YOUR GOD WON'T SAVE YOU NOW, CHRISTIAN.
CRASH

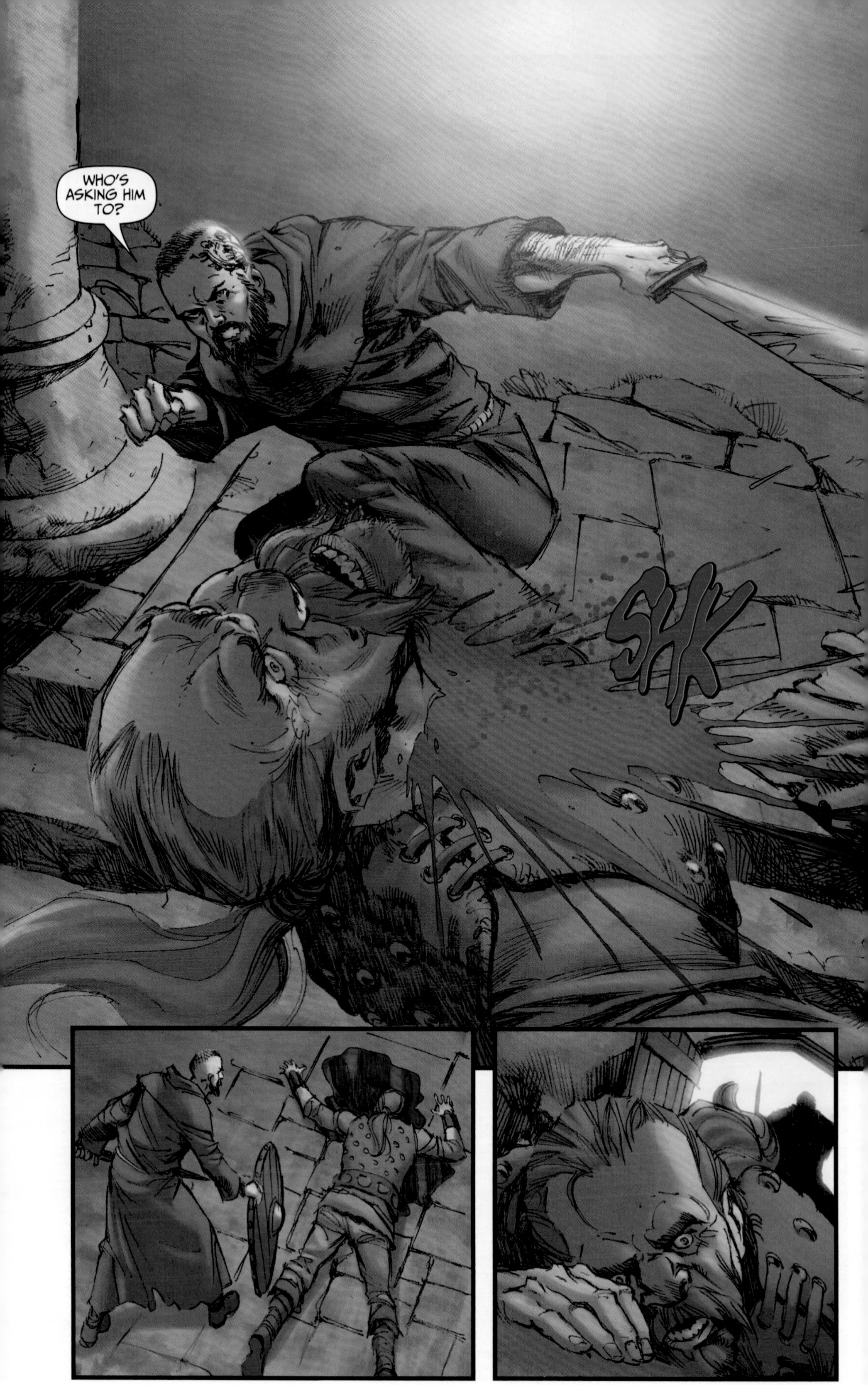
WHO'S ASKING HIM TO?
SHK

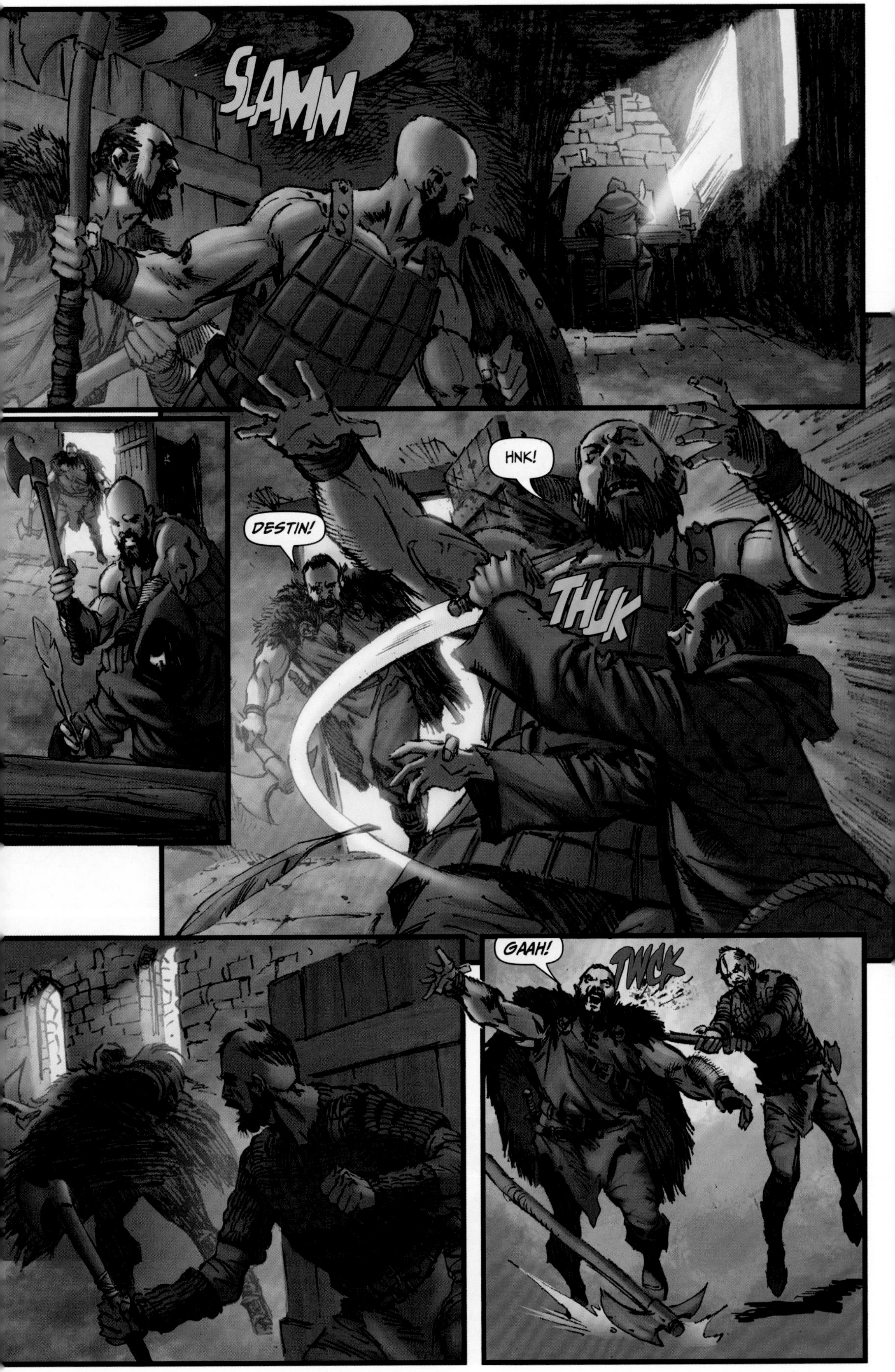
SLAMM
DESTIN!
HNK!
THUK
GAAH!
TWCK

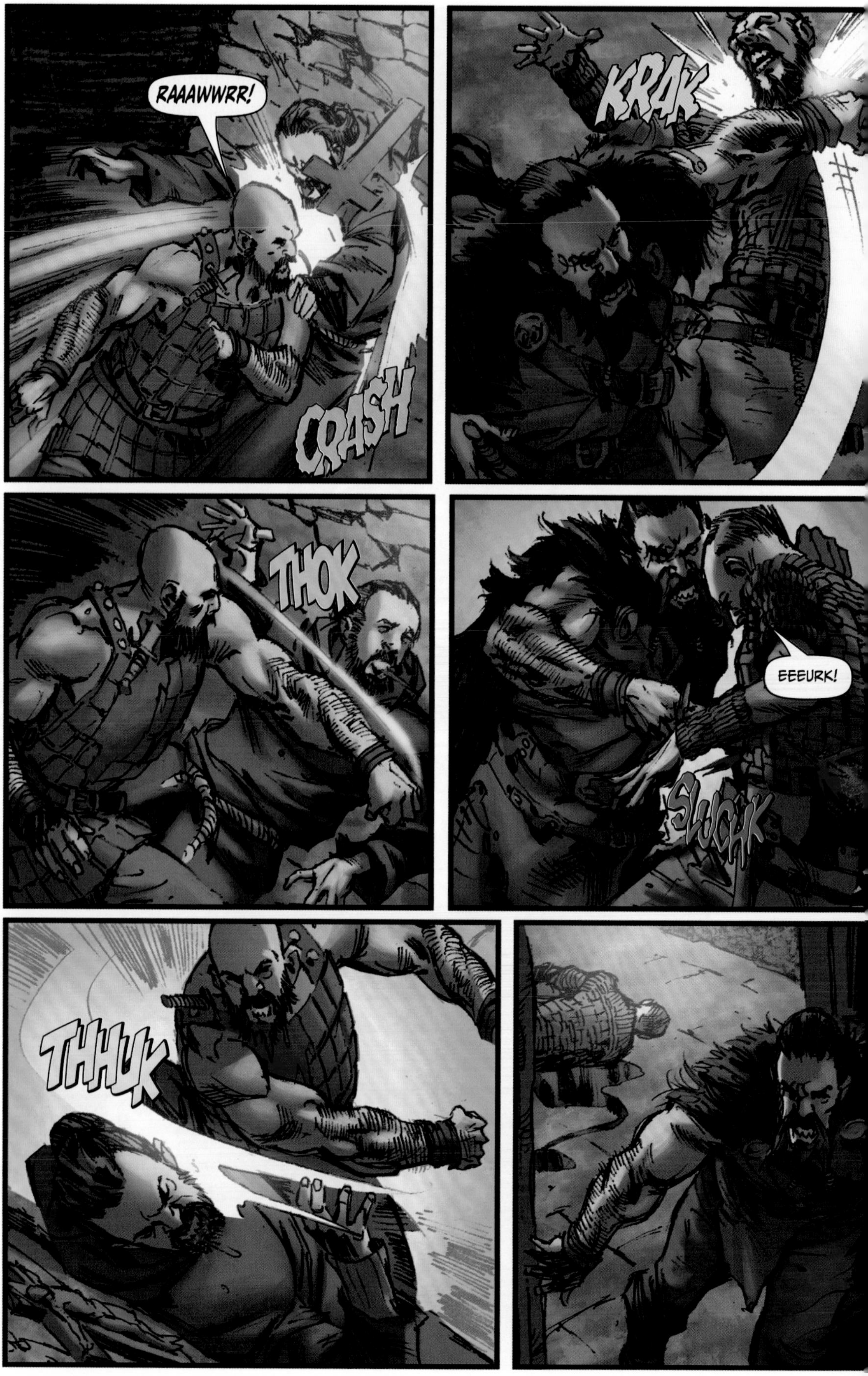
RAAAWWRR!
CRASH
KRAK
THOK
EEEURK!
SLUCHK
THHUK

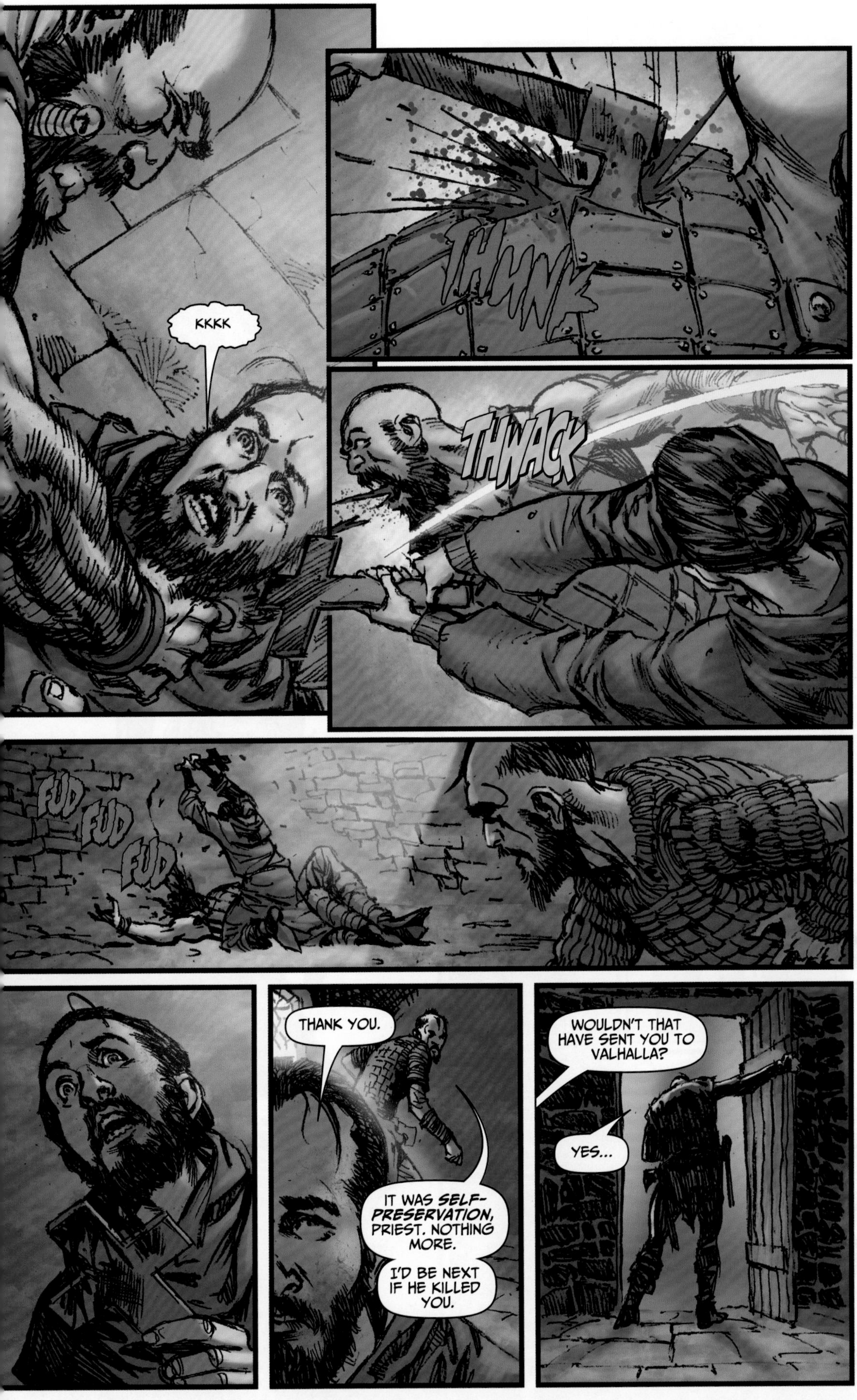
KKKK
THUNK
THWACK
FUD
FUD
FUD
THANK YOU.
IT WAS SELF-PRESERVATION, PRIEST. NOTHING MORE.
I'D BE NEXT IF HE KILLED YOU.
WOULDN'T THAT HAVE SENT YOU TO VALHALLA?
YES...

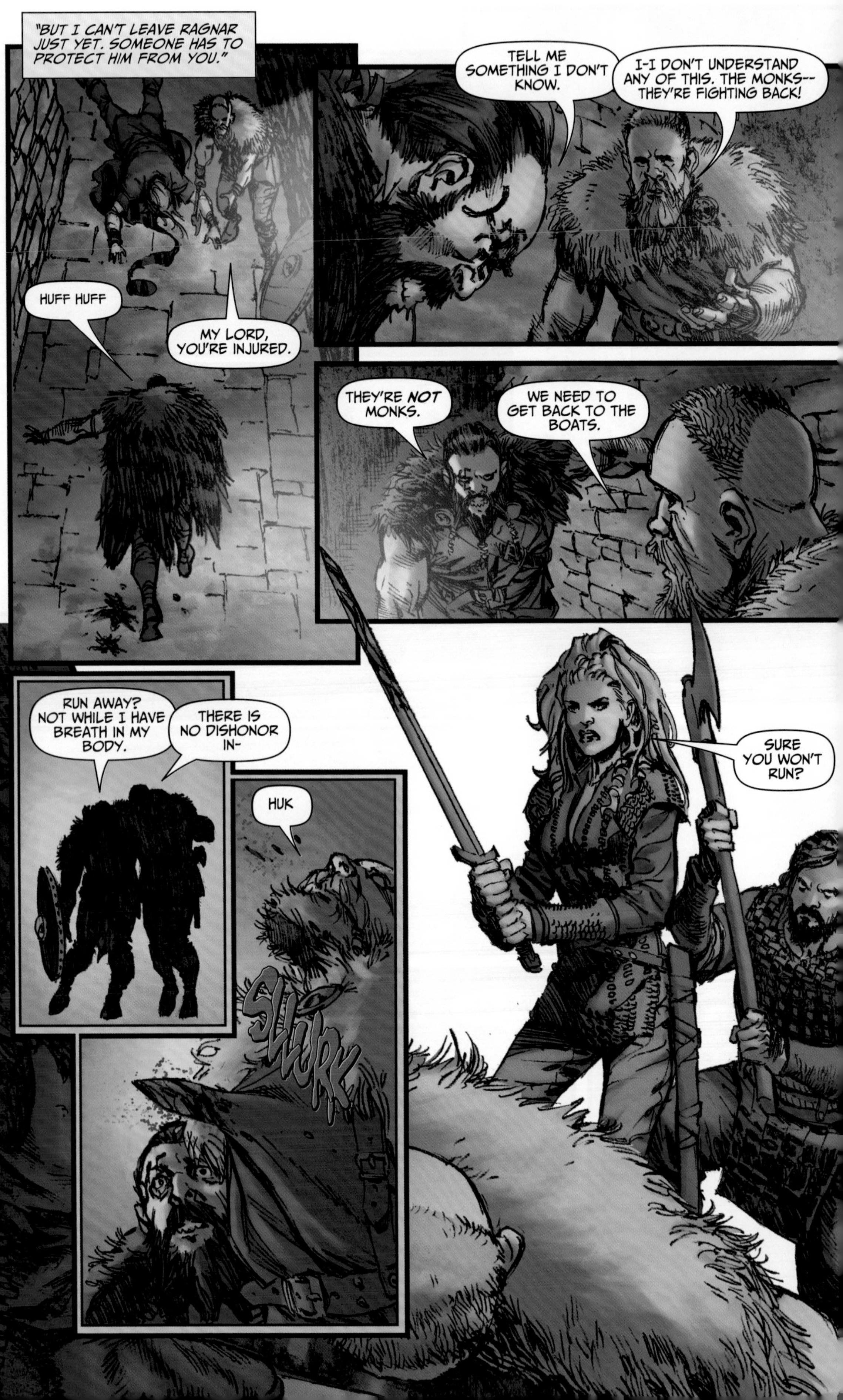
"BUT I CAN'T LEAVE RAGNAR JUST YET. SOMEONE HAS TO PROTECT HIM FROM YOU."
TELL ME SOMETHING I DON'T KNOW.
I-I DON'T UNDERSTAND ANY OF THIS. THE MONKS--THEY'RE FIGHTING BACK!
HUFF HUFF
MY LORD, YOU'RE INJURED.
THEY'RE *NOT* MONKS.
WE NEED TO GET BACK TO THE BOATS.
RUN AWAY? NOT WHILE I HAVE BREATH IN MY BODY.
THERE IS NO DISHONOR IN-
HUK
SHLORK
SURE YOU WON'T RUN?

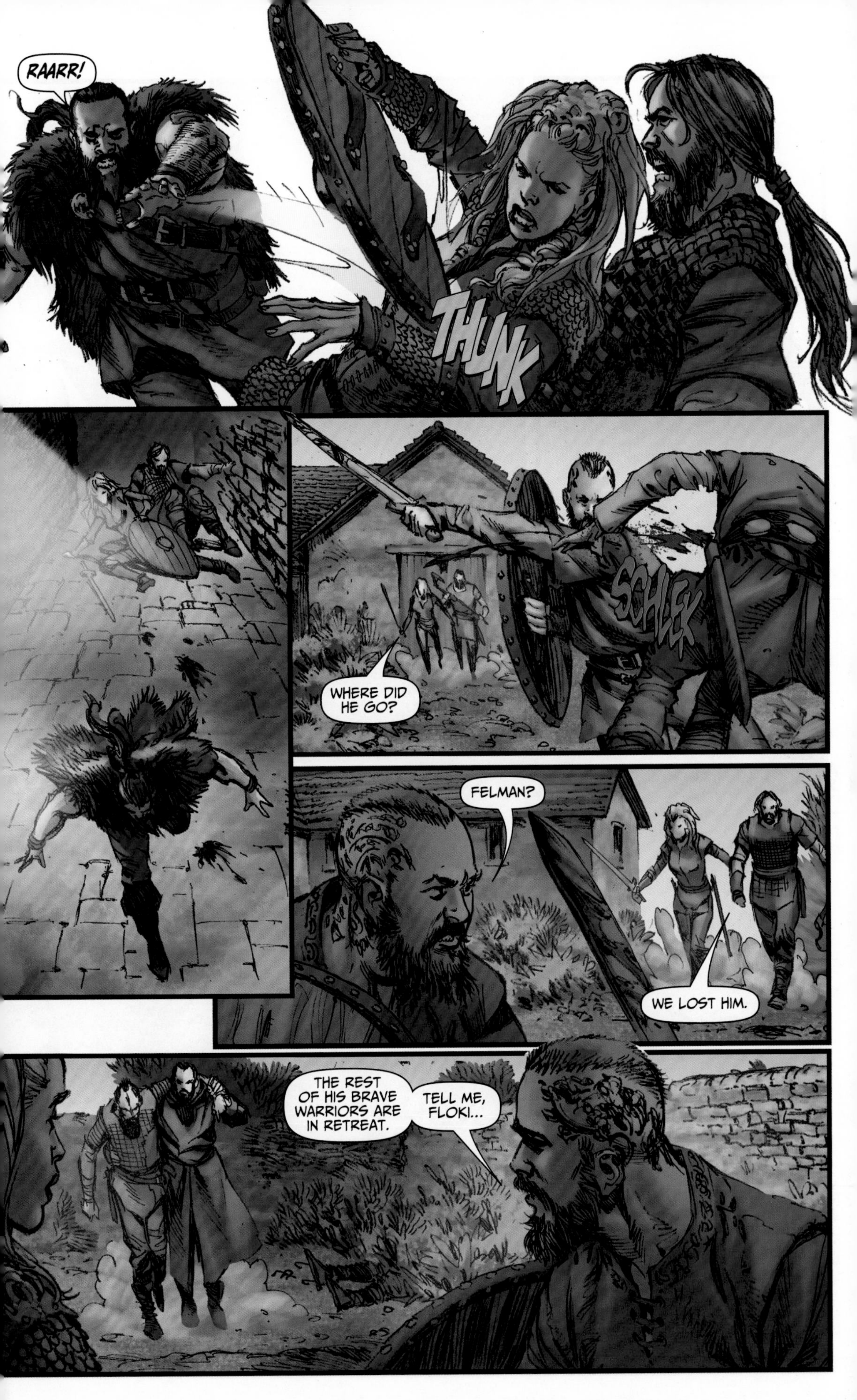
RAARR!
THUNK
SCHLEK
WHERE DID HE GO?
FELMAN?
WE LOST HIM.
THE REST OF HIS BRAVE WARRIORS ARE IN RETREAT.
TELL ME, FLOKI...

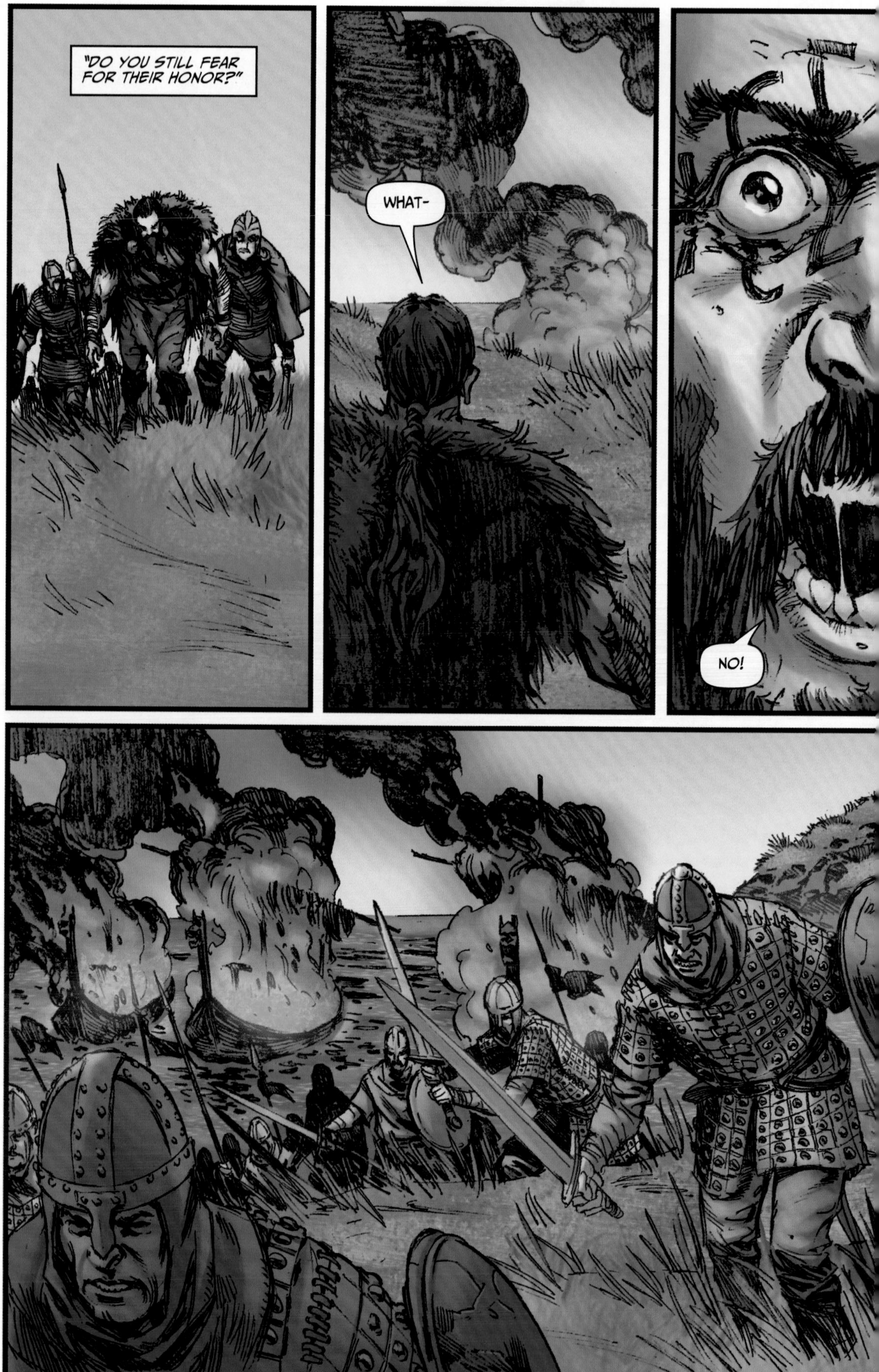
"DO YOU STILL FEAR FOR THEIR HONOR?"
WHAT-
NO!

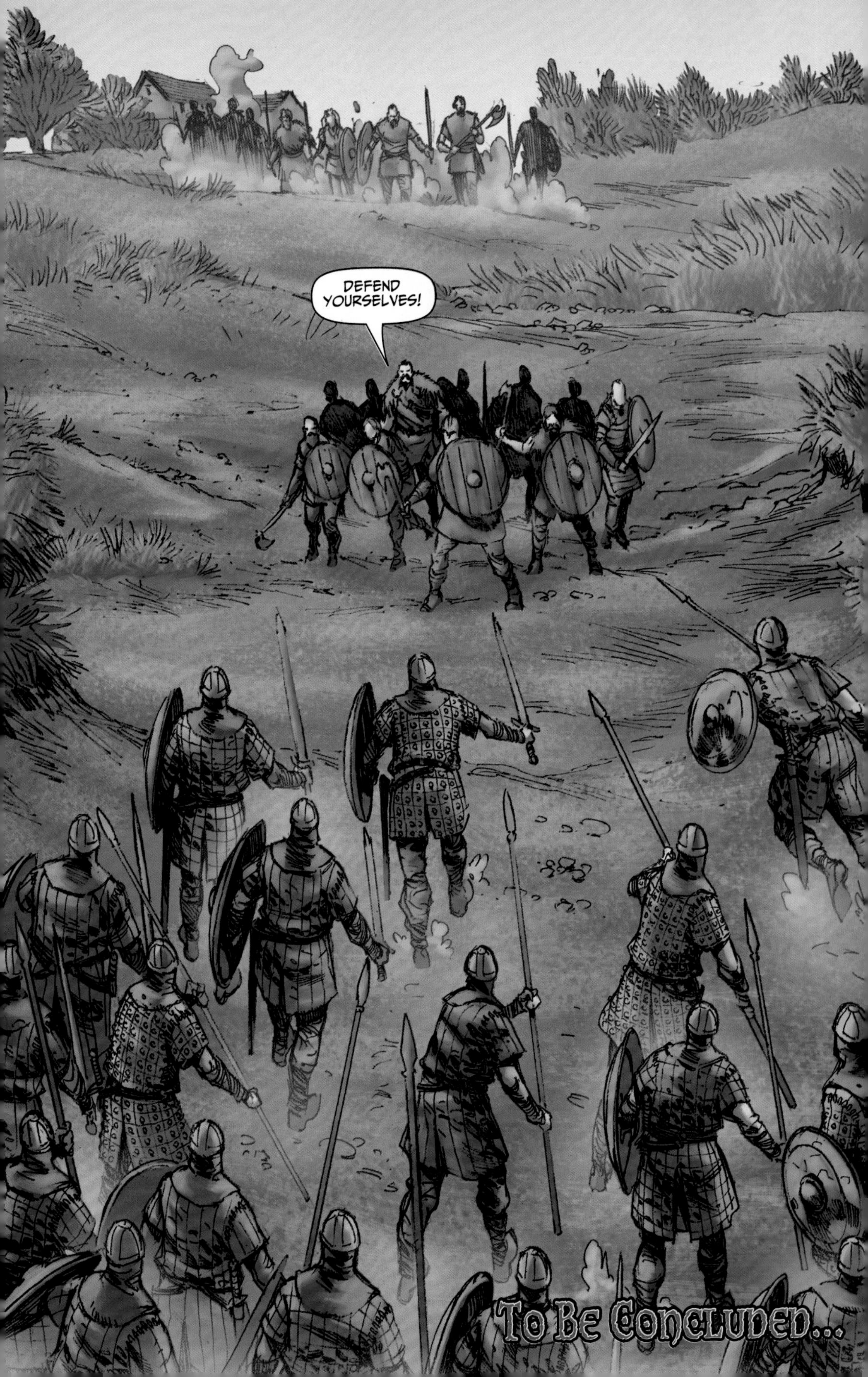
DEFEND YOURSELVES!
To Be Concluded...

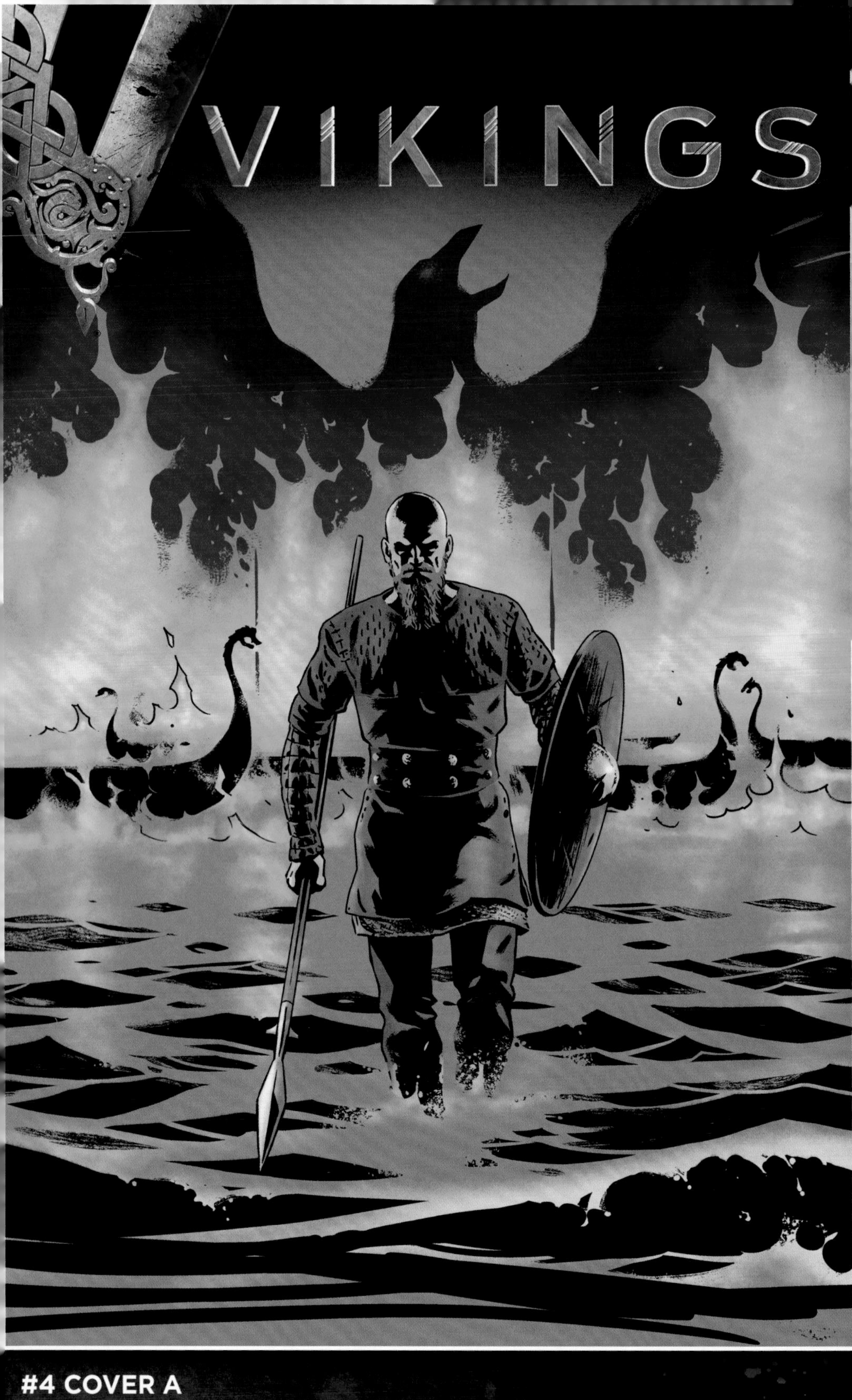
VIKINGS

#4 COVER A
ARTIST PETER SNEJBJERG

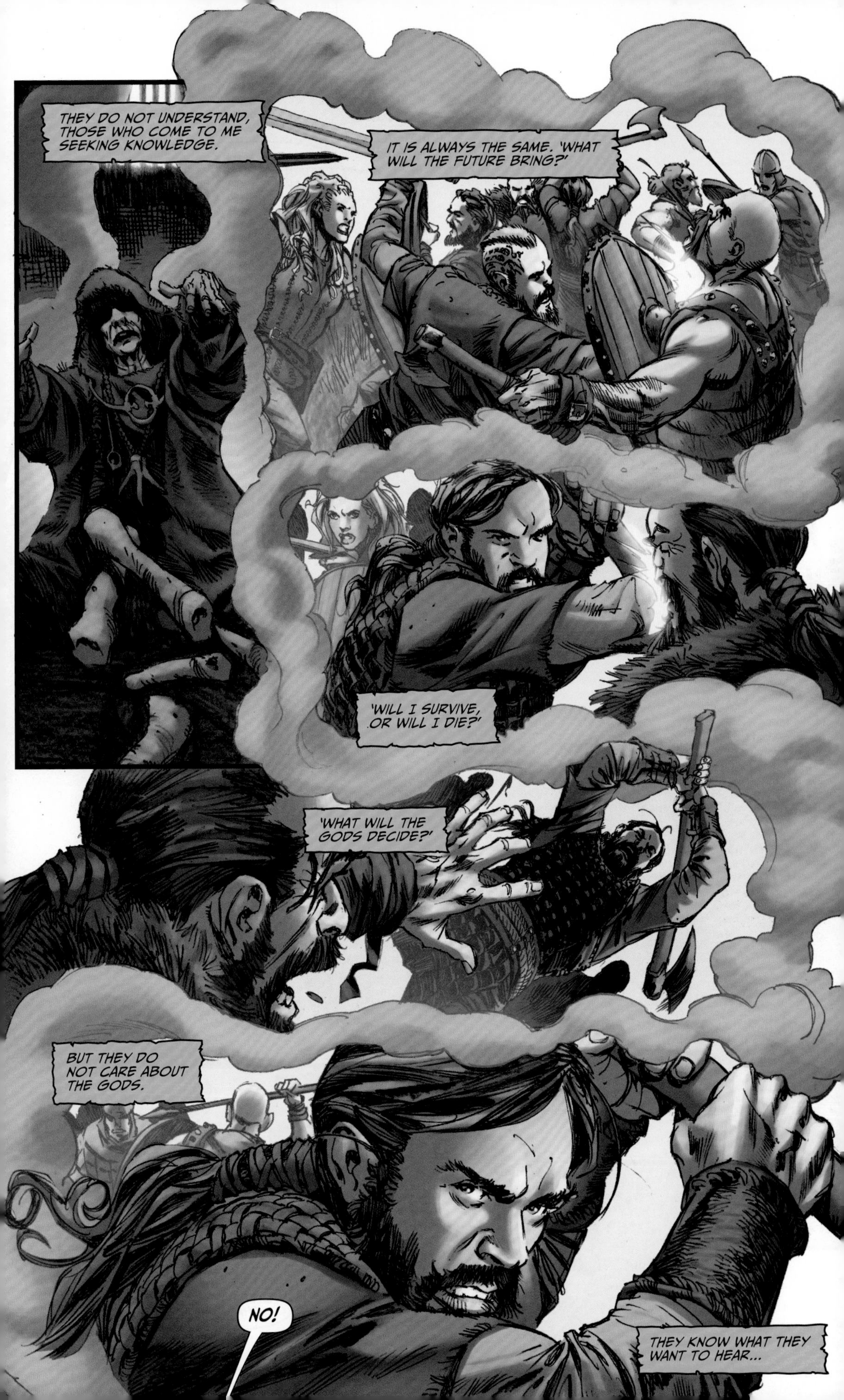

THEY DO NOT UNDERSTAND, THOSE WHO COME TO ME SEEKING KNOWLEDGE.
IT IS ALWAYS THE SAME. 'WHAT WILL THE FUTURE BRING?'
'WILL I SURVIVE, OR WILL I DIE?'
'WHAT WILL THE GODS DECIDE?'
BUT THEY DO NOT CARE ABOUT THE GODS.
NO!
THEY KNOW WHAT THEY WANT TO HEAR...

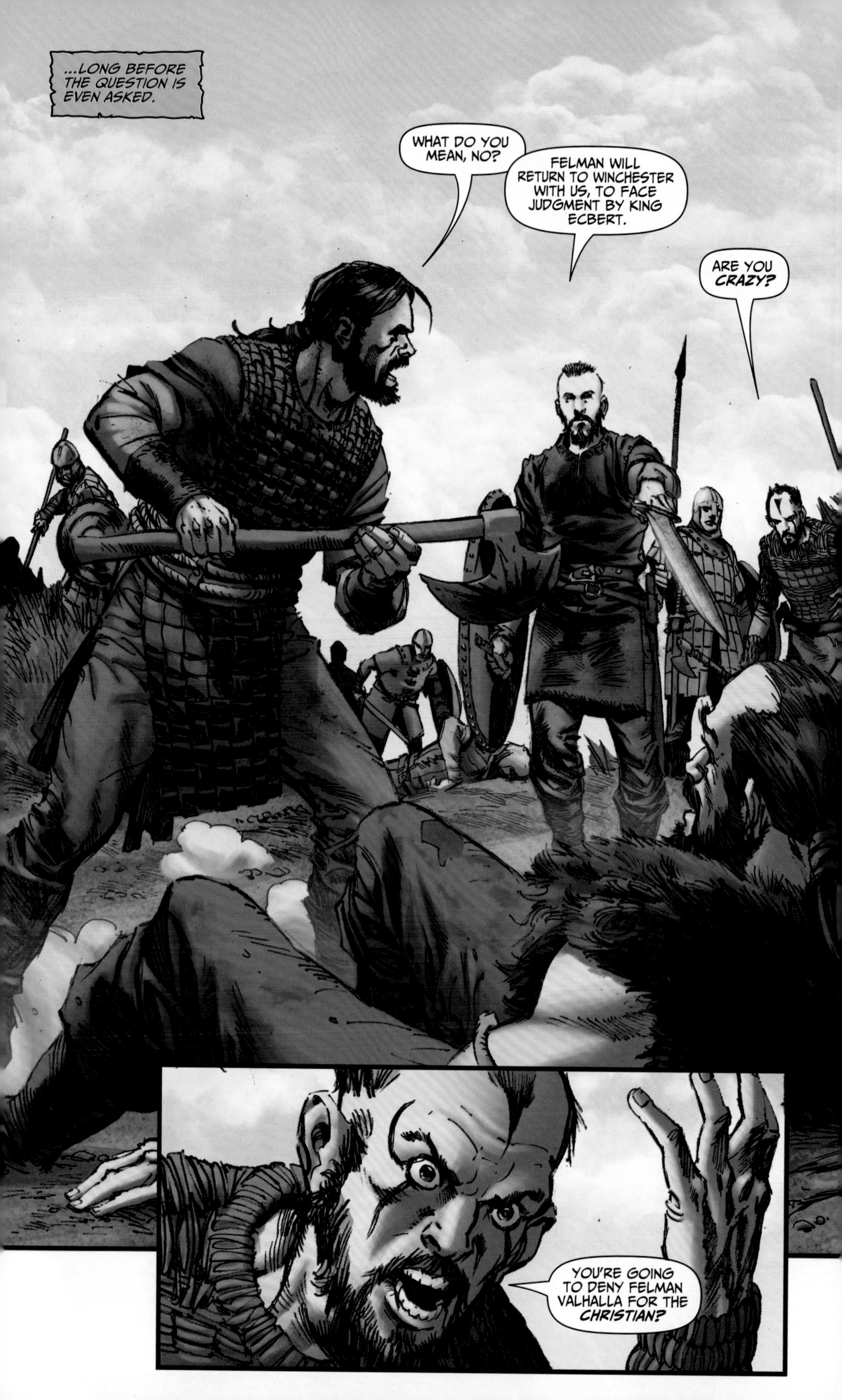
...LONG BEFORE THE QUESTION IS EVEN ASKED.
WHAT DO YOU MEAN, NO?
FELMAN WILL RETURN TO WINCHESTER WITH US, TO FACE JUDGMENT BY KING ECBERT.
ARE YOU *CRAZY?*
YOU'RE GOING TO DENY FELMAN VALHALLA FOR THE *CHRISTIAN?*

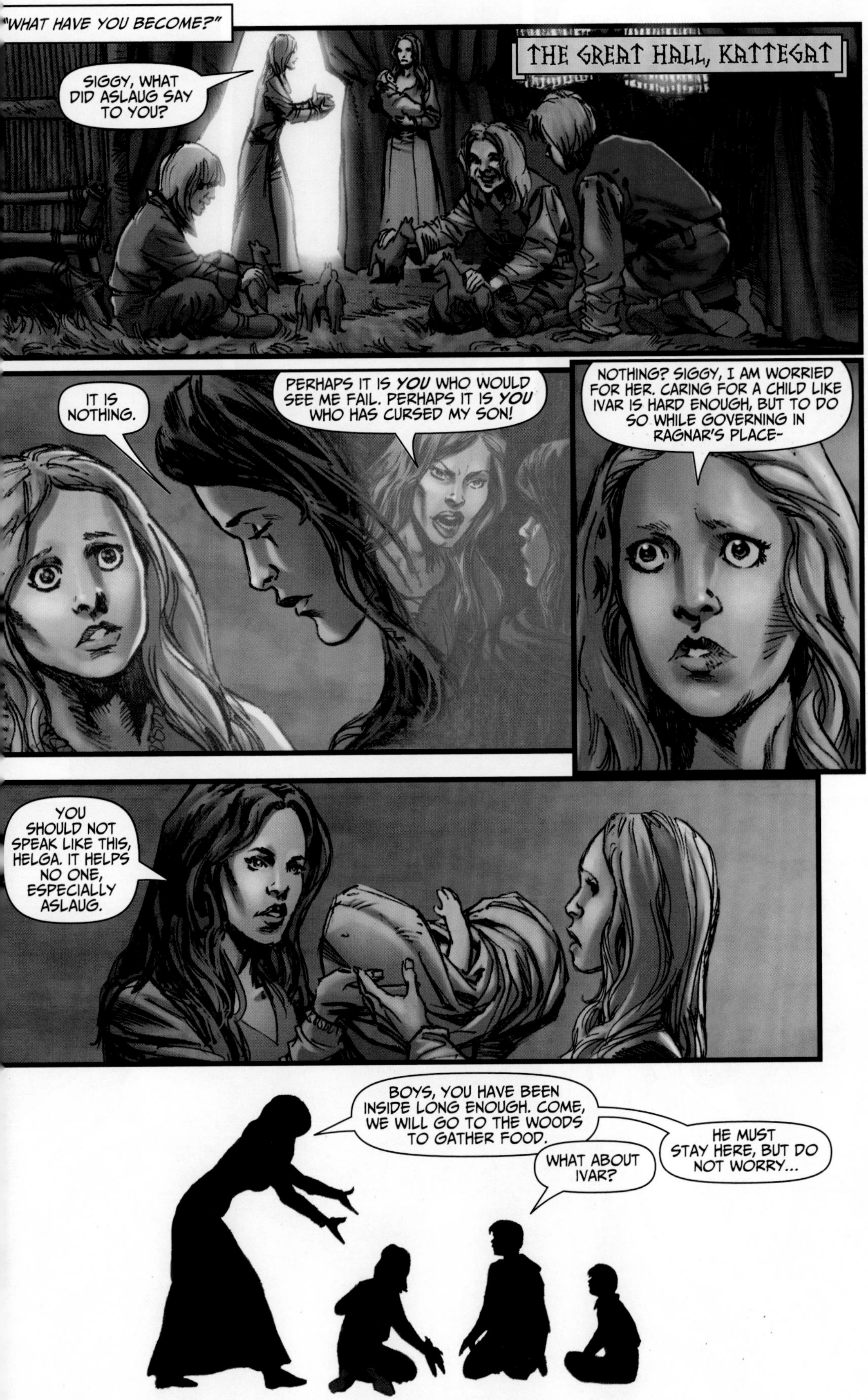
"WHAT HAVE YOU BECOME?"
THE GREAT HALL, KATTEGAT
SIGGY, WHAT DID ASLAUG SAY TO YOU?
IT IS NOTHING.
PERHAPS IT IS *YOU* WHO WOULD SEE ME FAIL. PERHAPS IT IS *YOU* WHO HAS CURSED MY SON!
NOTHING? SIGGY, I AM WORRIED FOR HER. CARING FOR A CHILD LIKE IVAR IS HARD ENOUGH, BUT TO DO SO WHILE GOVERNING IN RAGNAR'S PLACE-
YOU SHOULD NOT SPEAK LIKE THIS, HELGA. IT HELPS NO ONE, ESPECIALLY ASLAUG.
BOYS, YOU HAVE BEEN INSIDE LONG ENOUGH. COME, WE WILL GO TO THE WOODS TO GATHER FOOD.
WHAT ABOUT IVAR?
HE MUST STAY HERE, BUT DO NOT WORRY...

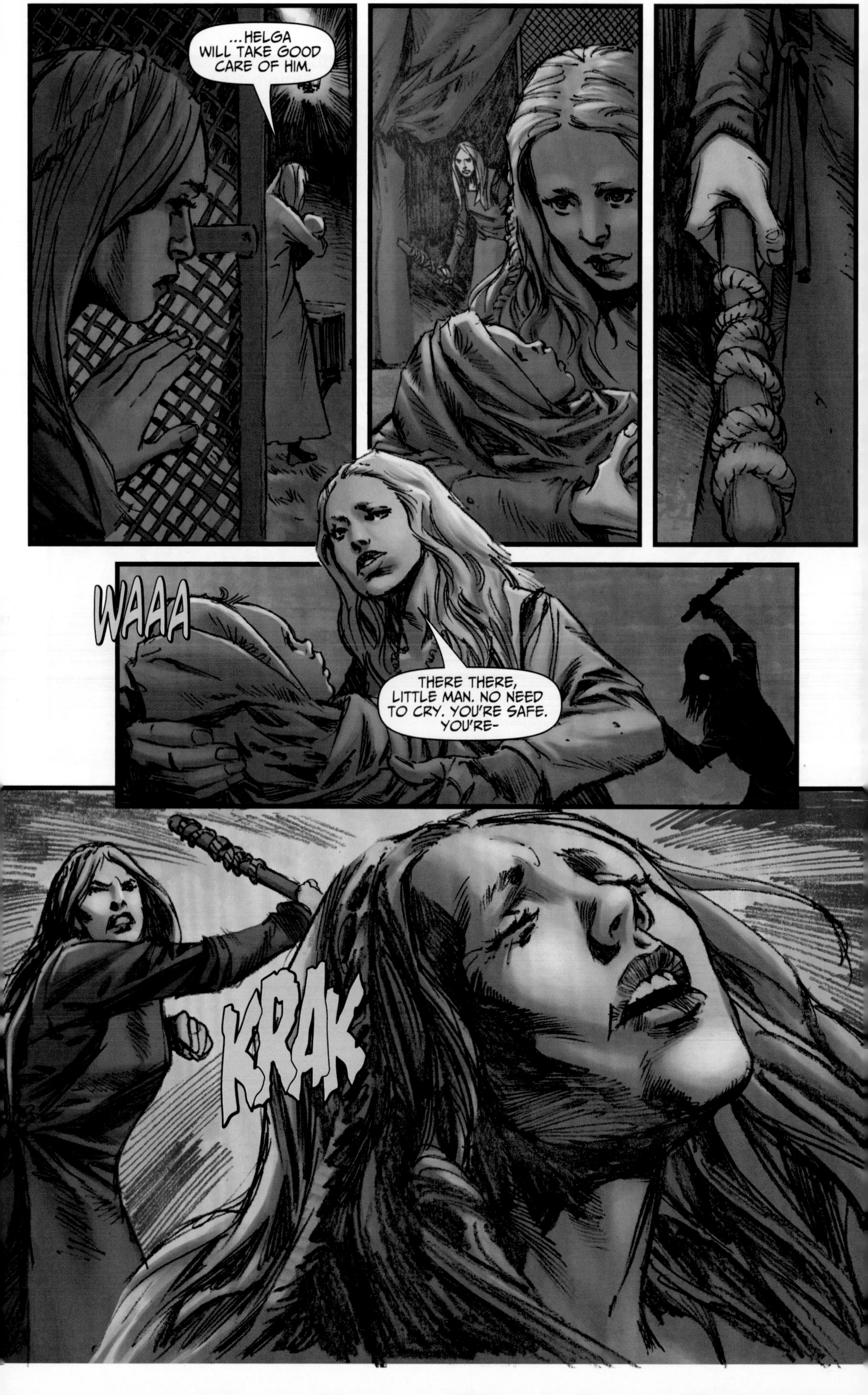
...HELGA WILL TAKE GOOD CARE OF HIM.
WAAA
THERE THERE, LITTLE MAN. NO NEED TO CRY. YOU'RE SAFE. YOU'RE-
KRAK

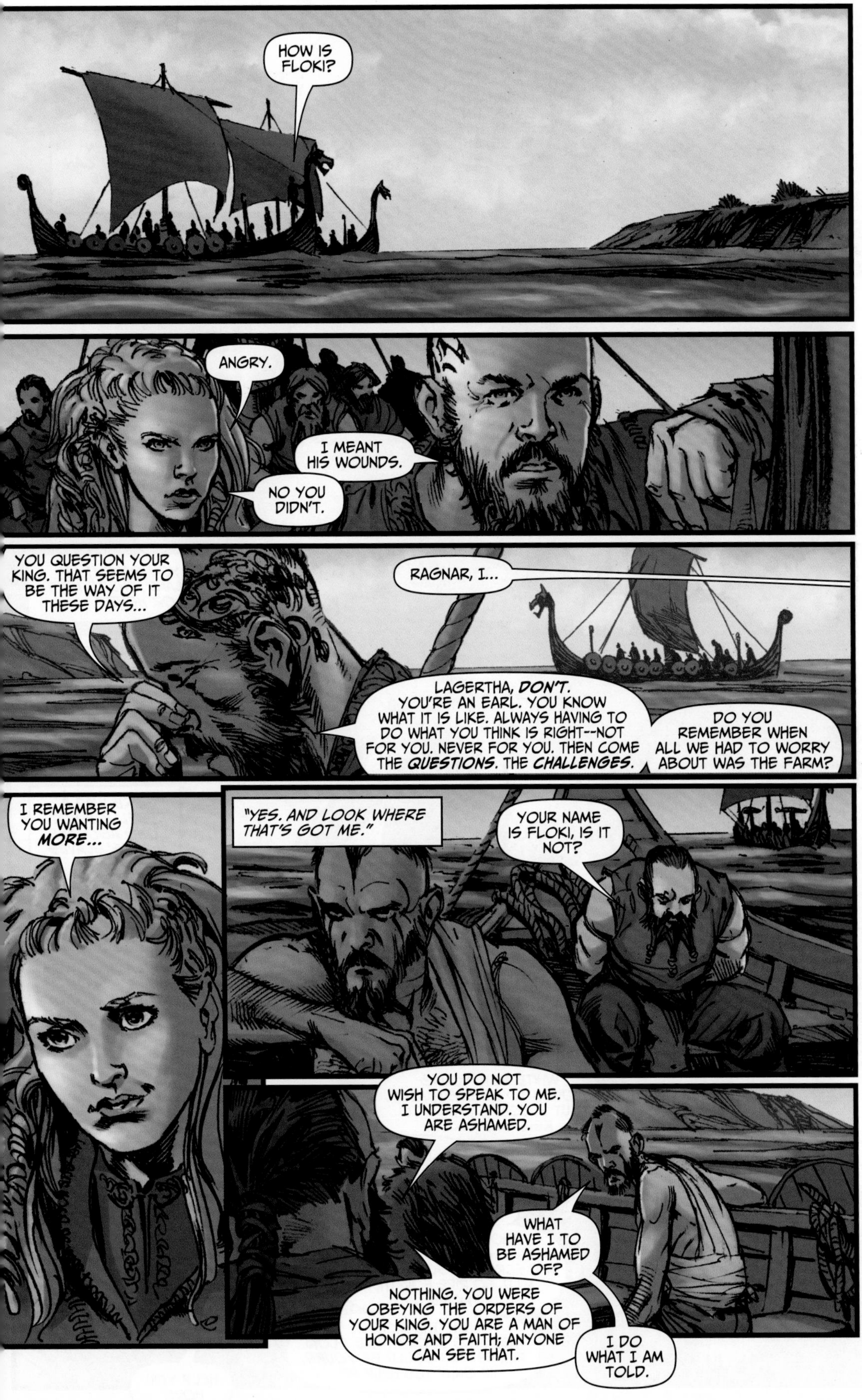
HOW IS FLOKI?
ANGRY.
I MEANT HIS WOUNDS.
NO YOU DIDN'T.
YOU QUESTION YOUR KING. THAT SEEMS TO BE THE WAY OF IT THESE DAYS...
RAGNAR, I...
LAGERTHA, *DON'T*. YOU'RE AN EARL. YOU KNOW WHAT IT IS LIKE. ALWAYS HAVING TO DO WHAT YOU THINK IS RIGHT--NOT FOR YOU. NEVER FOR YOU. THEN COME THE *QUESTIONS*. THE *CHALLENGES*.
DO YOU REMEMBER WHEN ALL WE HAD TO WORRY ABOUT WAS THE FARM?
I REMEMBER YOU WANTING *MORE...*
"YES. AND LOOK WHERE THAT'S GOT ME."
YOUR NAME IS FLOKI, IS IT NOT?
YOU DO NOT WISH TO SPEAK TO ME. I UNDERSTAND. YOU ARE ASHAMED.
WHAT HAVE I TO BE ASHAMED OF?
NOTHING. YOU WERE OBEYING THE ORDERS OF YOUR KING. YOU ARE A MAN OF HONOR AND FAITH; ANYONE CAN SEE THAT.
I DO WHAT I AM TOLD.

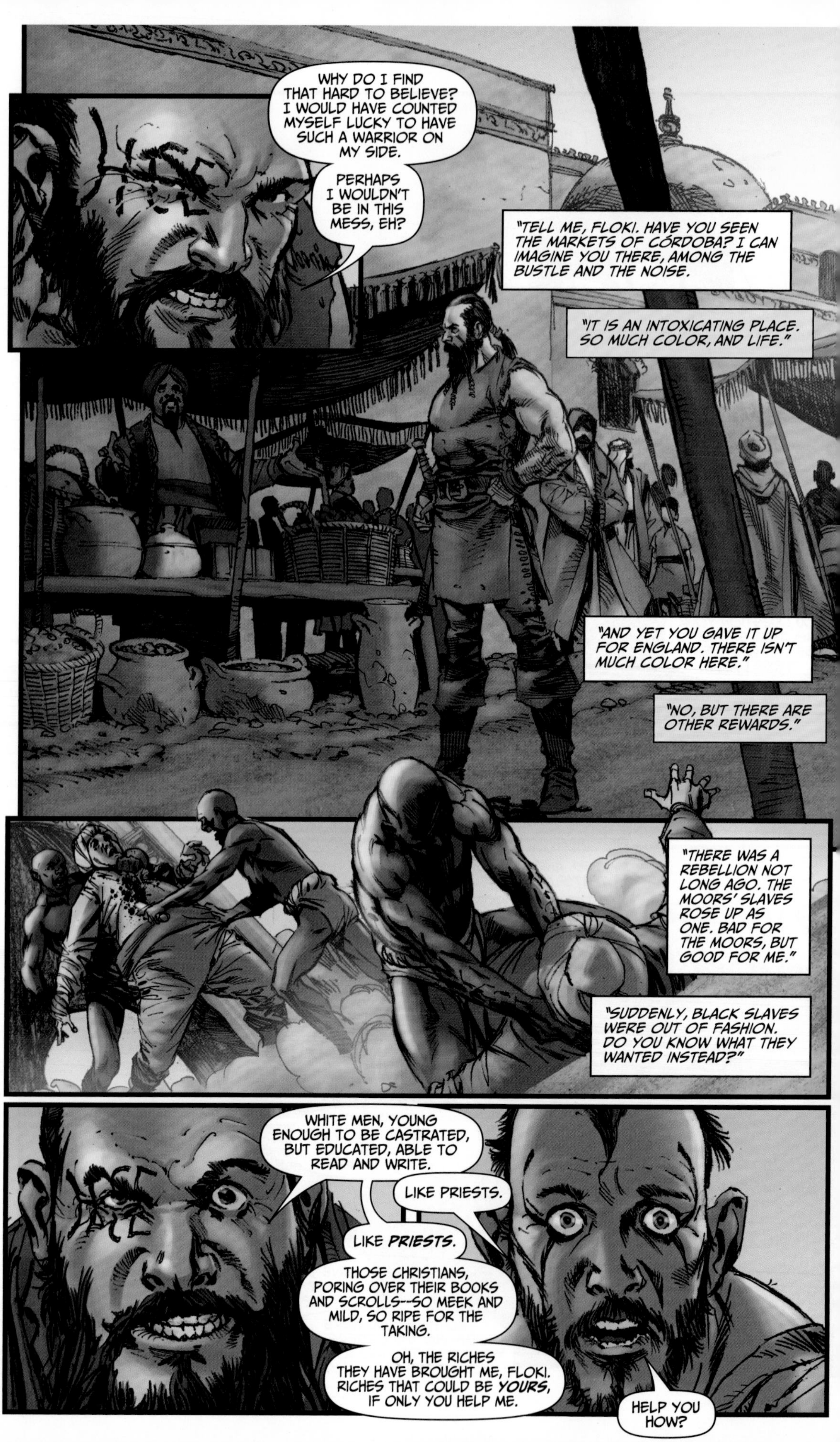
WHY DO I FIND THAT HARD TO BELIEVE? I WOULD HAVE COUNTED MYSELF LUCKY TO HAVE SUCH A WARRIOR ON MY SIDE.
PERHAPS I WOULDN'T BE IN THIS MESS, EH?
"TELL ME, FLOKI. HAVE YOU SEEN THE MARKETS OF CÓRDOBA? I CAN IMAGINE YOU THERE, AMONG THE BUSTLE AND THE NOISE.
"IT IS AN INTOXICATING PLACE. SO MUCH COLOR, AND LIFE."
"AND YET YOU GAVE IT UP FOR ENGLAND. THERE ISN'T MUCH COLOR HERE."
"NO, BUT THERE ARE OTHER REWARDS."
"THERE WAS A REBELLION NOT LONG AGO. THE MOORS' SLAVES ROSE UP AS ONE. BAD FOR THE MOORS, BUT GOOD FOR ME."
"SUDDENLY, BLACK SLAVES WERE OUT OF FASHION. DO YOU KNOW WHAT THEY WANTED INSTEAD?"
WHITE MEN, YOUNG ENOUGH TO BE CASTRATED, BUT EDUCATED, ABLE TO READ AND WRITE.
LIKE PRIESTS.
LIKE *PRIESTS*.
THOSE CHRISTIANS, PORING OVER THEIR BOOKS AND SCROLLS--SO MEEK AND MILD, SO RIPE FOR THE TAKING.
OH, THE RICHES THEY HAVE BROUGHT ME, FLOKI. RICHES THAT COULD BE *YOURS*, IF ONLY YOU HELP ME.
HELP YOU HOW?

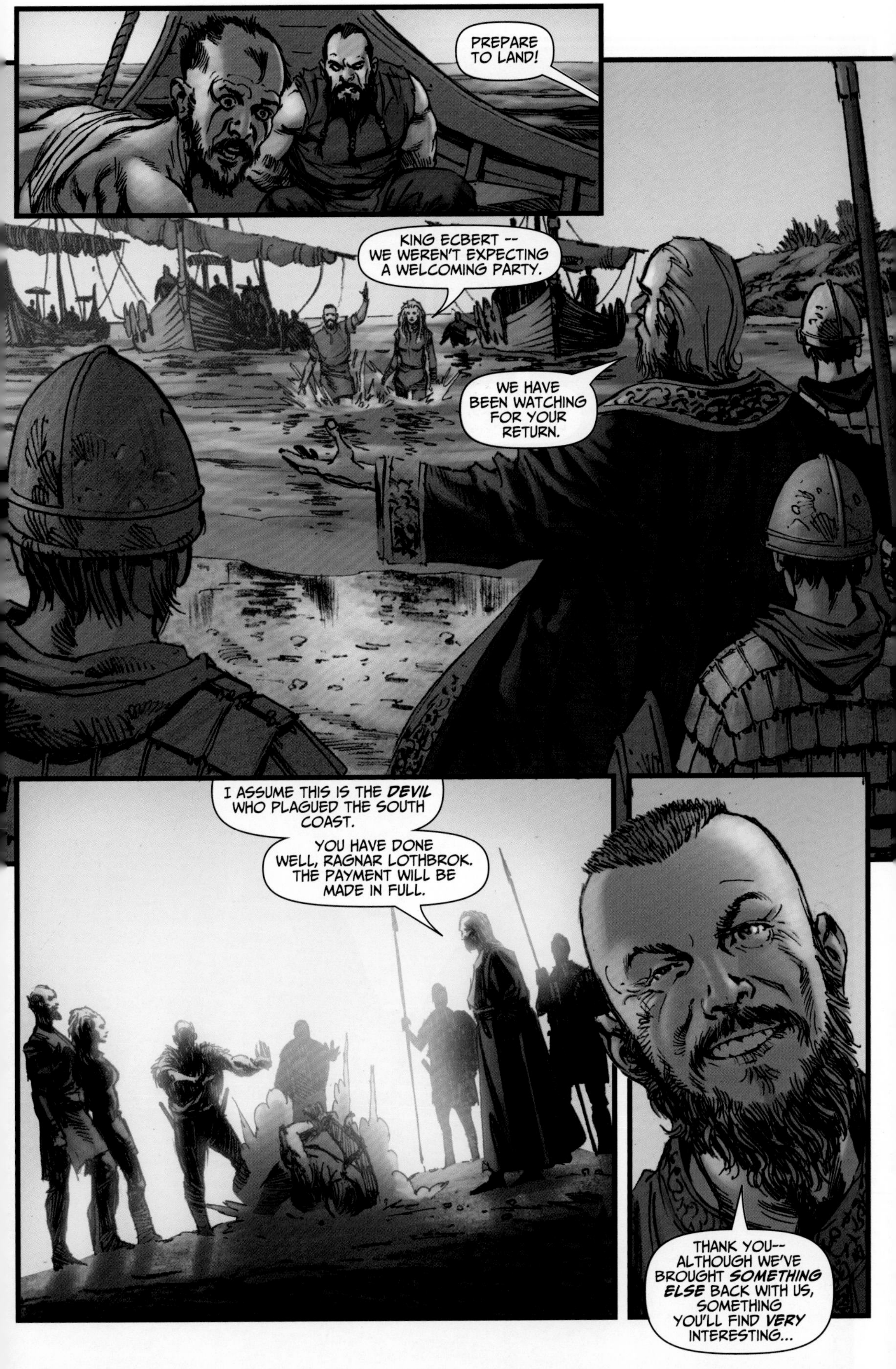
PREPARE TO LAND!
KING ECBERT -- WE WEREN'T EXPECTING A WELCOMING PARTY.
WE HAVE BEEN WATCHING FOR YOUR RETURN.
I ASSUME THIS IS THE *DEVIL* WHO PLAGUED THE SOUTH COAST.
YOU HAVE DONE WELL, RAGNAR LOTHBROK. THE PAYMENT WILL BE MADE IN FULL.
THANK YOU-- ALTHOUGH WE'VE BROUGHT *SOMETHING ELSE* BACK WITH US, SOMETHING YOU'LL FIND *VERY* INTERESTING...

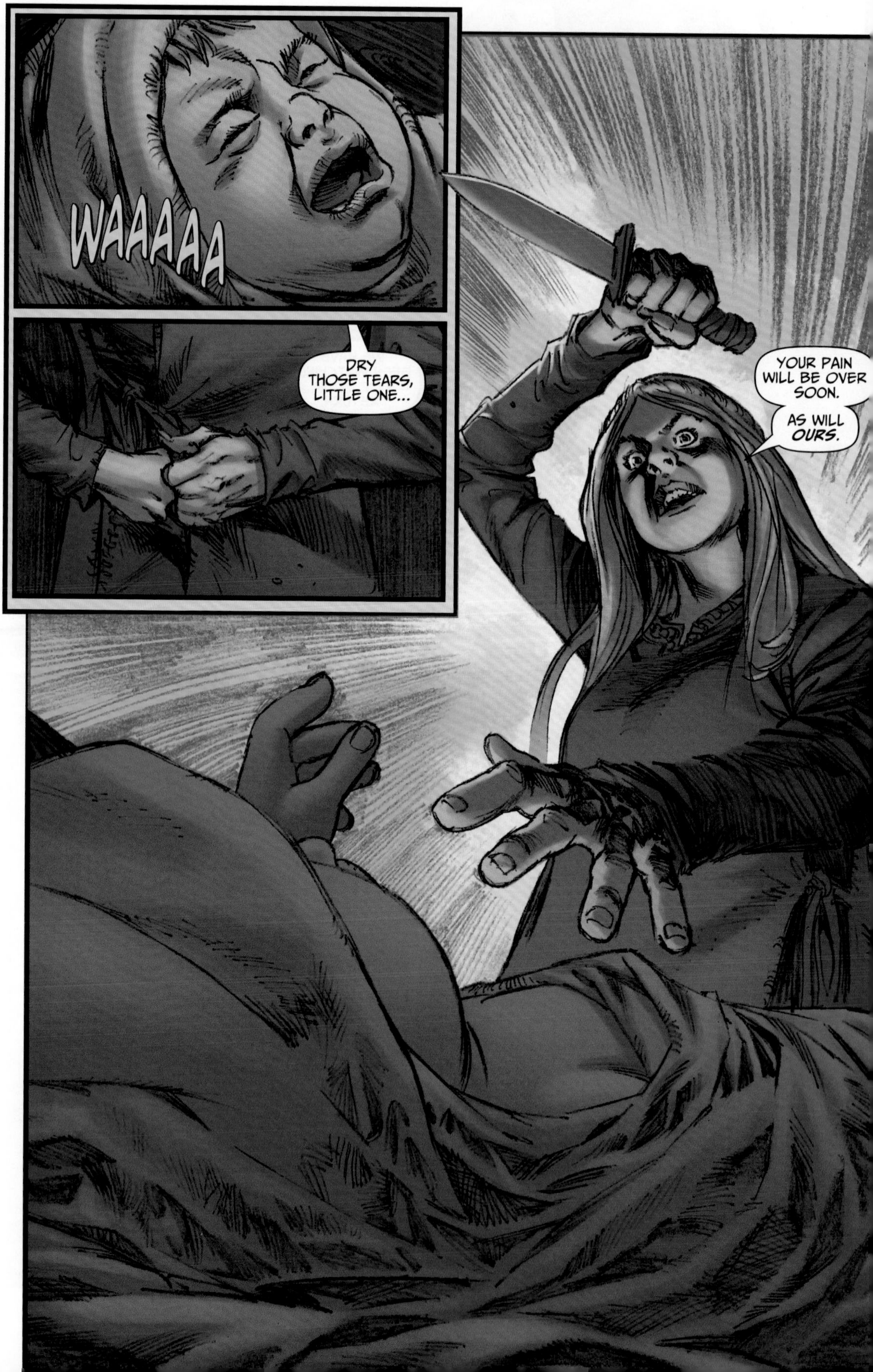
WAAAAA
DRY THOSE TEARS, LITTLE ONE...
YOUR PAIN WILL BE OVER SOON.
AS WILL OURS.

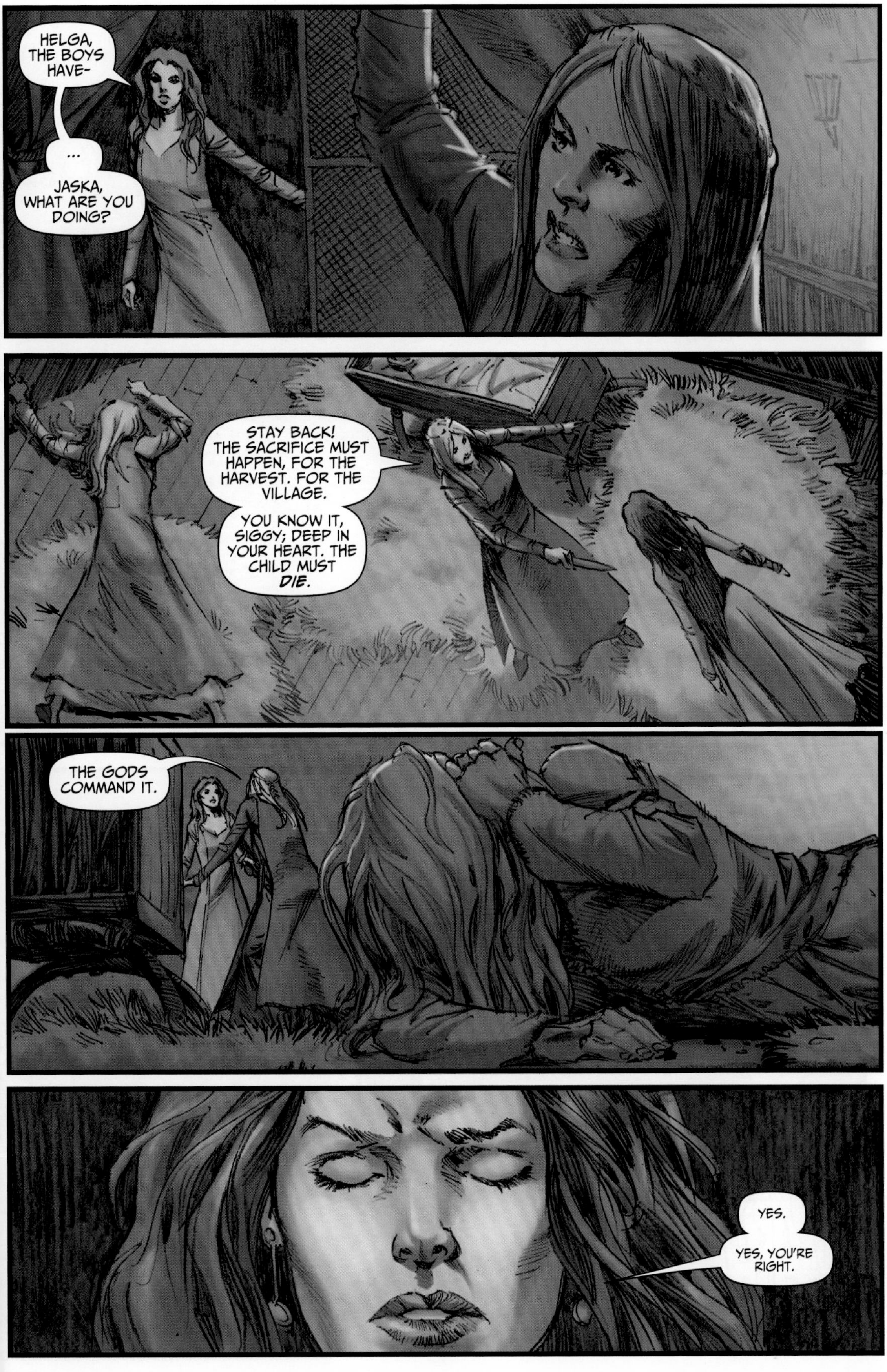
HELGA, THE BOYS HAVE-
...
JASKA, WHAT ARE YOU DOING?
STAY BACK! THE SACRIFICE MUST HAPPEN, FOR THE HARVEST. FOR THE VILLAGE.
YOU KNOW IT, SIGGY; DEEP IN YOUR HEART. THE CHILD MUST DIE.
THE GODS COMMAND IT.
YES.
YES, YOU'RE RIGHT.

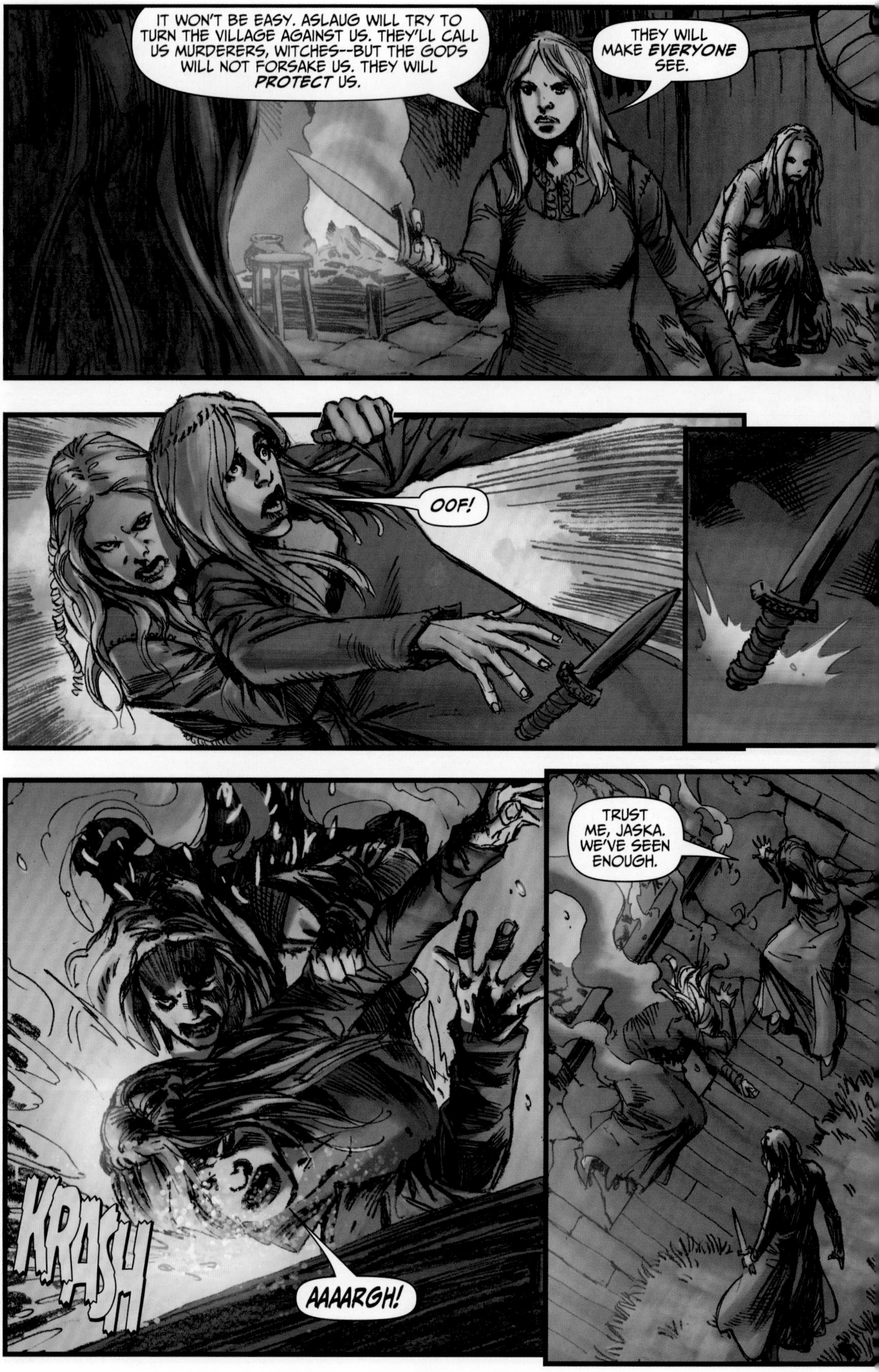
IT WON'T BE EASY. ASLAUG WILL TRY TO TURN THE VILLAGE AGAINST US. THEY'LL CALL US MURDERERS, WITCHES--BUT THE GODS WILL NOT FORSAKE US. THEY WILL *PROTECT* US.
THEY WILL MAKE ***EVERYONE*** SEE.
OOF!
KRASH
AAAARGH!
TRUST ME, JASKA. WE'VE SEEN ENOUGH.

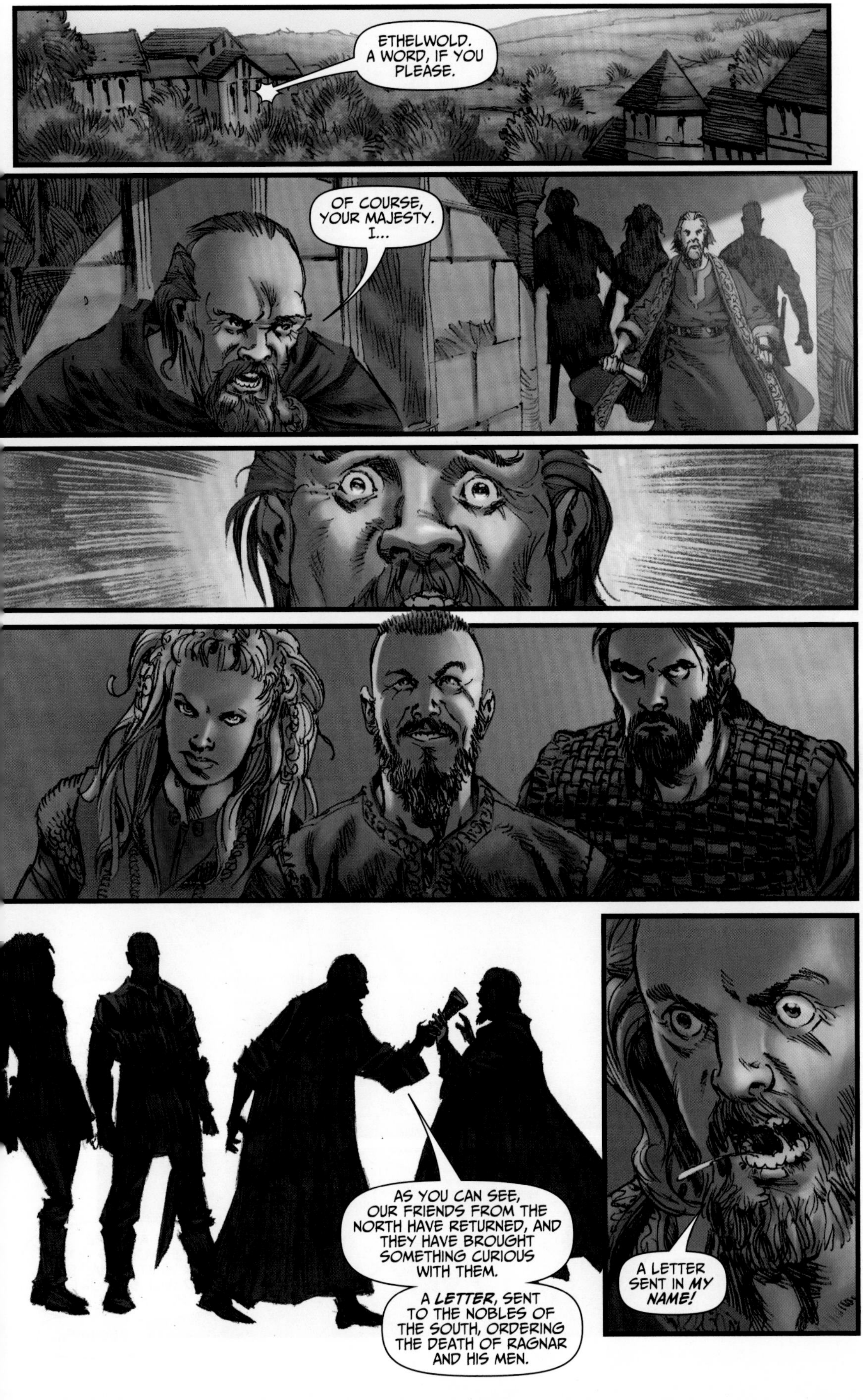

ETHELWOLD. A WORD, IF YOU PLEASE.
OF COURSE, YOUR MAJESTY. I...
AS YOU CAN SEE, OUR FRIENDS FROM THE NORTH HAVE RETURNED, AND THEY HAVE BROUGHT SOMETHING CURIOUS WITH THEM.
A LETTER, SENT TO THE NOBLES OF THE SOUTH, ORDERING THE DEATH OF RAGNAR AND HIS MEN.
A LETTER SENT IN MY NAME!

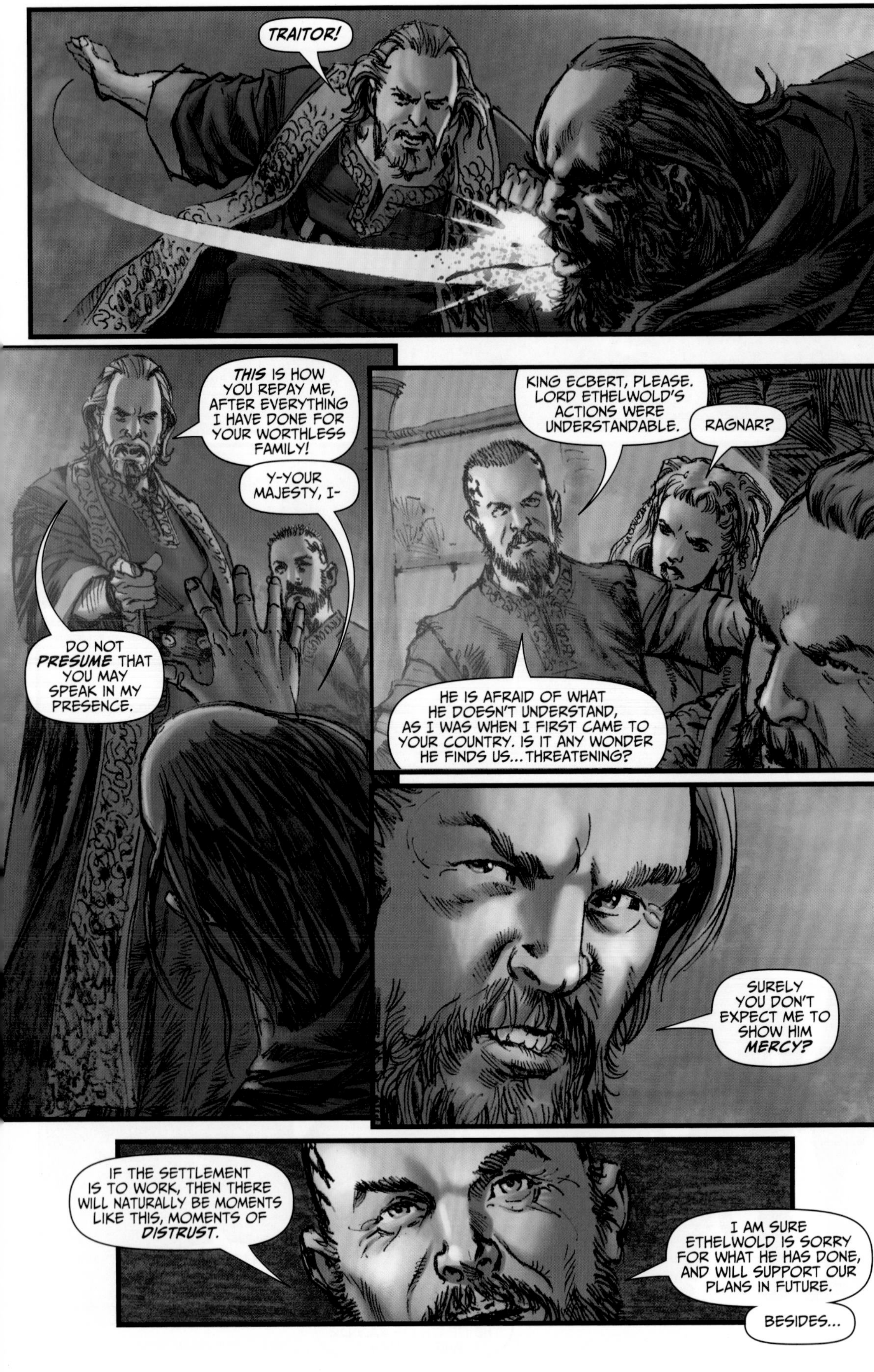
TRAITOR!
THIS IS HOW YOU REPAY ME, AFTER EVERYTHING I HAVE DONE FOR YOUR WORTHLESS FAMILY!
Y-YOUR MAJESTY, I-
DO NOT PRESUME THAT YOU MAY SPEAK IN MY PRESENCE.
KING ECBERT, PLEASE. LORD ETHELWOLD'S ACTIONS WERE UNDERSTANDABLE.
RAGNAR?
HE IS AFRAID OF WHAT HE DOESN'T UNDERSTAND, AS I WAS WHEN I FIRST CAME TO YOUR COUNTRY. IS IT ANY WONDER HE FINDS US... THREATENING?
SURELY YOU DON'T EXPECT ME TO SHOW HIM MERCY?
IF THE SETTLEMENT IS TO WORK, THEN THERE WILL NATURALLY BE MOMENTS LIKE THIS, MOMENTS OF DISTRUST.
I AM SURE ETHELWOLD IS SORRY FOR WHAT HE HAS DONE, AND WILL SUPPORT OUR PLANS IN FUTURE.
BESIDES...

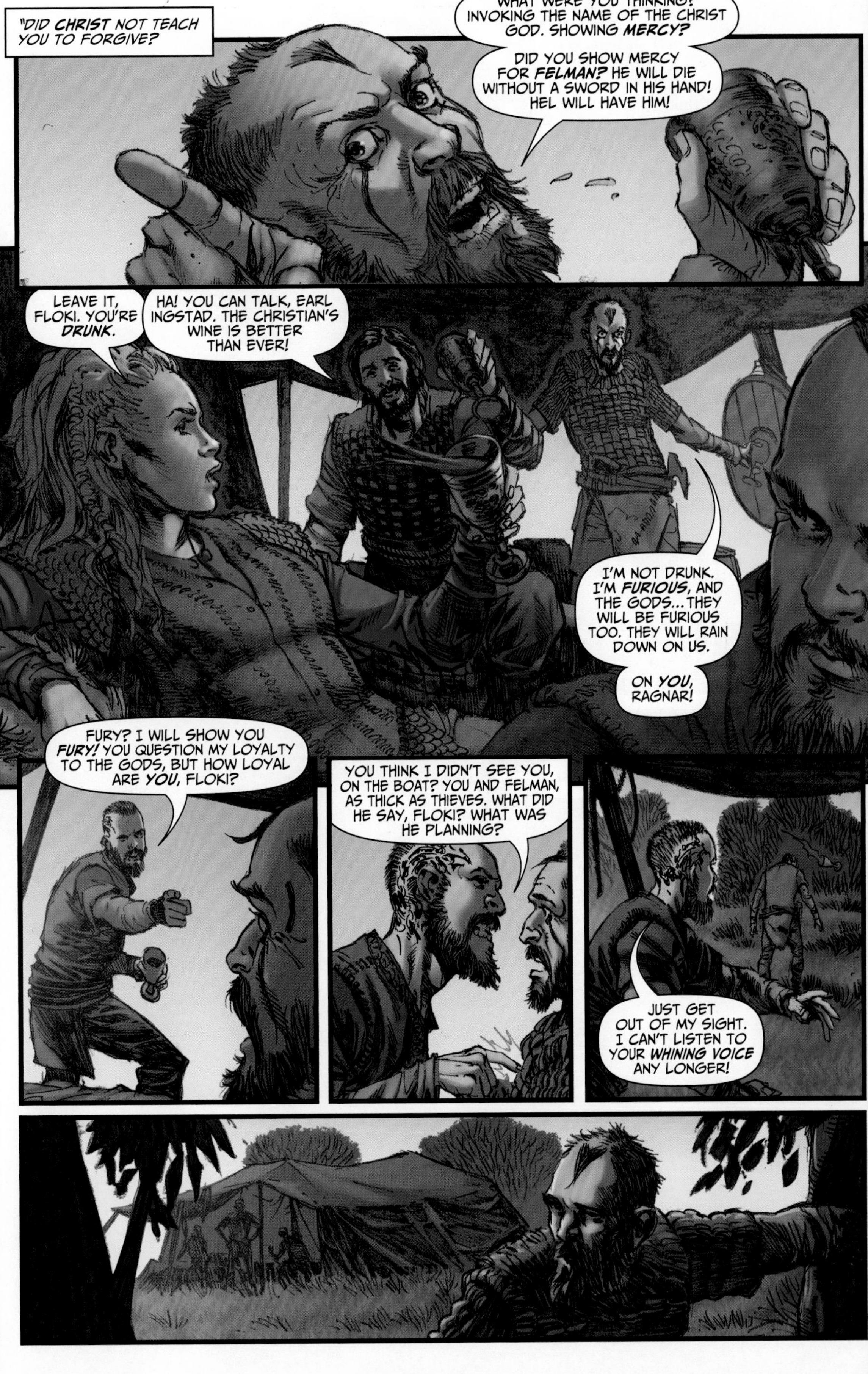
"DID CHRIST NOT TEACH YOU TO FORGIVE?
WHAT WERE YOU THINKING? INVOKING THE NAME OF THE CHRIST GOD. SHOWING MERCY?
DID YOU SHOW MERCY FOR FELMAN? HE WILL DIE WITHOUT A SWORD IN HIS HAND! HEL WILL HAVE HIM!
LEAVE IT, FLOKI. YOU'RE DRUNK.
HA! YOU CAN TALK, EARL INGSTAD. THE CHRISTIAN'S WINE IS BETTER THAN EVER!
I'M NOT DRUNK. I'M FURIOUS, AND THE GODS... THEY WILL BE FURIOUS TOO. THEY WILL RAIN DOWN ON US.
ON YOU, RAGNAR!
FURY? I WILL SHOW YOU FURY! YOU QUESTION MY LOYALTY TO THE GODS, BUT HOW LOYAL ARE YOU, FLOKI?
YOU THINK I DIDN'T SEE YOU, ON THE BOAT? YOU AND FELMAN, AS THICK AS THIEVES. WHAT DID HE SAY, FLOKI? WHAT WAS HE PLANNING?
JUST GET OUT OF MY SIGHT. I CAN'T LISTEN TO YOUR WHINING VOICE ANY LONGER!

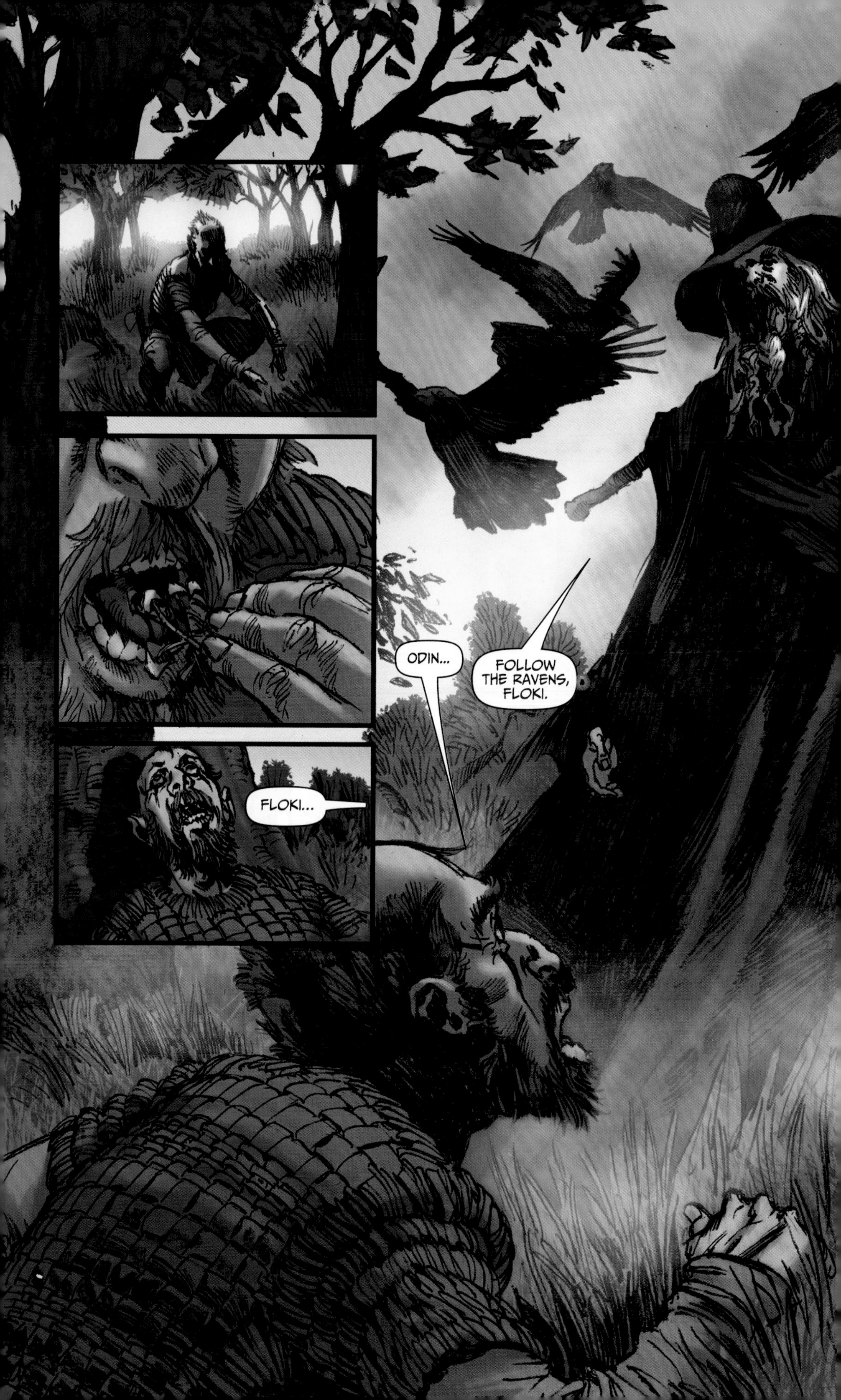
FLOKI...
ODIN...
FOLLOW THE RAVENS, FLOKI.

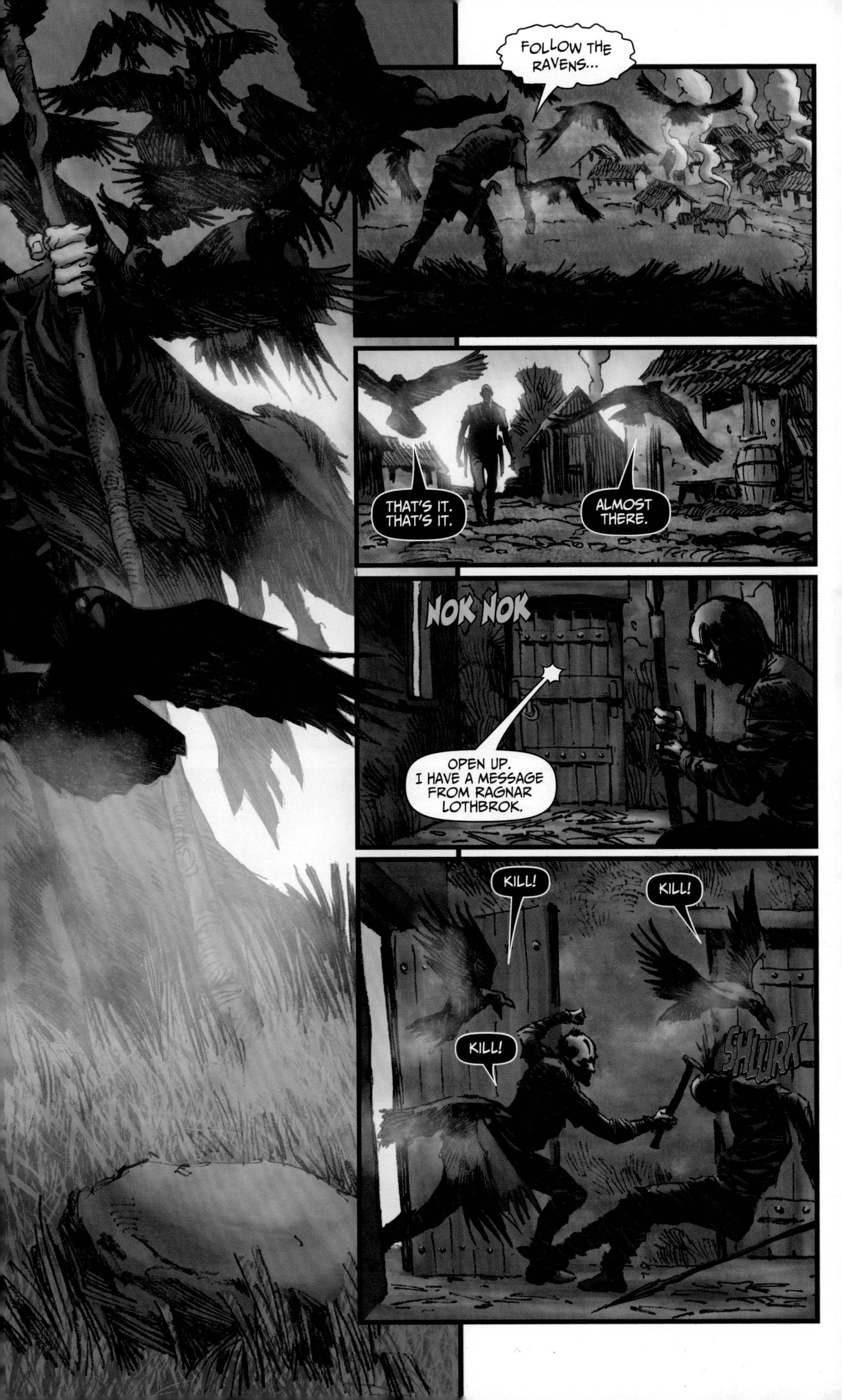
FOLLOW THE RAVENS...
THAT'S IT. THAT'S IT.
ALMOST THERE.
NOK NOK
OPEN UP. I HAVE A MESSAGE FROM RAGNAR LOTHBROK.
KILL!
KILL!
KILL!
SHLURK

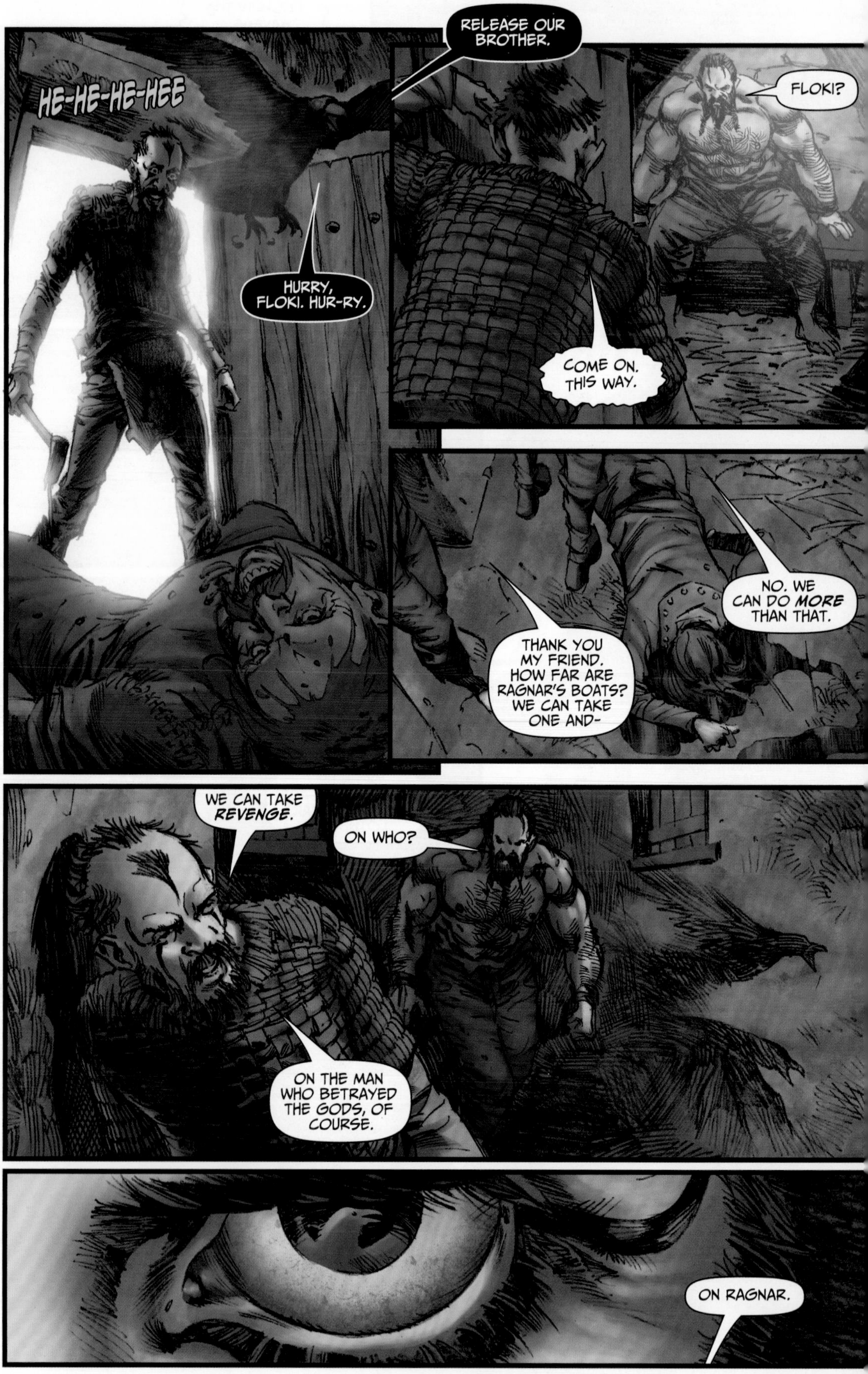
HE-HE-HE-HEE
RELEASE OUR BROTHER.
HURRY, FLOKI. HUR-RY.
COME ON. THIS WAY.
FLOKI?
THANK YOU MY FRIEND. HOW FAR ARE RAGNAR'S BOATS? WE CAN TAKE ONE AND-
NO. WE CAN DO MORE THAN THAT.
WE CAN TAKE REVENGE.
ON WHO?
ON THE MAN WHO BETRAYED THE GODS, OF COURSE.
ON RAGNAR.

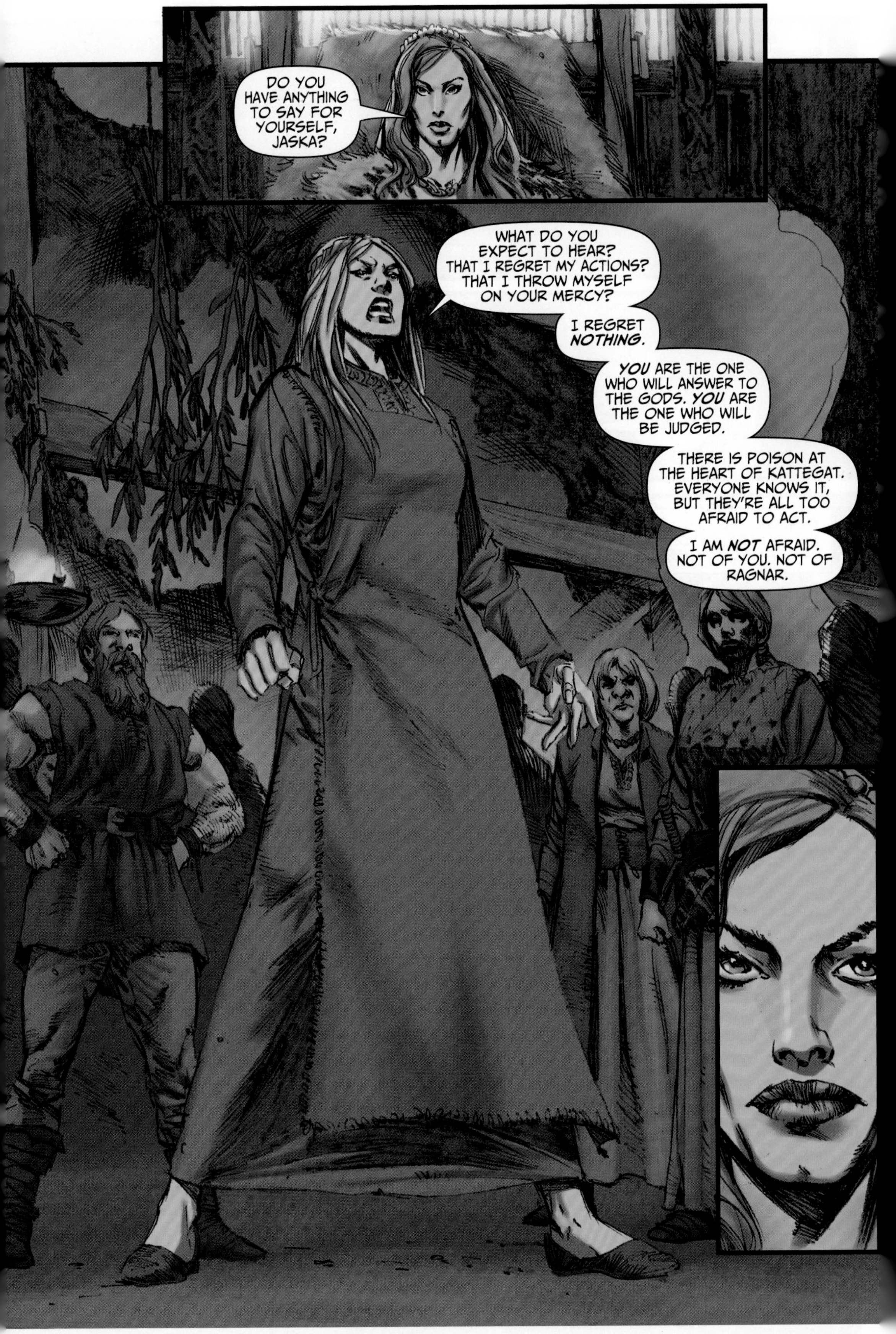
DO YOU HAVE ANYTHING TO SAY FOR YOURSELF, JASKA?
WHAT DO YOU EXPECT TO HEAR? THAT I REGRET MY ACTIONS? THAT I THROW MYSELF ON YOUR MERCY?
I REGRET *NOTHING*.
YOU ARE THE ONE WHO WILL ANSWER TO THE GODS. *YOU* ARE THE ONE WHO WILL BE JUDGED.
THERE IS POISON AT THE HEART OF KATTEGAT. EVERYONE KNOWS IT, BUT THEY'RE ALL TOO AFRAID TO ACT.
I AM *NOT* AFRAID. NOT OF YOU. NOT OF RAGNAR.

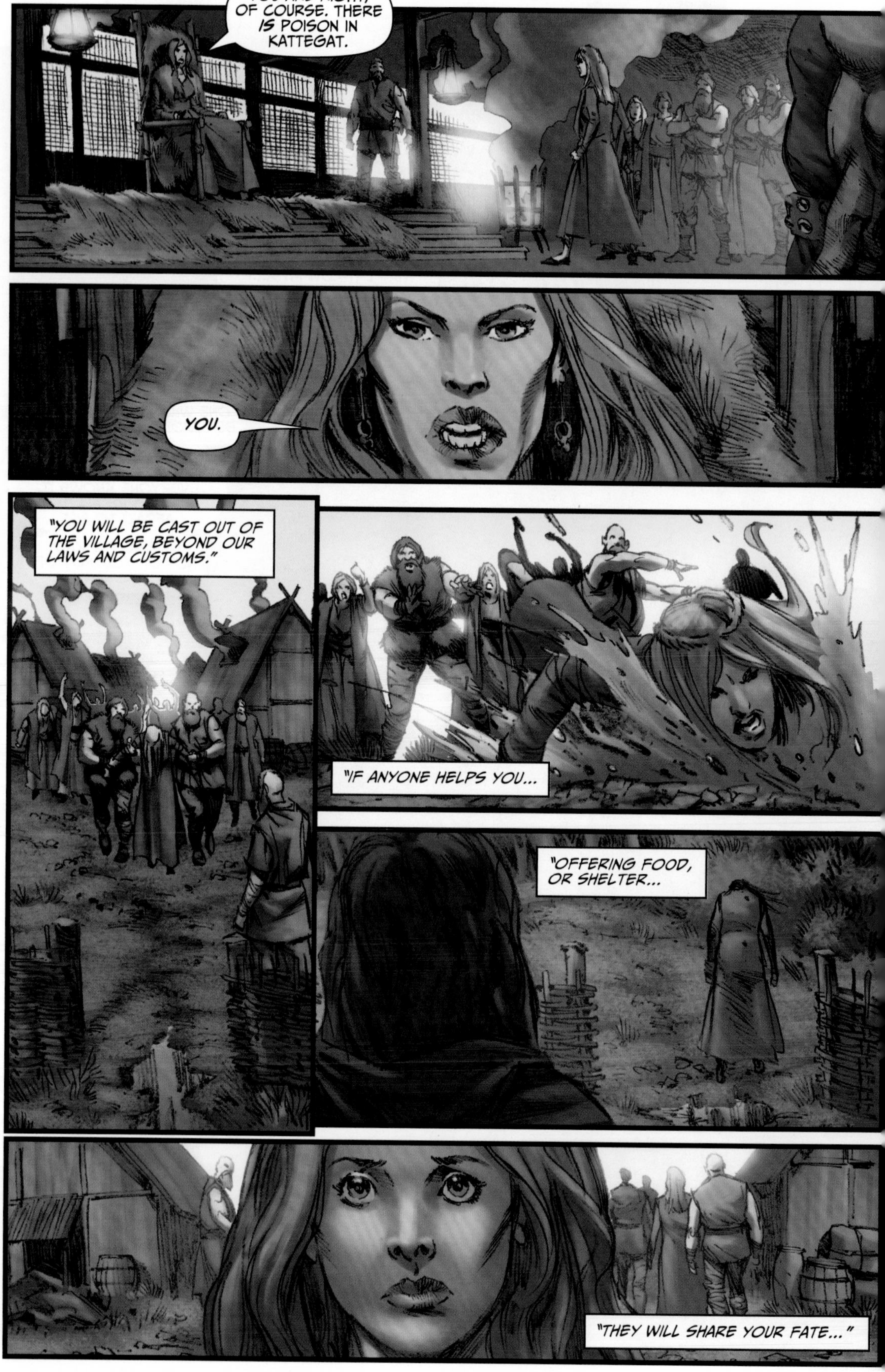
YOU ARE RIGHT, OF COURSE. THERE IS POISON IN KATTEGAT.
YOU.
"YOU WILL BE CAST OUT OF THE VILLAGE, BEYOND OUR LAWS AND CUSTOMS."
"IF ANYONE HELPS YOU...
"OFFERING FOOD, OR SHELTER...
"THEY WILL SHARE YOUR FATE..."

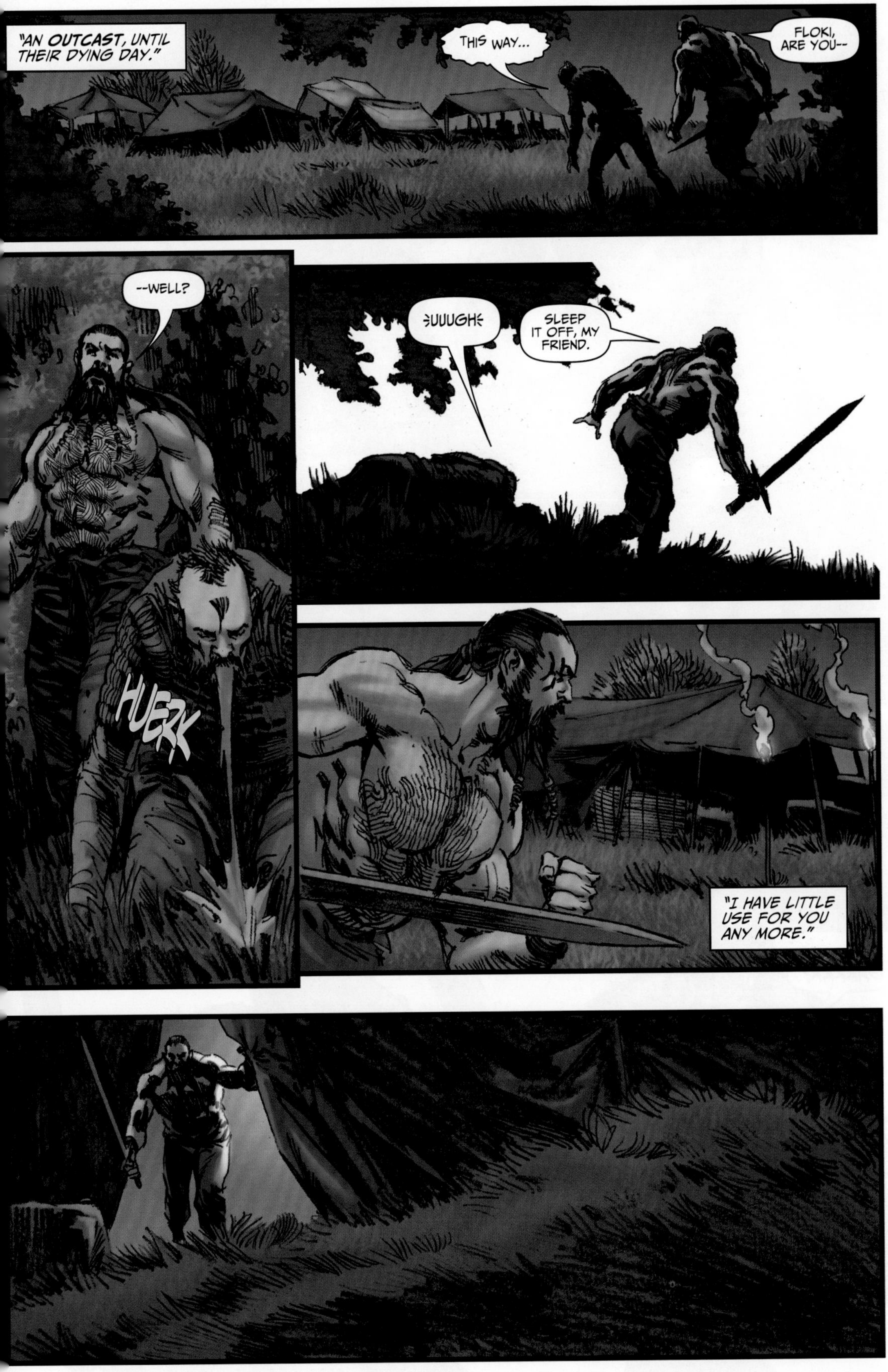
"AN OUTCAST, UNTIL THEIR DYING DAY."
THIS WAY...
FLOKI, ARE YOU--
--WELL?
UUUGH
SLEEP IT OFF, MY FRIEND.
HUERK
"I HAVE LITTLE USE FOR YOU ANY MORE."

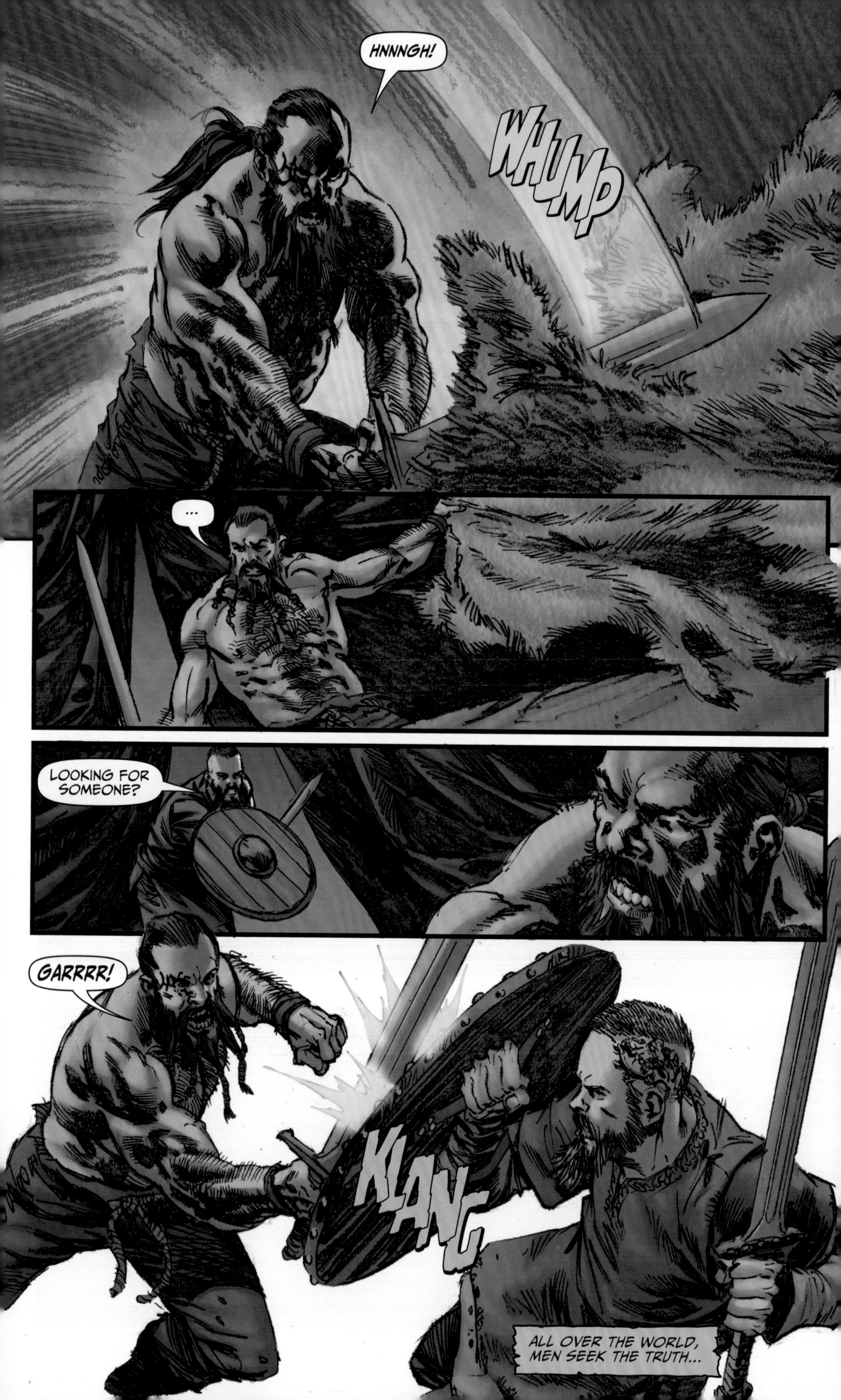
HNNNGH!
WHUMP
...
LOOKING FOR SOMEONE?
GARRRR!
KLANG
ALL OVER THE WORLD, MEN SEEK THE TRUTH...

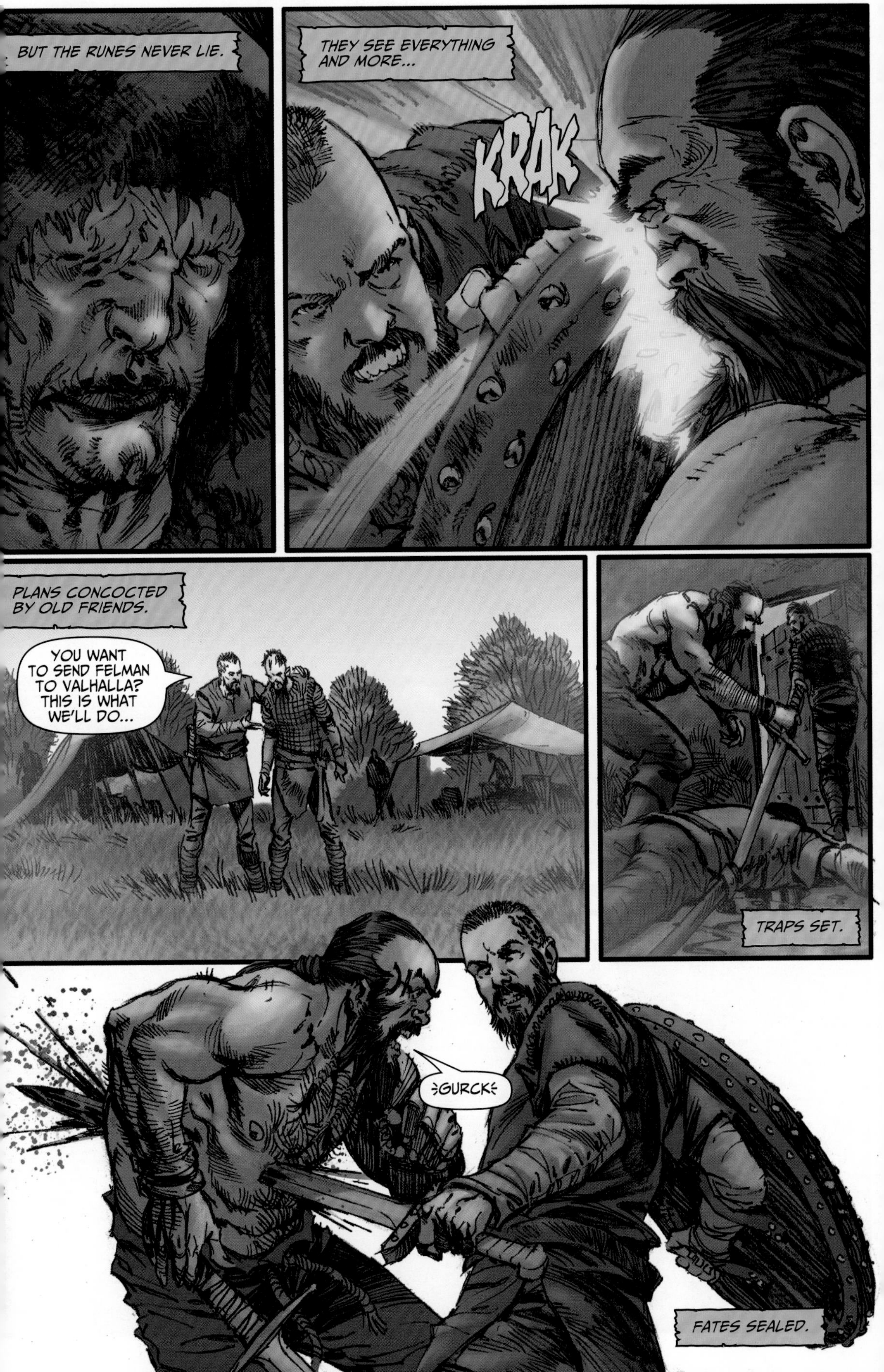
BUT THE RUNES NEVER LIE.
THEY SEE EVERYTHING AND MORE...
KRAK
PLANS CONCOCTED BY OLD FRIENDS.
YOU WANT TO SEND FELMAN TO VALHALLA? THIS IS WHAT WE'LL DO...
TRAPS SET.
GURCK
FATES SEALED.

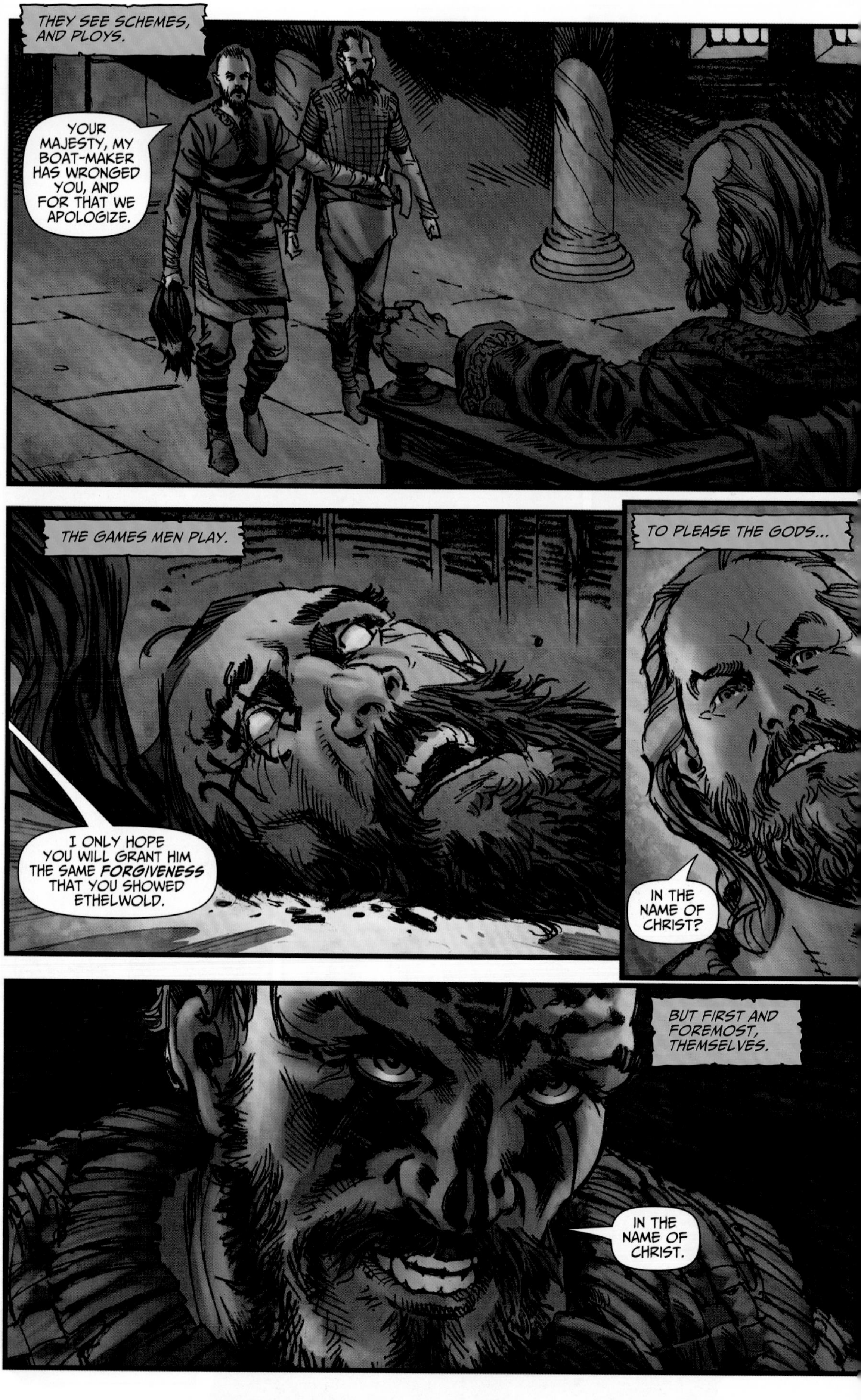
THEY SEE SCHEMES, AND PLOYS.
YOUR MAJESTY, MY BOAT-MAKER HAS WRONGED YOU, AND FOR THAT WE APOLOGIZE.
THE GAMES MEN PLAY.
I ONLY HOPE YOU WILL GRANT HIM THE SAME FORGIVENESS THAT YOU SHOWED ETHELWOLD.
TO PLEASE THE GODS...
IN THE NAME OF CHRIST?
BUT FIRST AND FOREMOST, THEMSELVES.
IN THE NAME OF CHRIST.

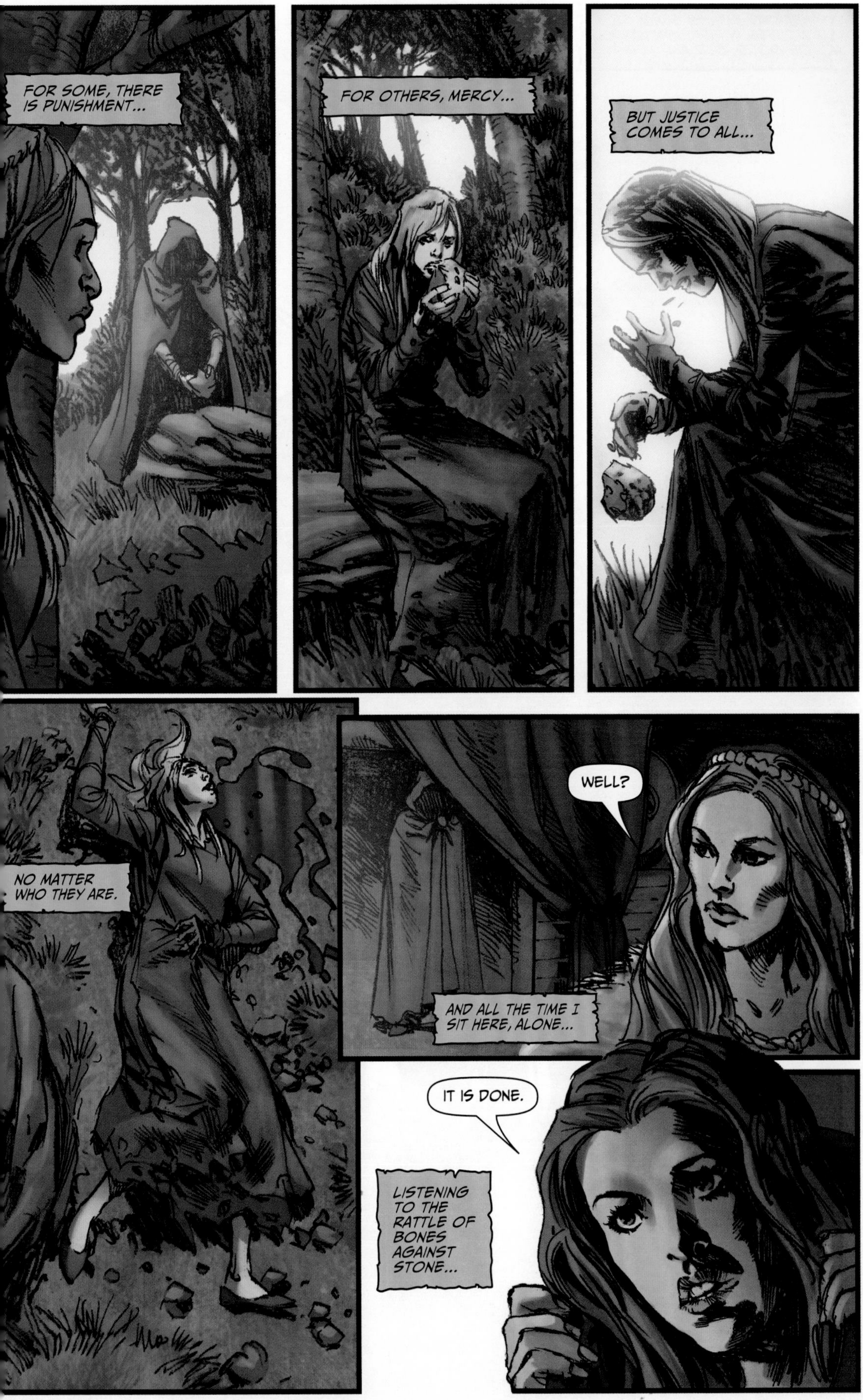

FOR SOME, THERE IS PUNISHMENT...
FOR OTHERS, MERCY...
BUT JUSTICE COMES TO ALL...
NO MATTER WHO THEY ARE.
WELL?
AND ALL THE TIME I SIT HERE, ALONE...
IT IS DONE.
LISTENING TO THE RATTLE OF BONES AGAINST STONE...

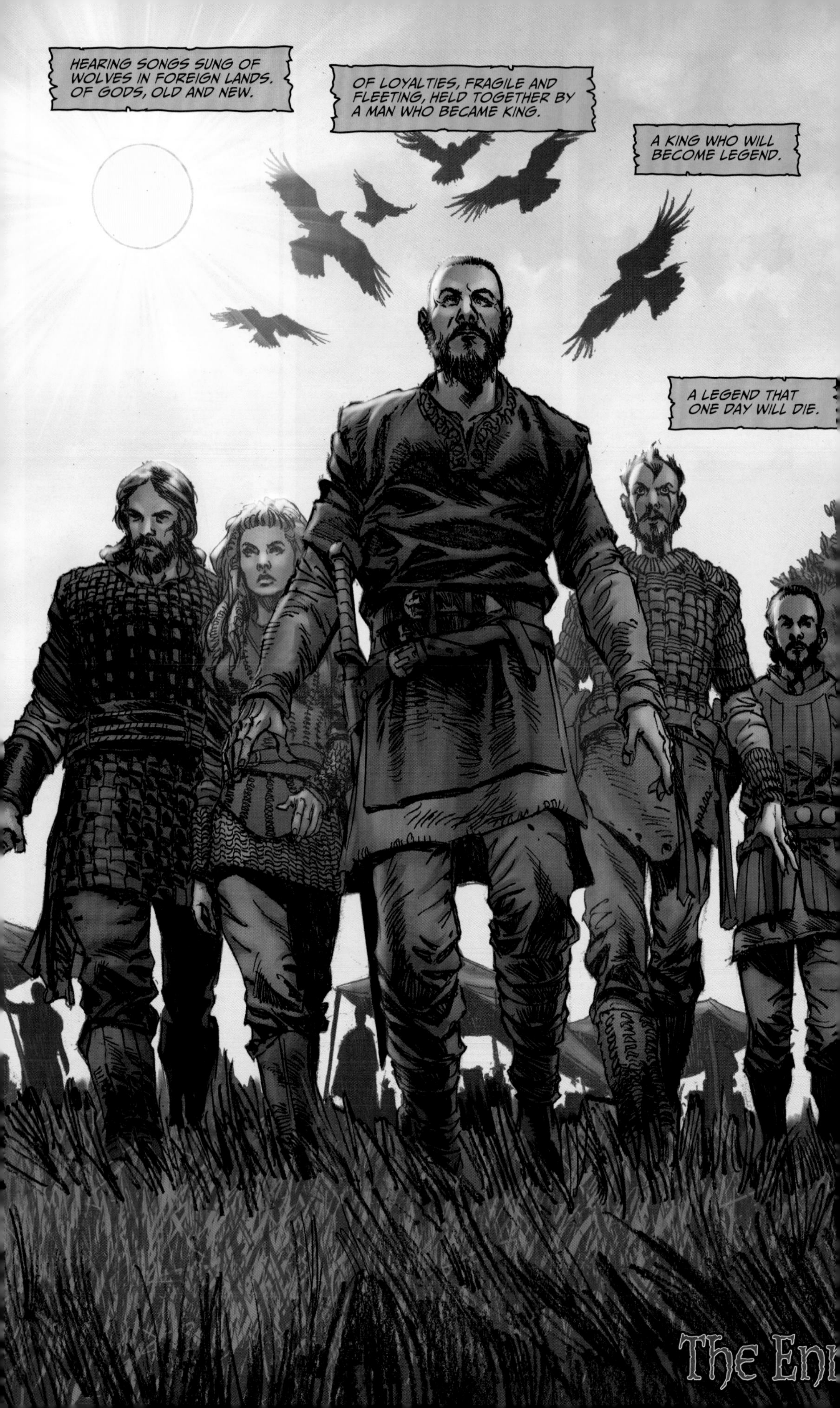
HEARING SONGS SUNG OF WOLVES IN FOREIGN LANDS. OF GODS, OLD AND NEW.
OF LOYALTIES, FRAGILE AND FLEETING, HELD TOGETHER BY A MAN WHO BECAME KING.
A KING WHO WILL BECOME LEGEND.
A LEGEND THAT ONE DAY WILL DIE.

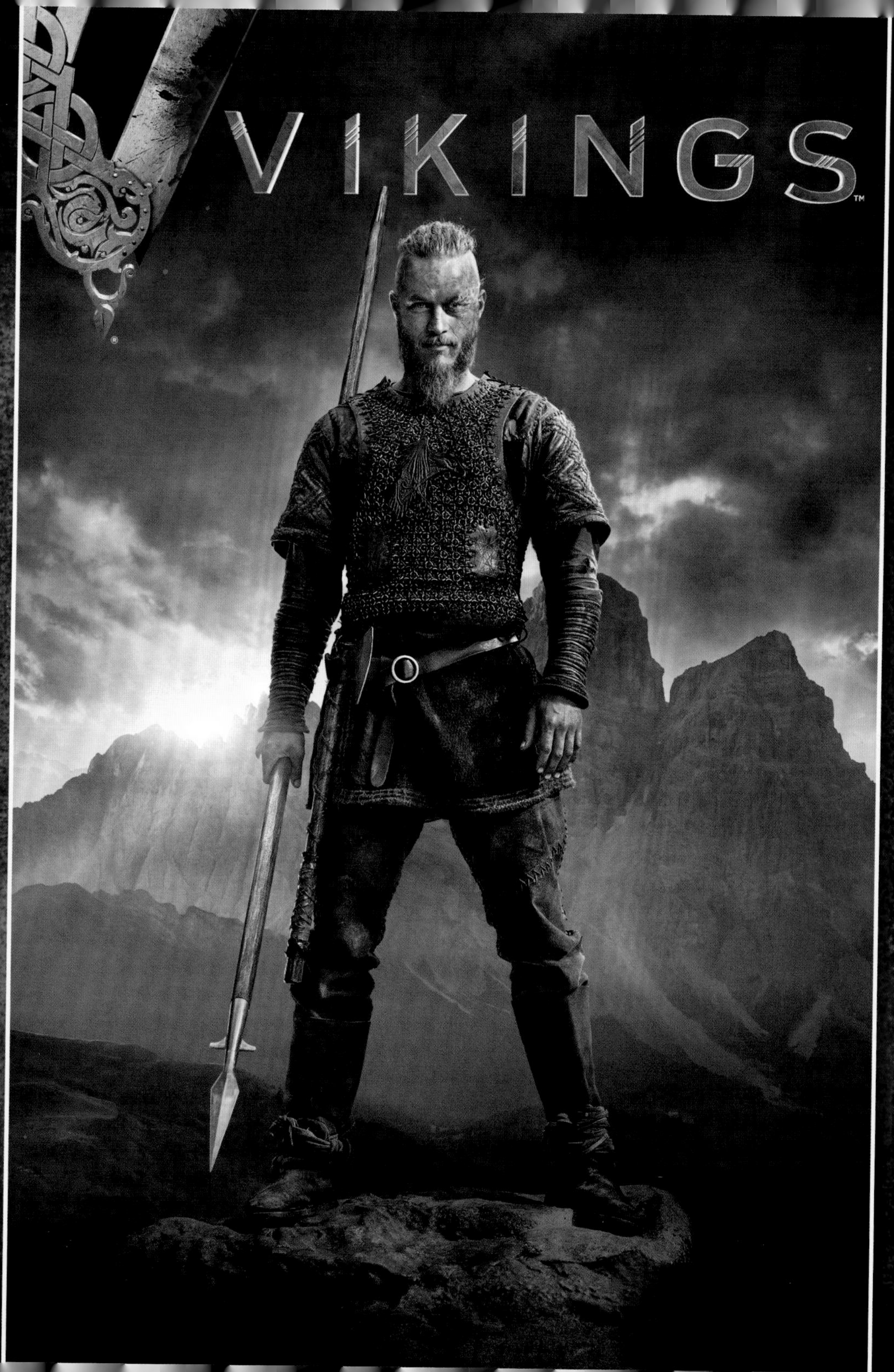
VIKINGS™

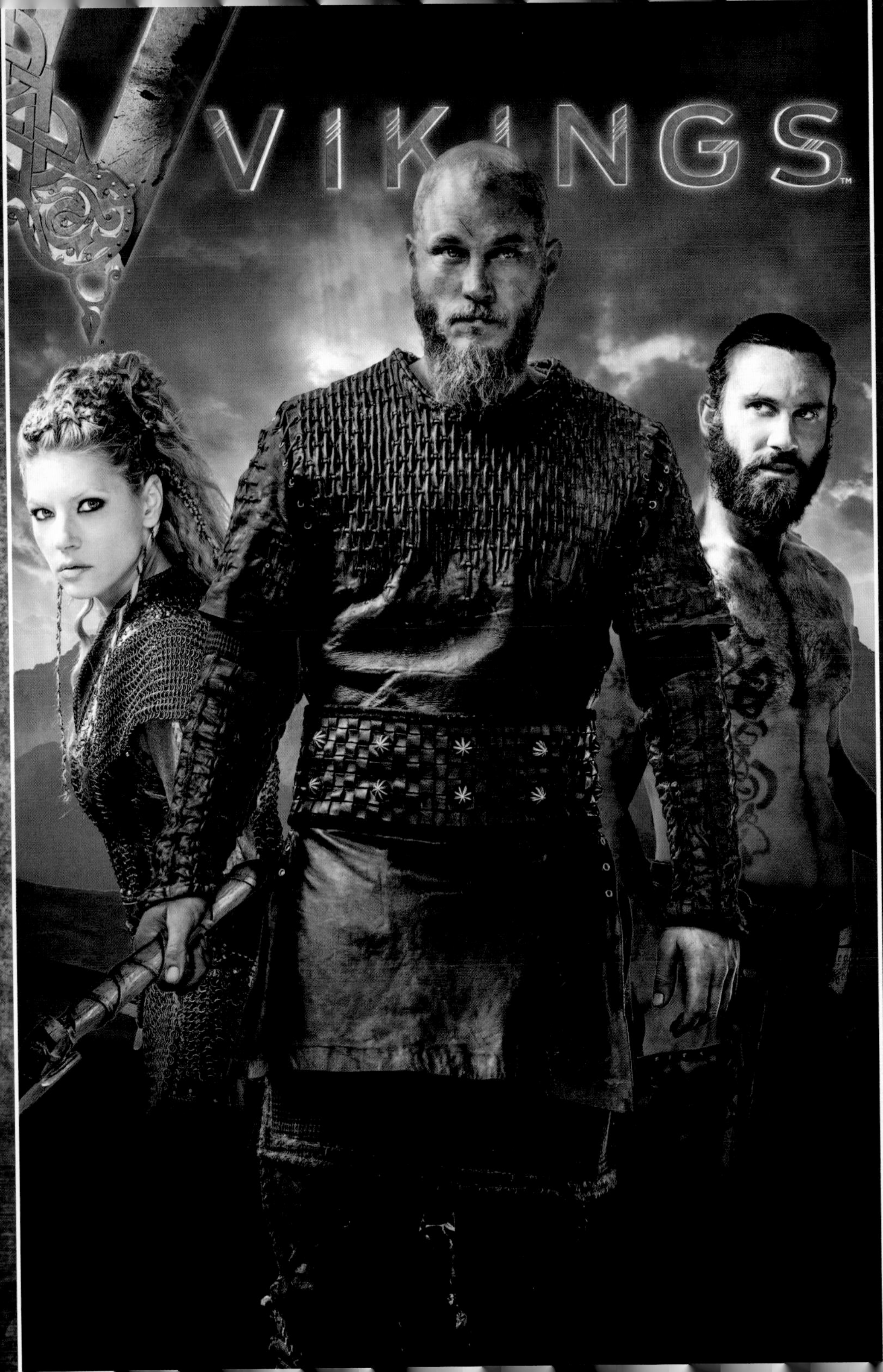
VIKINGS™

GALLERY

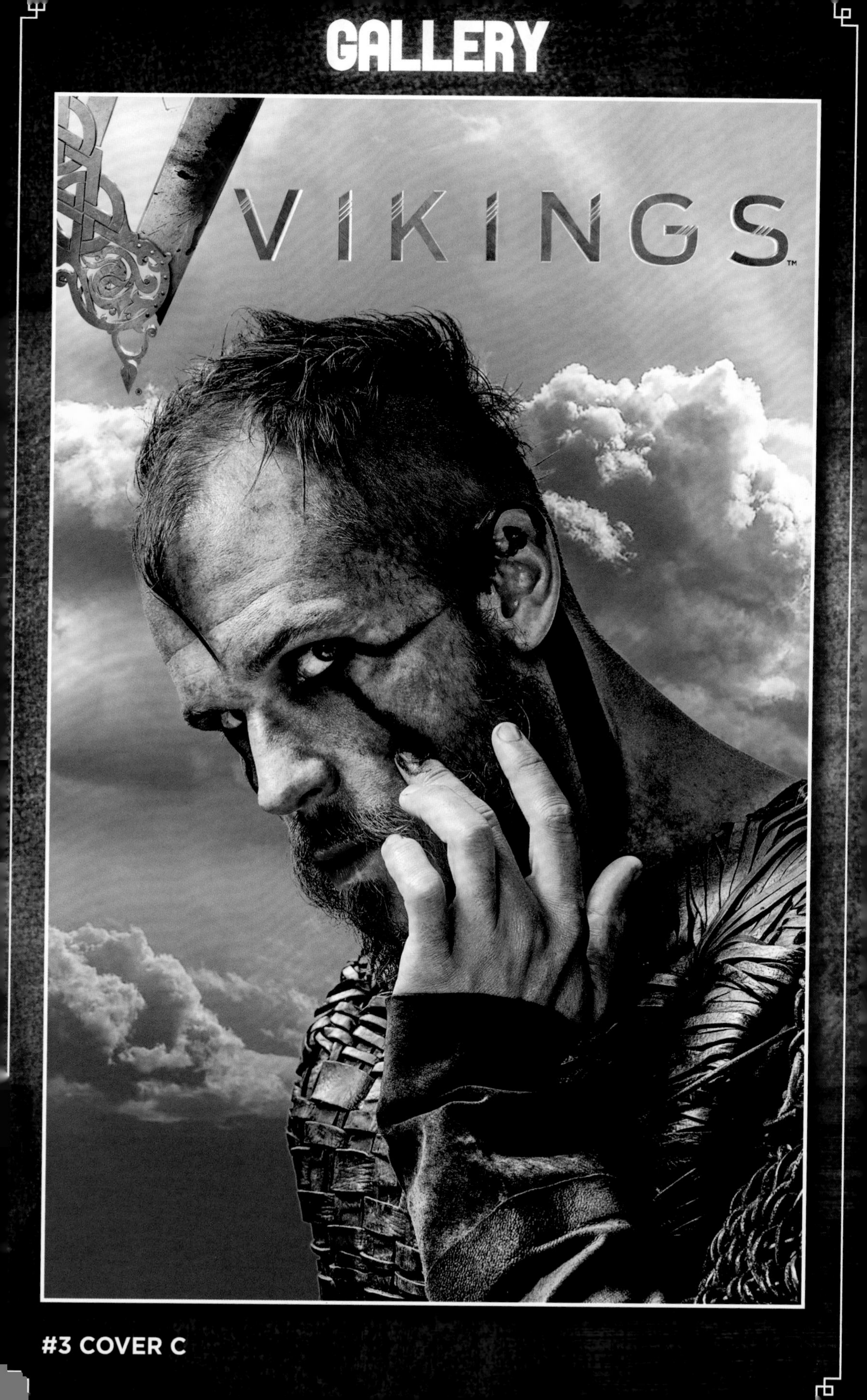
VIKINGS™

#3 COVER C

GALLERY

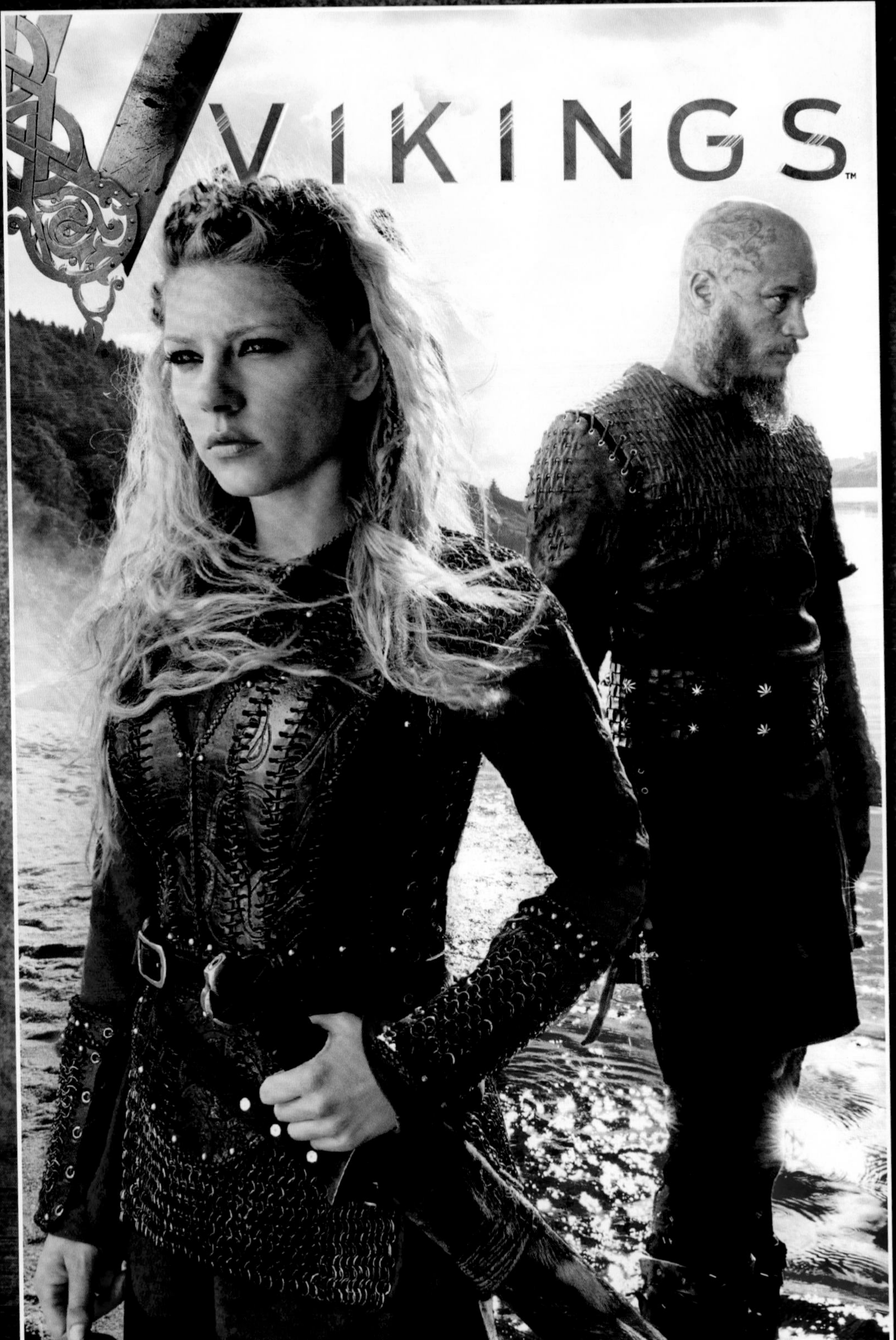

VIKINGS™

#4 COVER C

IN SEARCH OF HEROES

BY
CAVAN SCOTT

IN THE FIRST PART OF AN EXCLUSIVE INTERVIEW, CAVAN SCOTT TALKS TO *VIKINGS'* CREATOR AND SCREENWRITER MICHAEL HIRST ABOUT PILLAGING, PAGANISM AND FINDING RAGNAR LOTHBROK

You only have to look at your work on *Elizabeth* and *The Tudors* to see that you're a keen historian, but what about the Vikings? Have you always been interested in the Viking age and people?
Every Friday, my Dad would come home from work with a little toy soldier. Usually they were from the British Army or Civil War, but one day he brought back a Viking. It's strange that even saying the word summons up a visceral image of a warrior, and there

was certainly something charismatic about that little figure. However, it didn't become a real interest until after [I wrote] *Elizabeth*. Working Title wanted a movie about Alfred the Great. Through my research, I became fascinated by the Vikings' customs and beliefs. Nothing came of the Alfred the Great movie, but now I had the Vikings in my back pocket. Then, out of the blue, MGM asked whether I was interested in writing a Vikings TV series about four years ago.

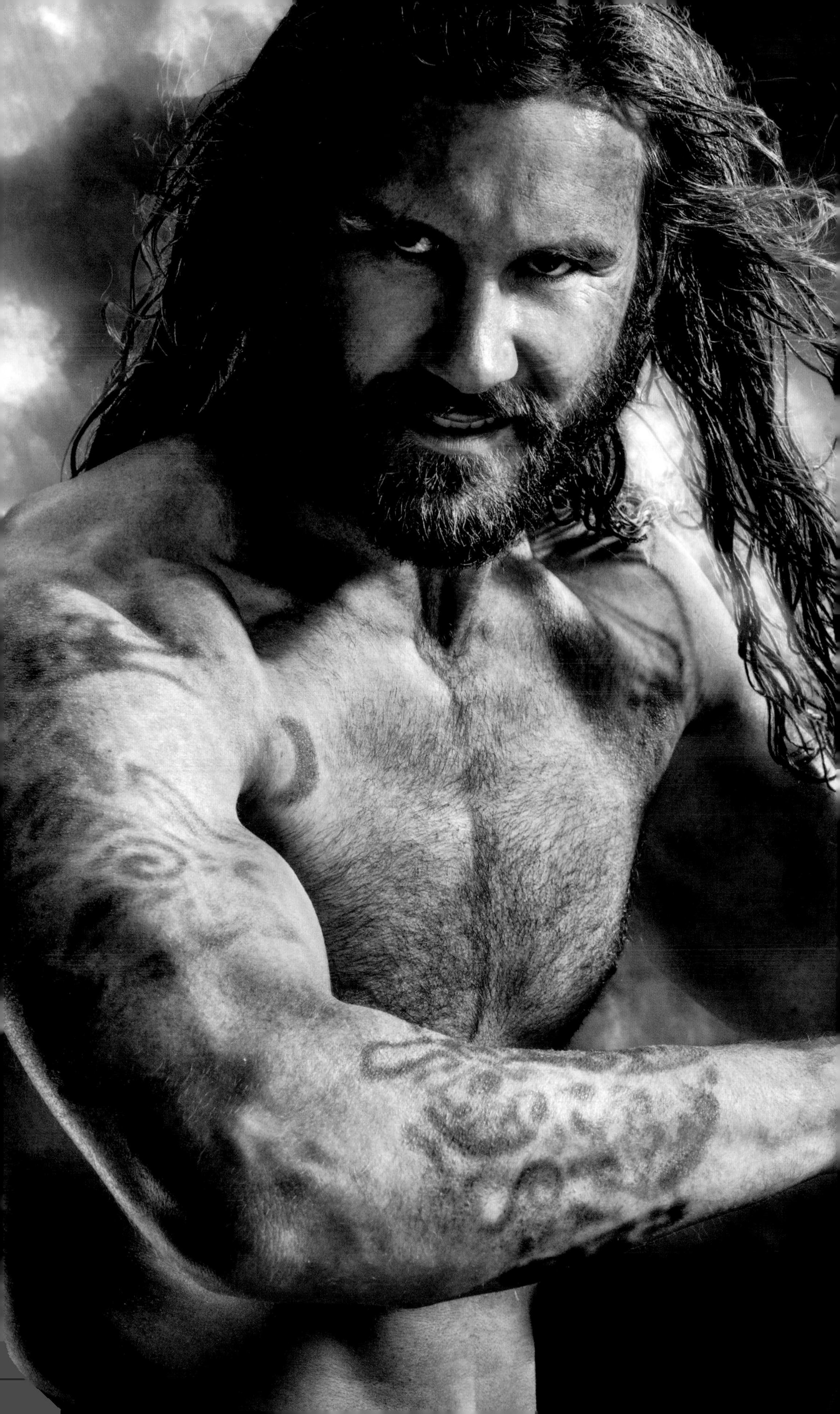

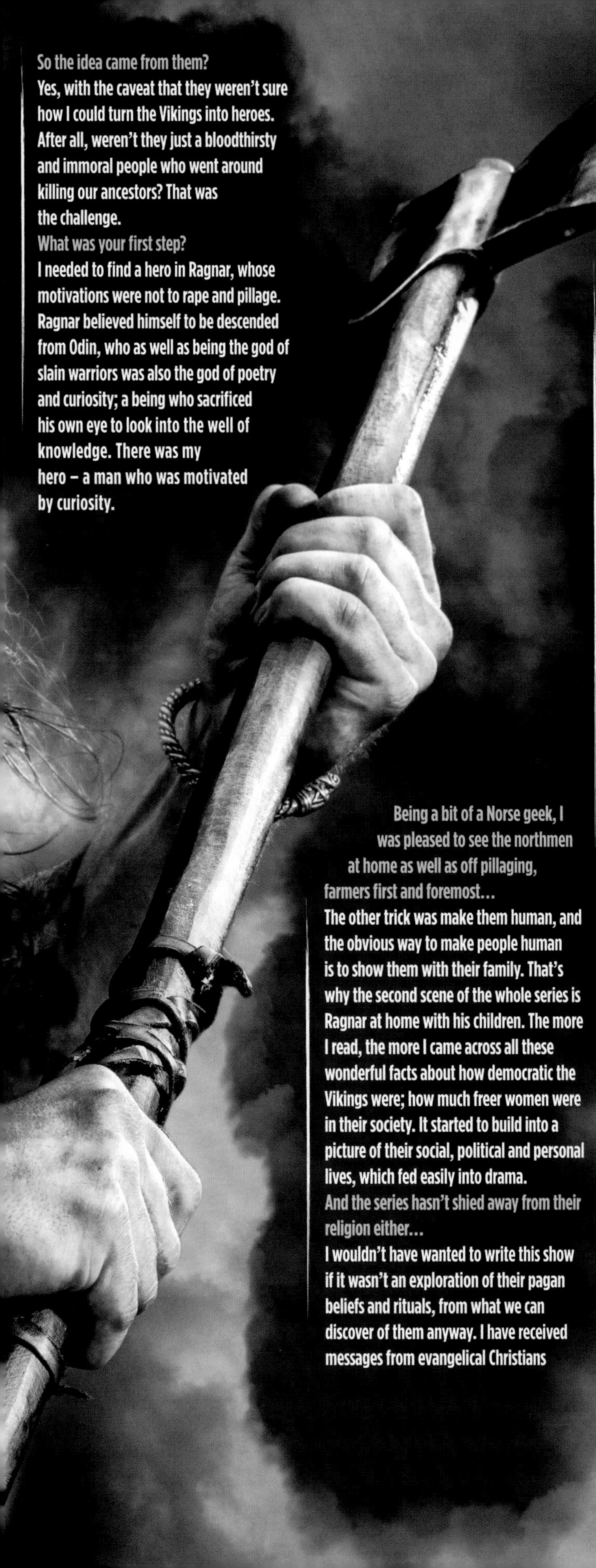

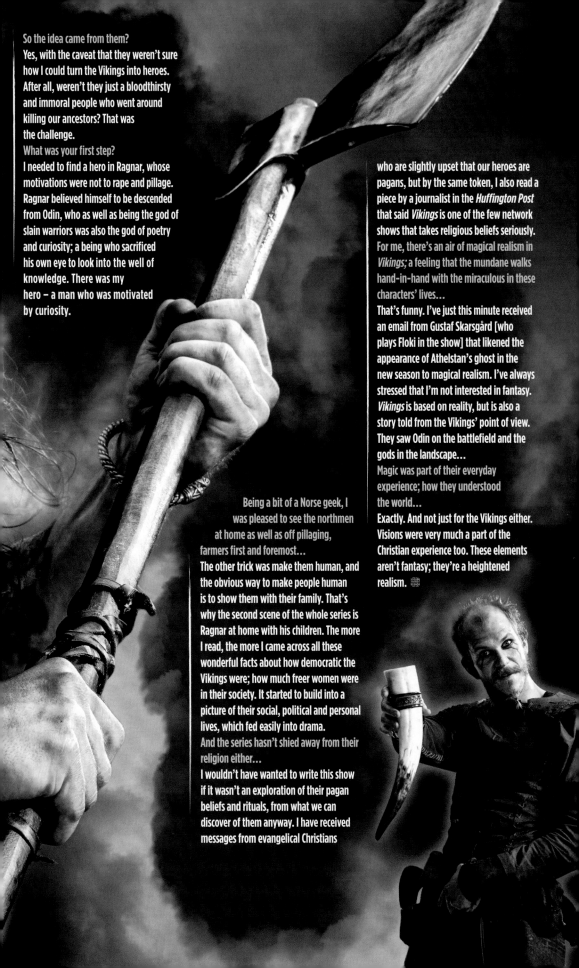

So the idea came from them?

Yes, with the caveat that they weren't sure how I could turn the Vikings into heroes. After all, weren't they just a bloodthirsty and immoral people who went around killing our ancestors? That was the challenge.

What was your first step?

I needed to find a hero in Ragnar, whose motivations were not to rape and pillage. Ragnar believed himself to be descended from Odin, who as well as being the god of slain warriors was also the god of poetry and curiosity; a being who sacrificed his own eye to look into the well of knowledge. There was my hero – a man who was motivated by curiosity.

Being a bit of a Norse geek, I was pleased to see the northmen at home as well as off pillaging, farmers first and foremost…

The other trick was make them human, and the obvious way to make people human is to show them with their family. That's why the second scene of the whole series is Ragnar at home with his children. The more I read, the more I came across all these wonderful facts about how democratic the Vikings were; how much freer women were in their society. It started to build into a picture of their social, political and personal lives, which fed easily into drama.

And the series hasn't shied away from their religion either…

I wouldn't have wanted to write this show if it wasn't an exploration of their pagan beliefs and rituals, from what we can discover of them anyway. I have received messages from evangelical Christians who are slightly upset that our heroes are pagans, but by the same token, I also read a piece by a journalist in the *Huffington Post* that said *Vikings* is one of the few network shows that takes religious beliefs seriously.

For me, there's an air of magical realism in *Vikings;* a feeling that the mundane walks hand-in-hand with the miraculous in these characters' lives…

That's funny. I've just this minute received an email from Gustaf Skarsgård [who plays Floki in the show] that likened the appearance of Athelstan's ghost in the new season to magical realism. I've always stressed that I'm not interested in fantasy. *Vikings* is based on reality, but is also a story told from the Vikings' point of view. They saw Odin on the battlefield and the gods in the landscape…

Magic was part of their everyday experience; how they understood the world…

Exactly. And not just for the Vikings either. Visions were very much a part of the Christian experience too. These elements aren't fantasy; they're a heightened realism.

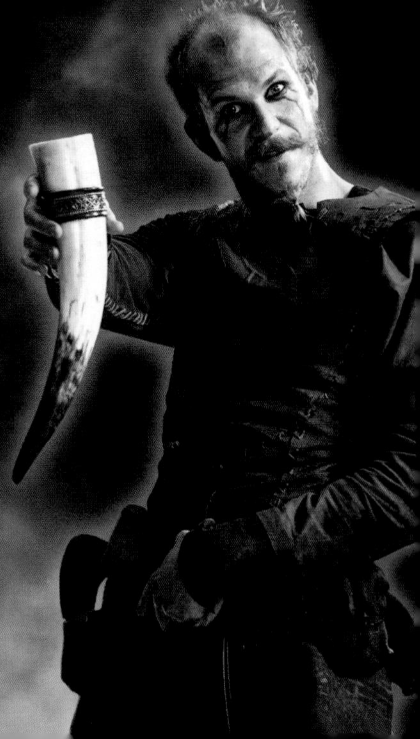

THE KING AND THE TRICKSTER

In the second part of our exclusive interview, Cavan Scott talks to *Vikings'* screenwriter Michael Hirst about quotes out of time, and the origins of Floki...

Vikings is made up of relationships; Ragnar and Floki, Ragnar and Lagertha... with Athelstan acting as a spoke in many of the relationships' wheels. Is there a particular character or pairing that fascinates you?

A lot of myself is invested in a lot of the characters. Athelstan started life as a device. I knew that the Vikings had taken captives on the first raid of Lindisfarne, so what if one of the monks went across the sea to see the Vikings' culture on our behalf? I thought he might be in two or three episodes, but like most of the central characters, he gained a slightly autonomous life that constantly surprised me. In many ways, he's more of an alter ego. I could never be Ragnar, but I *could* be Athelstan. I'm a writer and an observer. Athelstan was the outsider for a long time and continues to be, even in death.

I've also invested a lot in the relationship between Ecbert and Judith. I think it was very funny that Ecbert quotes quite a few lines of T.S. Eliot in series three.

I was going to say that he seems to have a library from the future...
They were lines relating to time – time past or time future – which a Harvard professor picked up on, saying he understood why I chose to include them. The script is full of quotes actually. I noticed an Andrew Marvell quote in an episode I watched recently, and I'm always slipping Beatles lyrics in there.

This is going to become a new *Vikings* drinking game. Take a sip when you spot a quote!
I should think so! But yes, I certainly identify with Ecbert and his agonies and issues. He's a really interesting character, played so well by Linus Roache. He makes it look effortless.

What about Floki? What were his origins?
I was determined to have a wild child or joker [in *Vikings*], because in any society, especially during the medieval period, there's always a mischief-maker, a Pan.

And the Vikings, of course, had Loki...
The Lord of Misrule, yes. Floki's name came out of a history book – the historical Floki discovered Iceland. So, I had the name and my wild card.

In most mythologies, knowledge comes through tricksters. In *Vikings*, the trickster gives Ragnar both his boats and his destiny...
That's right. Making him a boat builder centered him, and was connected to the idea that a boat was a living, magical thing for a Viking. It seemed fitting that a god would be involved in its building.

So, is Floki *actually* a god?
I've enjoyed teasing the audience, and myself, about whether Floki is even faintly a god or not, and what his powers actually are. But I try to root everything in reality.

Did you expect him to become such a popular character?
I honestly didn't know whether he would work. My wife didn't like the character at first, thinking he was over the top, but he's developed into part of the bedrock of the show. *Vikings* without Floki is unimaginable.

Out of all the characters, he's the one who has remained truest to his nature. With everyone else, the waters get muddied...
There are two viewpoints in the show. There is Ragnar, the pragmatist. Part of the reason for the Viking expansion was the search of good arable land to sustain a growing population. That brought with it commerce and deals with other kingdoms and people – which is why the Vikings are in most of our DNA.

Ragnar knows how important compromise is, not only to survive, but to thrive. And then, at the opposite end of the spectrum, there's Floki...
He believes that conflict between the pagan gods and the Christian God is irreconcilable. Compromise weakens the power of the faith, and as we know, the Viking age came to an end with the last Scandinavian country being Christianized. Both Ragnar and Floki are right, but Floki's view is the purest. He's a pagan fundamentalist.

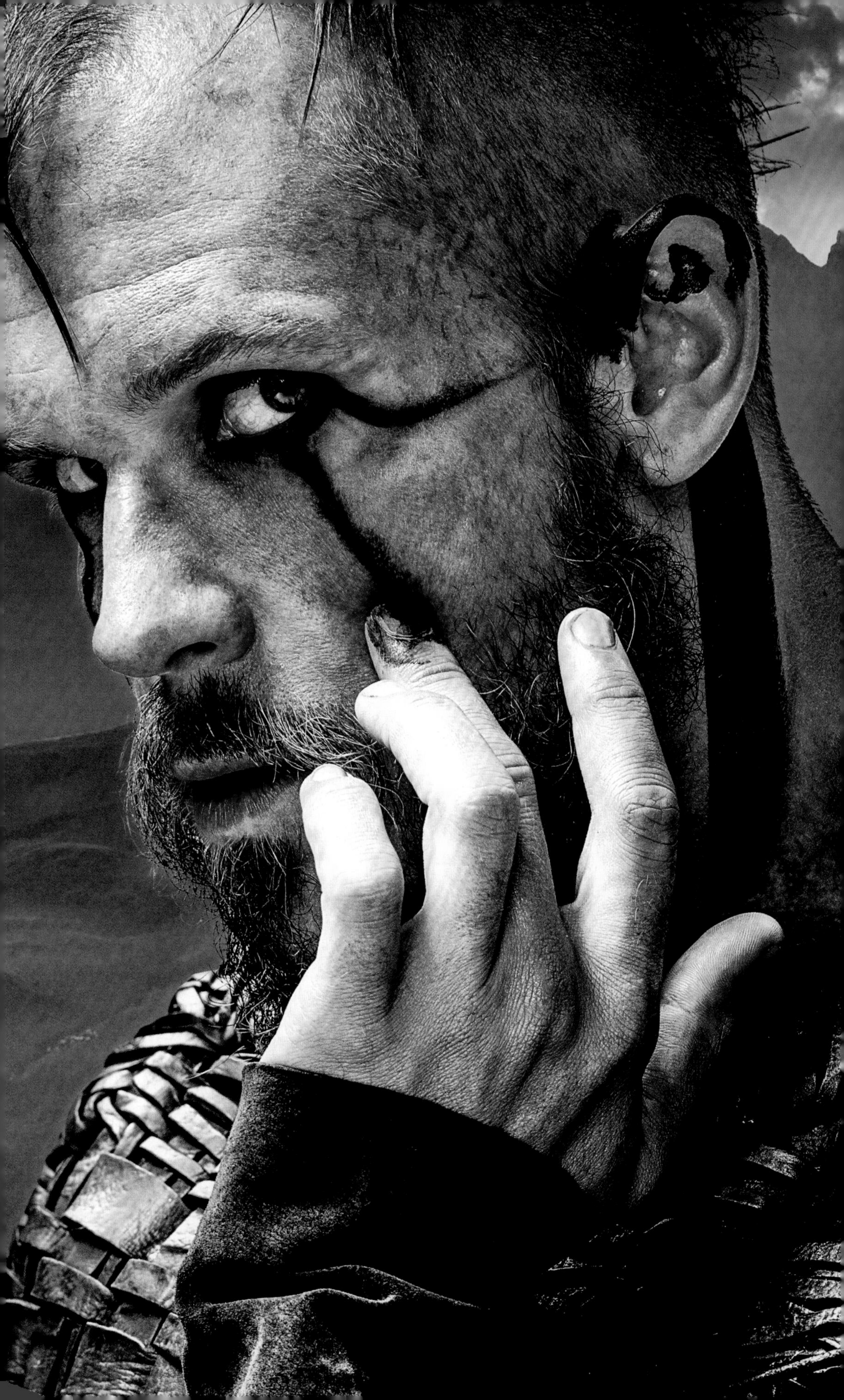

THE OUTSIDERS

In the third part of our exclusive interview, Cavan Scott talks to *Vikings* creator and screenwriter Michael Hirst about outsiders and the enduring popularity of Lagertha...

The latest season of *Vikings* seems to be largely about outsiders. You have Floki, alienated from Ragnar, and Bjorn off finding himself in the wilderness...
Michael Hirst: You're right. Whenever I've been asked about whether there's a theme for series four, I've said it's identity, because it starts with Bjorn heading off to the wilderness to try to find out who he is. Most of the characters have issues with their role. Ragnar hates being King and finds the burden intolerable. I think he really wants to understand why he has to carry that burden, and is questioning if he can ultimately escape from it. Identity is a big issue.

Meanwhile, Rollo is in a different country, trying to make sense of a culture that hates him...
Rollo is fascinating. I think he's the character you really want to hate in *Vikings*, but in fact you don't. And that's good. I would find it very hard to write about characters I hated.

One character everyone seems to love is Lagertha. Certainly, the news that our second *Vikings* comic series, *Uprising*, will be largely focused on her has been met with real enthusiasm.
She has a huge fanbase, hasn't she? Lagertha is easily as popular as Ragnar. I did get a note from a radical lesbian organisation in America that said they didn't care what I did to anyone, I could kill off as many male characters as I liked, but if I touched Lagertha I was in trouble!

Why do you think she's so popular?
I think Lagertha represents all the positive things I have discovered about Viking women. I certainly didn't realize how radical she would be on American TV. There isn't a character like her. She's a mother, she's a wife and she kicks ass – something that's apparently unique. Yes, she divorced Ragnar; yes, she rules and yes, she sits in judgment, but I wanted to continually make the point that she is still a woman. She's had to navigate through the power of men, and it's been a hell of a journey.

She certainly hasn't had an easy ride of it...
I remember very clearly Katheryn [Winnick, who plays Lagertha] was very upset when I told her that Lagertha was going to be married to an abusive husband in the second season. The character had begun to build this big fanbase, and she said that they simply wouldn't expect Lagertha to be in that situation. She really wasn't comfortable with any of it.

Did you manage to talk her round?
I said, "Look, for me this speaks to the experience of women throughout history, that powerful women can often find themselves in relationships like this. Lagertha has voluntarily walked out of her own life. At this point in time, she would need someone – someone with power, someone to bring up her son." None of that is a surprise. The difference in this situation is how Lagertha deals with it. I told Katheryn that Lagertha's solution would strengthen her as a role model, and I was right. The way she eventually dealt with the guy was shocking, and I believe spoke to women directly.

Have there been any other aspects of the show that have enraged audiences? You did, after all, crucify a priest...
Not that I know of. I don't always look at the papers, and I don't look at social media at all. I did get a [letter from a] plaintive evangelical minister who said it was a shame that Christianity was represented by someone who is neither powerful or virile. I said, "Just wait... Athelstan will surprise you; he's not as weak as you think he is."

In a show full of men and women solving problems by cleaving skulls, he remains one of the most influential characters.
Exactly. Even after his death.

Thanks for chatting, Michael.
No, thank you. I'm looking forward to seeing what you do with the comic. It's very exciting.

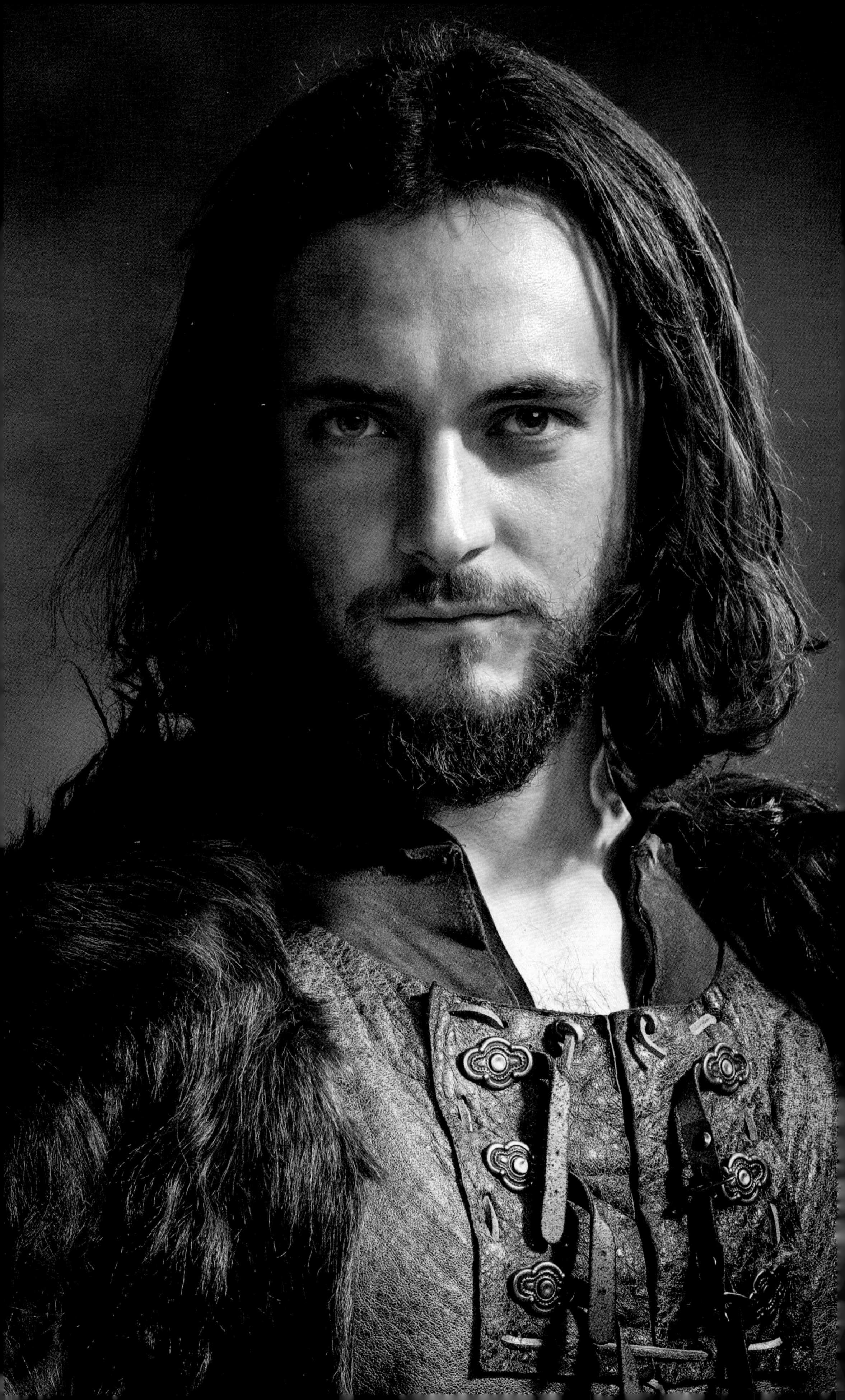

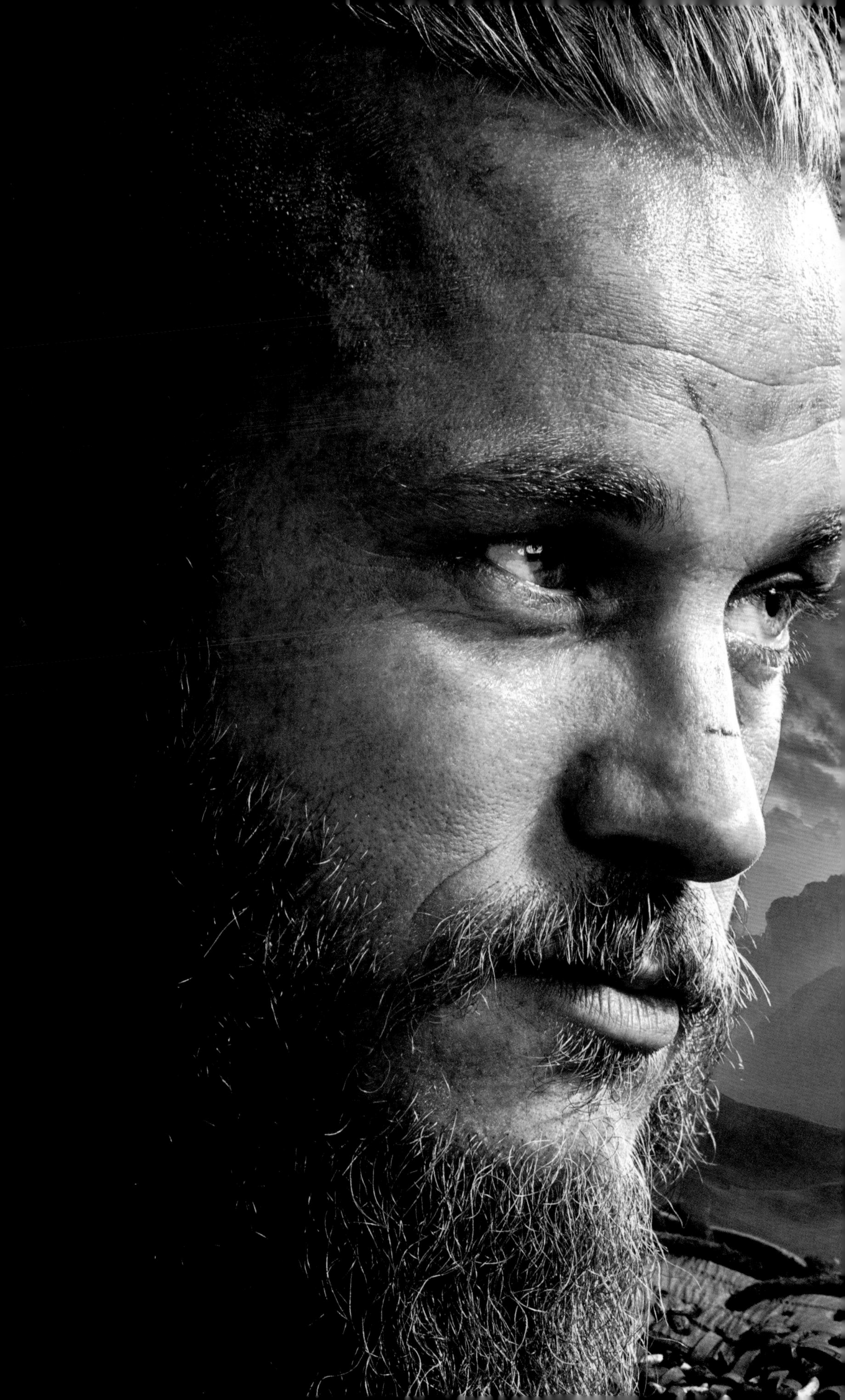

THE REAL RAGNAR LOTHBROK PLEASE STAND UP?

BY CAVAN SCOTT

Who was Ragnar Lothbrok? Well, that's a difficult question to answer. Certainly, he's a figure who is mentioned in numerous texts and sagas, offering many a contradiction and discrepancy along the way.

The first thing to tackle is that curious surname – which isn't actually a surname at all. More of a nickname, Lothbrok is usually interpreted as 'hairy breeches'. According to the *Saga of Ragnar Lodbrok*, the titular Viking warlord made himself shaggy

trousers and a fur coat. This wasn't just a fashion statement. The hirsute armor was boiled in pitch to protect the king as he battled a 'ring salmon-of-the-heath'. That's a dragon to you and me. And why did Ragnar get into the dragon-slaying business? Why, to win the hand of the beautiful Þóra Borgarhjǫrtr, of course.

One thing we do know about Ragnar was that he loved women. First there was the shield-maiden Lagertha, who, according to the 12th Century chronicler Saxo Grammaticus, fought alongside Ragnar to avenge his grandfather, Siward. Impressed by her courage and swordplay, Ragnar attempted to woo her by killing the bear and hound that protected her

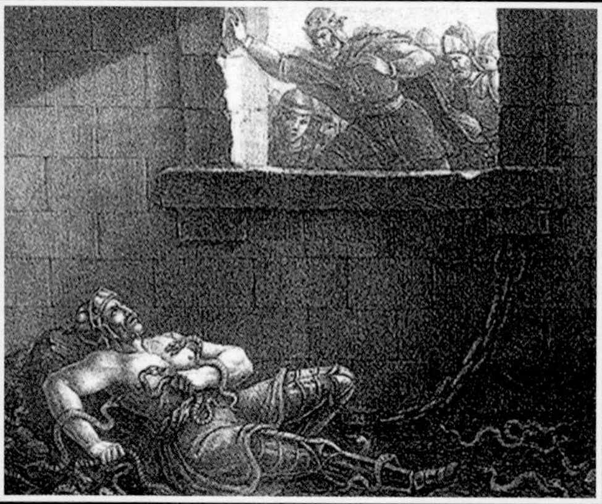

home. They had a son together, Fridleif, and two daughters, but the fact that she set her animals on him rankled Ragnar throughout their marriage.

Lagertha would later be divorced so that Ragnar could marry Þóra. This second union would bring two sons, Eiríkr and Agnar, although Þóra herself would sadly be struck down by a mysterious disease.

Never one to sit around on his hairy breeches, Ragnar would find love a third time. Aslaug possessed such beauty that she distracted Ragnar's bakers so much that the king's bread was burnt. Furious, Ragnar became intrigued with Aslaug, commanding her to visit him neither dressed nor undressed, neither hungry nor contented, and neither alone nor in the company of men. Aslaug appeared to him wearing a fishing net, snacking on an onion and accompanied by her dog. Suitably impressed by her wits – although presumably not her breath – Ragnar took Aslaug as his bride. Together they had five children including Ivar the Boneless, and Sigurd, born with the image of a snake in his eye.

Unfortunately, Ragnar's sons would prove to be his undoing. They grew into fine warriors, and Ragnar, worried that their fame would eclipse his own, set out on a foolhardy mission to England. He was captured by King Ælla of Northumberland and thrown into a pit of venomous snakes. After singing a heroic song – this is a Viking saga after all – Ragnar succumbed to the poison and died. Ivar the Boneless, in turn, ransacked England in a bloodthirsty act of revenge.

Of course, there is a different account of his death. According to some sources, Ragnar conquered Paris in 845AD, hanged 111 Christians and demanded a quite literal King's ransom to return the city to the Franks. This Ragnar – also known as Reginheri - would die an ignoble death, wracked by dysentery, his 'entrails spilling onto the ground'.

As *Vikings* proves, whatever fate took Ragnar to Valhalla, there is no doubt that the legendary warrior will intrigue both historians and storytellers for generations to come.

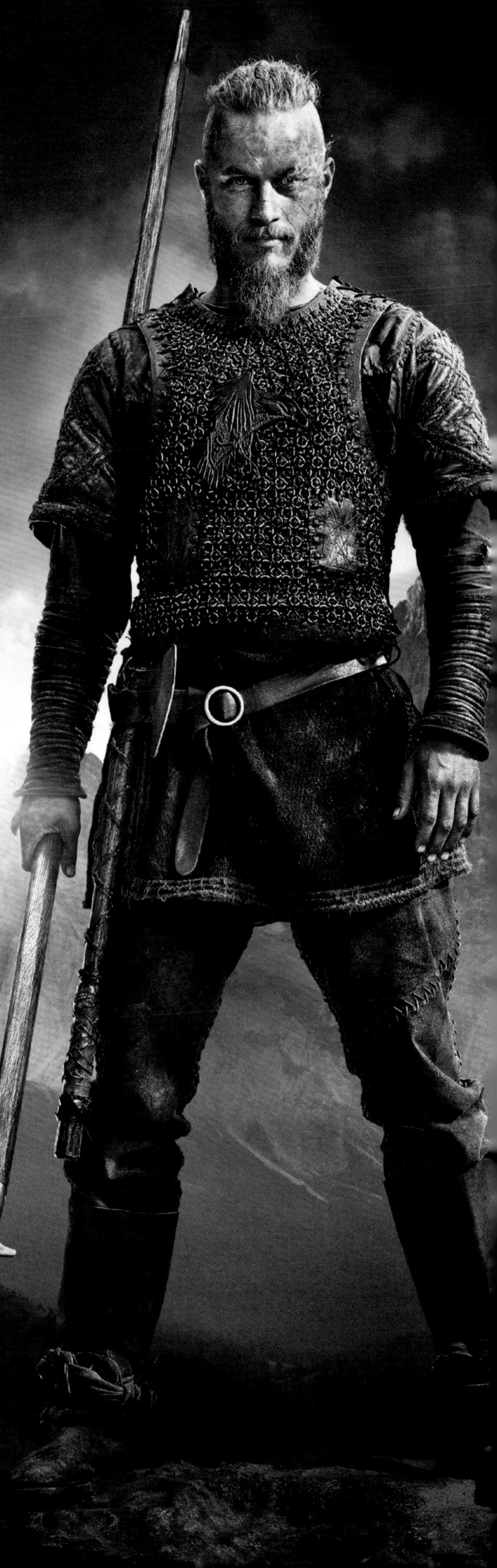

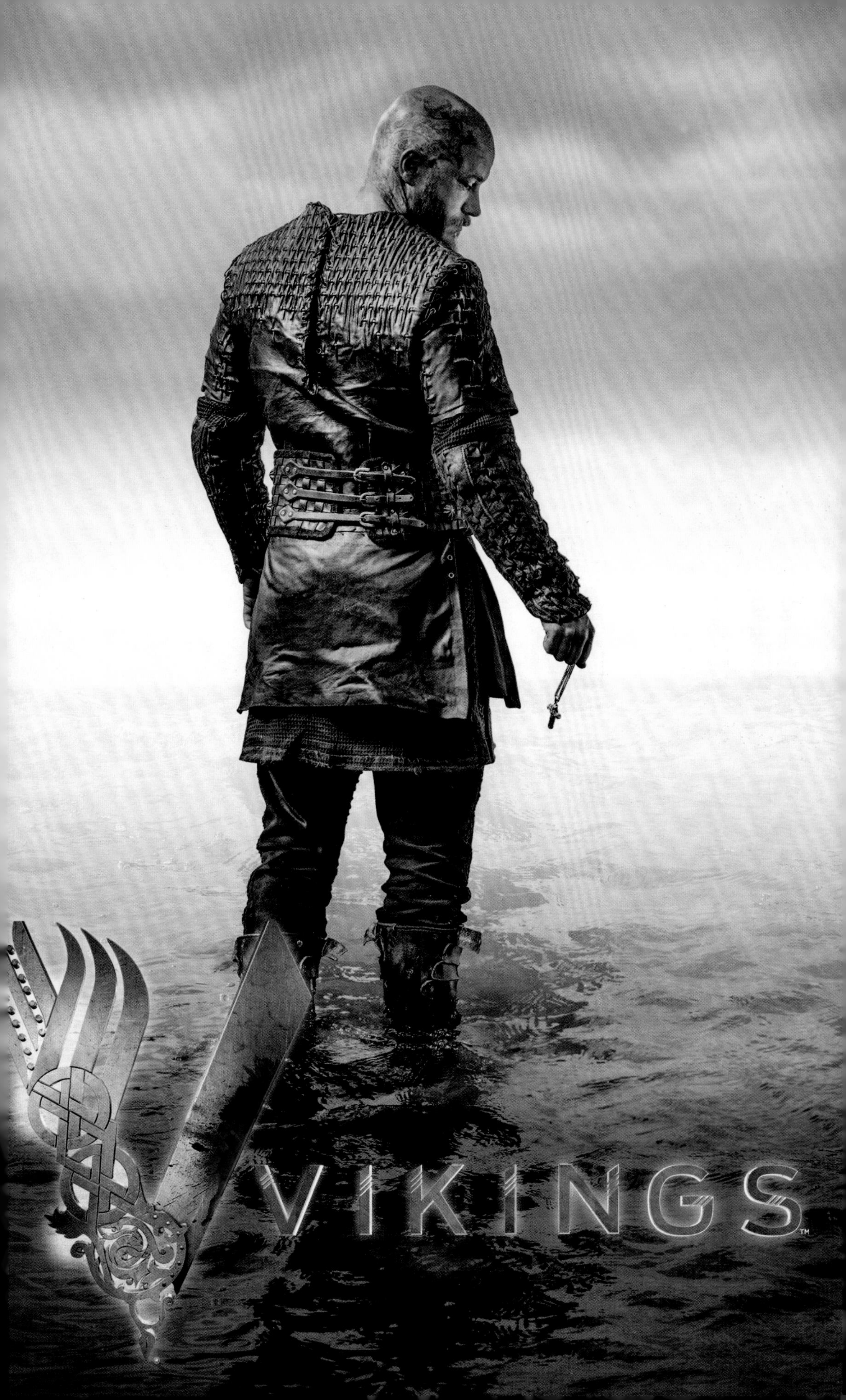
VIKINGS™

VIKING
UPRISING

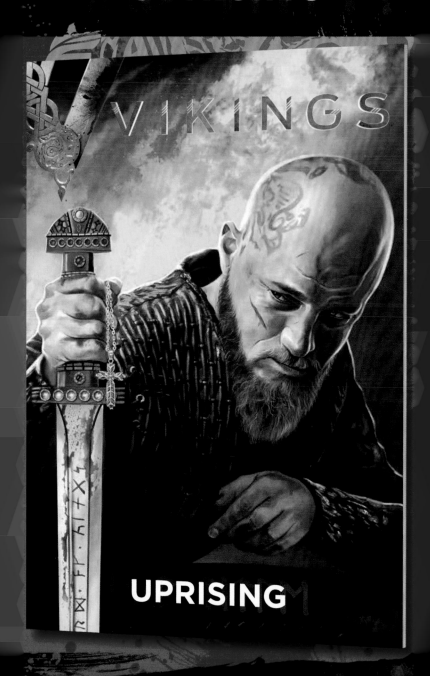

VIKINGS

UPRISING